declare [variadic] function

```
func sum (nums ...int) {
    fmt.Print (nums, " ")
    total := 0
    for _, num := range (nums) {
        total += num
    }
    fmt.Println (total)
```

invoke variadic function

```
sum (1, 2)                      [1,2]  3
sum (1, 2, 3)                   [1,2,3] 6

vals := [] int{1, 2, 3, 4}
sum (vals...)                   [1,2,3,4] 10
```

Go in Action

WILLIAM KENNEDY

WITH BRIAN KETELSEN
AND ERIK ST. MARTIN

MANNING
SHELTER ISLAND

Manning Publications Co.
20 Baldwin Road
PO Box 761
Shelter Island, NY 11964

Development editor: Jennifer Stout
Technical development editor: Kim Shrier
Copyeditor: Jodie Allen
Proofreader: Katie Tennant
Technical proofreader: Jimmy Frasché
Typesetter: Dottie Marsico
Cover designer: Marija Tudor

ISBN 9781617291784
Printed in the United States of America
2 3 4 5 6 7 8 9 10 – EBM – 20 19 18 17

brief contents

1 ■ Introducing Go 1

2 ■ Go quick-start 9

3 ■ Packaging and tooling 39

4 ■ Arrays, slices, and maps 57

5 ■ Go's type system 88

6 ■ Concurrency 128

7 ■ Concurrency patterns 158

8 ■ Standard library 184

9 ■ Testing and benchmarking 211

contents

foreword   xi
preface   xiii
acknowledgments   xiv
about this book   xvi
about the cover illustration   xix

1 Introducing Go   1

   1.1 Solving modern programming challenges with Go   2

      Development speed   3 ▪ *Concurrency   3* ▪ *Go's type system   5*
      Memory management   7

   1.2 Hello, Go   7

      Introducing the Go Playground   8

   1.3 Summary   8

2 Go quick-start   9

   2.1 Program architecture   10

   2.2 Main package   11

   2.3 Search package   13

      search.go   14 ▪ *feed.go   22* ▪ *match.go/default.go   26*

   2.4 RSS matcher   32

   2.5 Summary   38

3 Packaging and tooling 39

3.1 Packages 40

Package-naming conventions 40 • Package main 40

3.2 Imports 42

Remote imports 42 • Named imports 43

3.3 init 44

3.4 Using Go tools 45

3.5 Going farther with Go developer tools 47

go vet 47 • Go format 48 • Go documentation 48

3.6 Collaborating with other Go developers 51

Creating repositories for sharing 51

3.7 Dependency management 52

Vendoring dependencies 52 • Introducing gb 54

3.8 Summary 56

4 Arrays, slices, and maps 57

4.1 Array internals and fundamentals 57

Internals 58 • Declaring and initializing 58 • Working with arrays 60 • Multidimensional arrays 62 • Passing arrays between functions 64

4.2 Slice internals and fundamentals 65

Internals 65 • Creating and initializing 65 • Working with slices 68 • Multidimensional slices 79 • Passing slices between functions 80

4.3 Map internals and fundamentals 81

Internals 81 • Creating and initializing 83 • Working with maps 84 • Passing maps between functions 86

4.4 Summary 87

5 Go's type system 88

5.1 User-defined types 89

5.2 Methods 92

5.3 The nature of types 96

Built-in types 96 • Reference types 97 • Struct types 98

5.4   Interfaces   101

Standard library   102 • Implementation   104 • Method
sets   105 • Polymorphism   109

5.5   Type embedding   111

5.6   Exporting and unexporting identifiers   119

5.7   Summary   127

6   Concurrency   128

6.1   Concurrency versus parallelism   129

6.2   Goroutines   132

6.3   Race conditions   139

6.4   Locking shared resources   142

Atomic functions   142 • Mutexes   145

6.5   Channels   147

Unbuffered channels   148 • Buffered channels   153

6.6   Summary   157

7   Concurrency patterns   158

7.1   Runner   158

7.2   Pooling   167

7.3   Work   177

7.4   Summary   183

8   Standard library   184

8.1   Documentation and source code   185

8.2   Logging   187

Log package   187 • Customized loggers   191
Conclusion   195

8.3   Encoding/Decoding   196

Decoding JSON   196 • Encoding JSON   201
Conclusion   202

8.4   Input and output   203

Writer and Reader interfaces   203 • Working together   205
Simple curl   208 • Conclusion   210

8.5   Summary   210

9 Testing and benchmarking 211

9.1 Unit testing 212

Basic unit test 212 ▪ Table tests 216 ▪ Mocking calls 219
Testing endpoints 223

9.2 Examples 228

9.3 Benchmarking 232

9.4 Summary 236

index 237

foreword

In computer science, when you think of exceptional people, a few names come to mind. Among them are Rob Pike, Robert Griesmier, and Ken Thompson, who are responsible for UNIX, Plan 9, B, Java's JVM HotSpot, V8, Strongtalk, Sawzall, Ed, Acme, and UTF8, among many other creations. In 2007, they came together to experiment with a very powerful idea, combining their decades of experience to create a new systems language inspired by existing languages but truly unlike anything that came before. They released their creation as open source and named it "Go." If Go continues on the course it is now on, it may indeed prove to be the most impactful of their many notable creations.

Humanity is at its best when people join together with the pure intention of making the world a better place. In 2013, Brian and Erik formed the Gopher Academy and were soon joined by Bill and a few other similar-minded people, united in the pursuit of building a better community around the Go language. They first noticed that the community needed a place to gather and share material online so they set up the Go discussion board (slack) and the Gopher Academy blog. As time went on and the community continued to grow, they established the world's first global Go conference, GopherCon. Through their deep experience with the community, they knew that a resource was needed to guide the many thousands of programmers into this new language, so they began to write the book that you now hold in your hands.

This book is a labor of love from three individuals who have given so much of their time and talents to the Go community. I have been alongside Bill, Brian, and Erik to witness them writing and revising over the past year as they maintained their existing responsibilities as editors of the Gopher Academy blog, as conference organizers, in their day jobs, and in their roles as fathers and husbands. To them this is not a book, but a tribute to the language they love. They weren't content with producing a "good" book. They wrote and reviewed, rewrote and revised many drafts of each page, example, and chapter until they had a book worthy of the language they hold so dear.

It takes courage to leave a language of comfort and familiarity and try a language that is not only new to you but new to the world. This road less traveled is a bumpy one, lined with bugs that only early adopters are familiar with. It includes unexpected errors, spotty or missing documentation, and a lack of established libraries to use. This is the path of a trailblazer, a pioneer. If you are reading this now, you are likely on the beginning of this journey.

From the first chapter to the last, this book is crafted to provide you, the reader, a concise and comprehensive guide to exploring, learning, and using Go. In all the world, you couldn't hope to have better guides than Bill, Brian, and Erik. I'm excited for you to discover all the goodness that is Go and look forward to seeing you online and at the Go meetups and conferences.

STEVE FRANCIA
GOPHER AND CREATOR OF HUGO,
COBRA, VIPER, AND SPF13-VIM

preface

Back in October 2013 after writing the GoingGo.net blog for a few months, I received a call from Brian Ketelsen and Erik St. Martin. They were in the process of writing this book and asked if I would be a part of it. I jumped at the opportunity and started writing. I was still very new to Go at the time, so this was a great chance to learn more about the language, work with Brian and Erik and share what I learned at a greater scale than the blog.

After we finished the first four chapters, we released the book under the Manning Early Access Program (MEAP). Soon after, we received an email from a member of the language team. This person provided a review that contained a detailed set of changes plus a wealth of knowledge, advice, encouragement, and support. From there, we decided to rewrite chapter 2 from scratch and performed a major overhaul of chapter 4. We learned that rewriting chapters was not going to be the exception but the norm. That experience also taught us that it was going to take the help of the community to write this book, and we needed to make that happen immediately.

Ever since then, this book has been a community effort. We have tried to put a proper amount of time in researching each chapter, developing code samples, and working with the community to review, discuss, and edit the material and code. We have done our best to make sure this book is technically correct, shows only idiomatic code, and teaches you Go the way the community feels it should be written and thought about. We do have some of our own thoughts, practices, and guidelines sprinkled in as well.

We hope this book helps you learn Go and you find it a useful resource today and for many years to come. Brian, Erik, and I are always online and available to help anyone who reaches out to us. If you purchased the book, thank you, and don't be shy about saying "hi."

WILLIAM KENNEDY

acknowledgments

We have spent over 18 months writing this book, but none of our efforts would have been possible without the support of many people—our families, friends, colleagues, and mentors; the entire Go community; and our publisher, Manning.

When you're writing a book like this, you need an editor who will not only share the good but help you through the bad and be there for you at all cost. Jennifer Stout, you're a brilliant, nurturing, and amazing friend. Thank you for everything and for being there when we needed you the most. Thank you for making this book a reality. Thanks also to all the other folks at Manning who worked with us during the development and production of our book.

You can't know everything, so it requires a community of people to give their time and knowledge. We thank the Go community and everyone who participated in reviews and provided feedback on the manuscript at various stages of its development, especially Adam McKay, Alex Basile, Alex Jacinto, Alex Vidal, Anjan Bacchu, Benoît Benedetti, Bill Katz, Brian Hetro, Colin Kennedy, Doug Sparling, Jeffrey Lim, Jesse Evans, Kevin Jackson, Mark Fisher, Matt Zulak, Paulo Pires, Peter Krey, Philipp K. Janert, Sam Zaydel, and Thomas O'Rourke. Thanks also to Jimmy Frasché for his careful technical review of the final manuscript shortly before it went into production.

There are a few other people who need to be acknowledged in particular.

Kim Shrier was there from the very beginning, providing reviews, and giving of his time to teach. We learned so many things from you and we are grateful. The book is better technically because of you.

Bill Hathaway got involved heavily in the last year of writing the book, shaping each chapter; his thoughts and opinions were invaluable. We must give Bill credit as a coauthor of chapter 9. It would not exist without Bill's time, talent, and effort.

We would also like to recognize Cory Jacobson, Jeffery Lim, Chetan Conikee, and Nan Xiao, who consistently provided time for reviews, opinions, and guidance. Thanks to Gabriel Aszalos, Fatih Arslan, Kevin Gillette, and Jason Waldrip for help with sample code and reviews. And special thanks to Steve Francia for contributing the foreword and endorsing our work.

We end by sincerely thanking our families and friends. Anything that takes this level of commitment and time always has an effect on the ones you love.

WILLIAM KENNEDY

I would like to thank Lisa, my beautiful wife, and my five children: Brianna, Melissa, Amanda, Jarrod, and Thomas. Lisa, I know you and the kids spent way too many days, nights, and weekends without your husband and father. Thank you for letting me take all the time I needed to work on the book: I love each and every one of you.

I would also like to thank my business partner Ed Gonzalez, creative director Erick Zelaya, and the entire team at Ardan Studios. Ed, thanks for supporting me from the beginning. I could not have done this without you. You are more than just a business partner, you are a friend and brother: thank you. Erick, thanks for everything you do to support me and the company. Not sure what we would do without you.

BRIAN KETELSEN

I would like to thank my family for their patience during this four-year-long process of producing a book. Christine, Nathan, Lauren, and Evelyn: thank you for putting up with me as I wrote chapters in a lounge chair by the pool while you were swimming. Thank you for believing that this book could and would be published.

ERIK ST. MARTIN

I would like to thank my fiancée Abby, and my three children Halie, Wyatt, and Allie for being so patient and understanding how much time writing a book and organizing conferences demand. I love you all so very much and am lucky to have you.

I would also like to thank Bill Kennedy for the tremendous effort he has poured into this book—we asked him to help us write it, and he steered the ship most of the way due to the demands of our jobs and organizing GopherCon. I also want to thank the community for all their reviews and words of encouragement.

about this book

Go is an open source programming language that makes it easy to build simple, reliable, and efficient software. Although it borrows ideas from existing languages, it has a unique and simple nature that makes Go programs different in character from programs written in other languages. It balances the capabilities of a low-level systems language with some high-level features you see in modern languages today. This creates a programming environment that allows you to be incredibly productive, performant, and fully in control; in Go, you can write less code and do so much more.

Who should read this book?

This book was written for an intermediate-level developer who has some experience with other programming languages and wants to learn Go. Our goal in writing this book is to provide you an intensive, comprehensive, and idiomatic view of the language. We focus on both the specification and implementation of the language, including topics that range from language syntax, Go's type system, concurrency, channels, testing, and more. We believe this book is perfect for anyone who wants a jump-start in learning Go as well as for those who want a more thorough understanding of the language and its internals.

Roadmap

The book consists of nine chapters, briefly described here:

- Chapter 1 is a quick introduction to what the language is, why it was created, and the problems it solves. It also briefly introduces some of Go's core concepts such as concurrency.

- Chapter 2 walks you through a complete Go program, teaching you all that Go has to offer as a language along the way.
- Chapter 3 introduces the concept of packaging and how to best set up your Go workspace and development environment. It also shows how to use the Go tooling, including fetching and building your code.
- Chapter 4 provides a detailed view of Go's built-in data types: arrays, slices, and maps. It explains the implementation and mechanics behind these data structures.
- Chapter 5 is a detailed view of Go's type system, from struct types to named types to interfaces and type embedding. It also covers how all these things come together to allow you to structure and write complex software in a simpler way.
- Chapter 6 dives deeply into how the Go scheduler, concurrency, and channels work. It teaches the mechanics behind this aspect of the language.
- Chapter 7 takes what you learn from chapter 6 and shows more practical code around concurrency patterns. You will learn how to implement goroutine pools to manage work and how to pool reusable resources to be shared.
- Chapter 8 explores the standard library and goes deep into three packages: log, json, and io. The chapter focuses on some of the intricacies of these three packages.
- Chapter 9 closes the book by showing how to use the testing and benchmarking framework. You will learn how to write unit and table tests and benchmarks, and how to add examples to your documentation and use the examples as tests.

About the code

All source code in the book is presented in a mono-spaced typeface like this, which sets it off from the surrounding text. In many listings, the code is annotated to point out key concepts, and numbered bullets are sometimes used in the text to provide additional information about the code.

Source code for the examples in the book is available for download from the publisher's website at www.manning.com/books/go-in-action and from GitHub at https://github.com/goinaction/code.

Author Online

Purchase of *Go in Action* includes free access to a private web forum run by Manning Publications where you can make comments about the book, ask technical questions, and receive help from the authors and from other users. To access the forum and subscribe to it, point your web browser to www.manning.com/books/go-in-action. This page provides information on how to get on the forum once you're registered, what kind of help is available, and the rules of conduct on the forum.

Manning's commitment to our readers is to provide a venue where a meaningful dialog between individual readers and between readers and the authors can take place. It is not a commitment to any specific amount of participation on the part of the authors, whose contributions to the AO remain voluntary (and unpaid). We suggest you ask the authors challenging questions, lest their interest stray.

The Author Online forum and the archives of previous discussions will be accessible from the publisher's website as long as the book is in print.

About the authors

WILLIAM KENNEDY (@goinggodotnet) is a managing partner at Ardan Studio in Miami, Florida, a mobile, web, and systems development company. He is also the author of the blog GoingGo.Net, and the organizer for the Go meetup in Miami. Bill is focused on Go education through his training company, Ardan Labs. He can often be found talking at conferences and giving workshops both locally and over hangouts. He always finds time to work with individuals and groups who want to take their Go knowledge, blogging, and coding skills to the next level.

BRIAN KETELSEN (@bketelsen) is the CIO and cofounder of XOR Data Exchange. Brian is a co-organizer of GopherCon, the annual Go conference, and the founder of GopherAcademy—a community-focused organization created for the promotion of the Go language and the education of Go developers. He's been using Go since 2010.

ERIK ST. MARTIN (@erikstmartin) is the Director of Software Development at XOR Data Exchange, a big data and analytics company located in Austin, Texas, but resides in Tampa, Florida. Erik is a long-time contributor to open source and its communities. He's an organizer for GopherCon, an annual Go conference, and the organizer of the Go Tampa meetup group. He's very passionate about Go and the community and eager to find new ways to foster its growth.

about the cover illustration

The figure on the cover of *Go in Action* is captioned "Man from the East Indies." The illustration is taken from Thomas Jefferys' *A Collection of the Dresses of Different Nations, Ancient and Modern* (four volumes), London, published between 1757 and 1772. The title page states that these are hand-colored copperplate engravings, heightened with gum arabic. Thomas Jefferys (1719–1771) was called "Geographer to King George III." He was an English cartographer who was the leading map supplier of his day. He engraved and printed maps for government and other official bodies and produced a wide range of commercial maps and atlases, especially of North America. His work as a map maker sparked an interest in local dress customs of the lands he surveyed and mapped, and which are brilliantly displayed in this collection.

Fascination with faraway lands and travel for pleasure were relatively new phenomena in the late eighteenth century, and collections such as this one were popular, introducing both the tourist as well as the armchair traveler to the inhabitants of other countries. The diversity of the drawings in Jefferys' volumes speaks vividly of the uniqueness and individuality of the world's nations some 200 years ago. Dress codes have changed since then, and the diversity by region and country, so rich at the time, has faded away. It is now often hard to tell the inhabitants of one continent from another. Perhaps, trying to view it optimistically, we have traded a cultural and visual diversity for a more varied personal life—or a more varied and interesting intellectual and technical life.

At a time when it is hard to tell one computer book from another, Manning celebrates the inventiveness and initiative of the computer business with book covers based on the rich diversity of regional life of two centuries ago, brought back to life by Jeffreys' pictures.

Introducing Go

In this chapter

- Solving modern computing challenges with Go
- Using the Go tools

Computers have evolved, but programming languages haven't kept up the same pace of evolution. The cell phones we carry might have more CPU cores than the first computer we used. High-powered servers now have 64, 128, or even more cores, but we're still programming using the techniques we were using for a single core.

The art of programming has evolved too. Most programs aren't written by a single developer any more: they're written by teams of people sitting in different time zones and working at different times of the day. Large projects are broken up into smaller pieces and assigned to programmers who then deliver their work back to the team in the form of a library or package that can be used across an entire suite of applications.

Today's programmers and companies believe more than ever in the power of open source software. Go is a programming language that makes sharing code easy. Go ships with tools that make it simple to use packages written by others, and Go makes it easy to share our own packages too.

1

In this chapter you'll see how Go is different from other programming languages. Go rethinks the traditional object-oriented development you might be used to, while still providing an efficient means for code reuse. Go makes it easier for you to effectively use all of the cores on your expensive server, and it takes away the penalty of compiling a very large project.

As you read this chapter, you'll get a feeling for the many decisions that shaped the creation of Go, from its concurrency model to its lightning-fast compiler. We mentioned it in the preface, but it bears repeating: this book has been written for an intermediate-level developer who has some experience with other programming languages and wants to learn Go. Our goal in writing this book is to provide you an intensive, comprehensive, and idiomatic view of the language. We focus on both the specification and implementation of the language, including the wide-ranging topics of language syntax, Go's type system, concurrency, channels, testing, and more. We believe this book is perfect for anyone who wants a jump-start in learning Go or who wants a more thorough understanding of the language and its internals.

The source code for the examples in the book is available at https://github.com/goinaction/code.

We hope you'll appreciate the tools that ship with Go to make your life as a developer easier. In the end, you'll appreciate why so many developers are choosing Go when they start up that new project.

1.1   *Solving modern programming challenges with Go*

The Go team went to great lengths to solve the problems facing software developers today. Developers have to make an uncomfortable choice between rapid development and performance when choosing a language for their projects. Languages like C and C++ offer fast execution, whereas languages like Ruby and Python offer rapid development. Go bridges these competing worlds and offers a high-performance language with features that make development fast.

As we explore Go, you'll find well-planned features and concise syntax. As a language, Go is defined not only by what it includes, but by what it doesn't include. Go has a concise syntax with few keywords to memorize. Go has a compiler that's so fast, sometimes you'll forget it's running. As a Go developer, you'll spend significantly less time waiting for your project to build. Because of Go's built-in concurrency features, your software will scale to use the resources available without forcing you to use special threading libraries. Go uses a simple and effective type system that takes much of the overhead out of object-oriented development and lets you focus on code reuse. Go also has a garbage collector, so you don't have to manage your own memory. Let's look quickly at these key features.

1.1.1 Development speed

Compiling a large application in C or C++ takes more time than getting a cup of coffee. Figure 1.1 shows an XKCD classic excuse for messing around in the office.

Go offers lightning-quick compiles by using a smart compiler and simplified dependency resolution algorithms. When you build a Go program, the compiler only needs to look at the libraries that you directly include, rather than traversing the dependencies of all the libraries that are included in the entire dependency chain like Java, C, and C++. Consequently, many Go applications compile in under a second. The entire Go source tree compiles in under 20 seconds on modern hardware.

Figure 1.1 Working hard? (via XKCD)

Writing applications in dynamic languages makes you productive quickly because there are no intermediate steps between writing code and executing it. The trade-off is that dynamic languages don't offer the type safety that static languages do and often need a comprehensive test suite to avoid discovering incorrect type bugs at runtime.

Imagine writing a large application in a dynamic language like JavaScript and coming across a function that expects to receive a field called ID. Is that an integer, a string, or a UUID? The way to find out is to look at the source. You could try to execute the function with a number or a string and see what happens. In Go, you wouldn't spend time wondering, because the compiler will catch type differences for you.

1.1.2 Concurrency

One of the hardest things to do as a programmer is to write an application that effectively uses the available resources of the hardware running it. Modern computers have many cores, but most programming languages don't have effective tools for utilizing those additional resources easily. They often require a lot of thread synchronization code, which is prone to errors.

Go's concurrency support is one of its strongest features. Goroutines are like threads, but use far less memory and require less code to use. Channels are data structures that let you send typed messages between goroutines with synchronization built in. This facilitates a programming model where you send data between goroutines, rather than letting the goroutines fight to use the same data. Let's look at these features in more detail now.

GOROUTINES

Goroutines are functions that run concurrently with other goroutines, including the entry point of your program. In other languages, you'd use threads to accomplish the same thing, but in Go many goroutines execute on a single thread. For example, if you write a web server and you want to handle different web requests simultaneously, you'd have to write a lot of extra code to use threads in C or Java. In Go, the net/http library

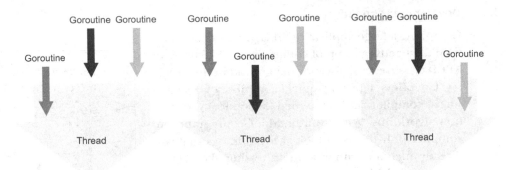

Figure 1.2   Many goroutines execute on a single OS thread

has concurrency built in using goroutines. Each inbound request automatically runs on its own goroutine. Goroutines use less memory than threads and the Go runtime will automatically schedule the execution of goroutines against a set of configured logical processors. Each logical processor is bound to a single OS thread (see figure 1.2). This makes your application much more efficient with significantly less development effort.

If you want to execute some code concurrently while you move on to accomplish other things, a goroutine is perfect for the job. Here's a quick example:

```
func log(msg string){
    ... some logging code here
}

// Elsewhere in our code after we've discovered an error.
go log("something dire happened")
```

That keyword go is all you need to schedule the log function to run as a goroutine and for that goroutine be run concurrently with other goroutines. This means you can continue executing the rest of your application while the logging happens concurrently, which often results in greater perceived performance for your end users. As stated before, goroutines have minimal overhead, so it isn't uncommon to spawn tens of thousands of them. We'll explore goroutines and concurrency more in-depth in chapter 6.

CHANNELS

Channels are data structures that enable safe data communication between goroutines. Channels help you to avoid problems typically seen in programming languages that allow shared memory access.

The hardest part of concurrency is ensuring that your data isn't unexpectedly modified by concurrently running processes, threads, or goroutines. When multiple threads change the same data without locks or synchronization, heartache always follows. In other languages, when you have global variables and shared memory, you're required to use complicated locking disciplines to prevent unsynchronized changes to the same variables.

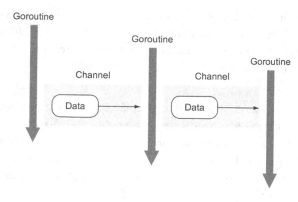

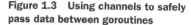

Figure 1.3 Using channels to safely pass data between goroutines

Channels help to solve this problem by providing a pattern that makes data safe from concurrent modification. Channels help to enforce the pattern that only one goroutine should modify the data at any time. You can see an example of this flow in figure 1.3, where channels are used to send data between several running goroutines. Imagine an application where many different processes need to know about or modify data sequentially. Using goroutines and channels, you can model this process safely.

In figure 1.3 you see three goroutines and two unbuffered channels. The first goroutine passes a data value through the channel to a second goroutine that's already waiting. The exchange of the data between both goroutines is synchronized, and once the hand-off occurs, both goroutines know the exchange took place. After the second goroutine performs its tasks with the data, it then sends the data to a third goroutine that's waiting. That exchange is also synchronized, and both goroutines can have guarantees the exchange has been made. This safe exchange of data between goroutines requires no other locks or synchronization mechanisms.

It's important to note that channels don't provide data access protection between goroutines. If copies of data are exchanged through a channel, then each goroutine has its own copy and can make any changes to that data safely. When pointers to the data are being exchanged, each goroutine still needs to be synchronized if reads and writes will be performed by the different goroutines.

1.1.3 Go's type system

Go provides a flexible hierarchy-free type system that enables code reuse with minimal refactoring overhead. It's still object-oriented development, but without the traditional headaches. If you've ever spent a week planning your abstract classes and interfaces in a complex Java or C++ program, you'll appreciate the simplicity of Go's type system. Go developers simply embed types to reuse functionality in a design pattern called *composition*. Other languages use composition, but it's often deeply tied to inheritance, which can make it complicated and difficult to use. In Go, types are *composed* of smaller types, which is in contrast to traditional inheritance-based models.

In addition Go has a unique interface implementation that allows you to model behavior, rather than model types. You don't need to declare that you're implementing an interface in Go; the compiler does the work of determining whether values of your types satisfy the interfaces you're using. Many interfaces in Go's standard library are very small, exposing only a few functions. In practice this takes some time to get used to, especially if you've been writing in object-oriented languages like Java.

TYPES ARE SIMPLE

Go has built-in types like `int` and `string` as well as user-defined types. A typical user-defined type in Go will have typed fields to store data. If you've seen structs in C, Go's user-defined types will look familiar and operate similarly. But types may also declare methods that operate on that data. Rather than building a long inheritance structure—Client extends User extends Entity—Go developers build small types—Customer and Admin—and embed them into larger ones. Figure 1.4 demonstrates the difference between inheritance and composition.

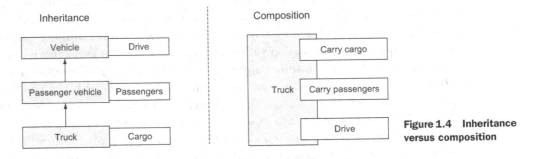

Figure 1.4   Inheritance versus composition

GO INTERFACES MODEL SMALL BEHAVIORS

Interfaces allow you to express the behavior of a type. If a value of a type implements an interface, it means the value has a specific set of behaviors. You don't even need to declare that you're implementing an interface; you just need to write the implementation. Other languages call this *duck typing*—if it quacks like a duck, then it can *be* a duck—and Go does it well. In Go, if your type implements the methods of an interface, a value of your type can be stored in a value of that interface type. No special declarations are required.

In a strictly object-oriented language like Java, interfaces are all-encompassing. You're often required to think through a large inheritance chain before you're able to even start writing code. Here's an example of a Java interface:

```
interface User {
    public void login();
    public void logout();
}
```

Implementing this interface in Java requires you to create a class that fulfills all of the promises made in the `User` interface and explicitly declare that you implement the interface. In contrast, a Go interface typically represents just a single action. One of the most common interfaces you'll use in Go is `io.Reader`. The `io.Reader` interface provides a simple way to declare that your type has data to be read in a way that other functions in the standard library understand. Here's the definition:

```
type Reader interface {
    Read(p []byte) (n int, err error)
}
```
slice of bytes   returns

To write a type that implements the io.Reader interface, you only need to implement a Read method that accepts a slice of bytes and returns an integer and possible error.

This is a radical departure from the interface systems used in other object-oriented programming languages. Go's interfaces are smaller and more aligned with single actions. In practice, this allows significant advantages in code reuse and composability. You can implement an io.Reader on nearly any type that has data available, and then pass it to any Go function that knows how to read from io.Reader.

The entire networking library in Go is built using the io.Reader interface, because it allows it to separate the network implementation required for each different network operation from the functionality of your application. It makes interfaces fun, elegant, and flexible. That same io.Reader enables simple operations with files, buffers, sockets, and any other data source. Using a single interface allows you to operate on data efficiently, regardless of the source.

1.1.4 Memory management

Improper memory management causes applications to crash and leak memory, and even crash the operating system. Go has a modern garbage collector that does the hard work for you. In other systems languages, like C or C++, you need to allocate a piece of memory before you can use it, and then free it when you're done. If you fail to do either of these correctly, you'll have program crashes or memory leaks. It isn't always easy to track a piece of memory when it's no longer needed; threads and heavy concurrency make it even harder. When you write code with garbage collection in mind, Go's garbage collection adds little overhead to program execution time, but reduces development effort significantly. Go takes the tedium out of programming and leaves the bean counting to the accountants.

1.2 Hello, Go

It's much easier to get the feel of a programming language by seeing it in action. Let's look at the traditional *Hello World!* application written in Go:

**Go programs are
organized as packages.**

```
package main

import "fmt"

func main(){
    fmt.Println("Hello World!")
}
```

The import statement allows you to use external code. The fmt package provided by the standard library allows you to format and output data.

The main function is what gets executed when you run your application—just like in C.

This sample program prints a familiar phrase on your screen when you run it. But how should you run it? Without installing Go on your computer, you can use almost all that Go provides right from your web browser.

1.2.1 Introducing the Go Playground

The Go Playground allows you to edit and run Go code from your web browser. Fire up a web browser and navigate to http://play.golang.org. The code in the browser window is editable right on the screen (see figure 1.5). Click Run and see what happens!

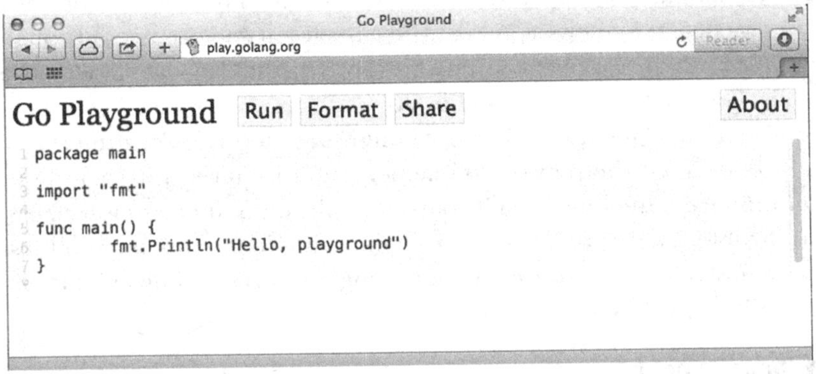

Figure 1.5 The Go Playground

You can even change the code to make the greeting text output in a different language. Go ahead and change the greeting inside the `fmt.Println()` function and hit Run again.

> **SHARING GO CODE**   Go developers use the Playground to share code ideas, test theories, and debug their code, as you soon will too. Every time you create a new application on the Playground, you can click Share to get a sharable URL that anyone else can open. Try this one: http://play.golang.org/p/EWIXicJdmz.

The Go Playground is the perfect way to demonstrate an idea to a coworker or friend who's trying to learn something, or to solicit help. On the Go IRC channels, Slack group, mailing lists, and countless emails sent among Go developers, you'll see Go Playground programs being created, modified, and shared.

1.3   Summary

- Go is modern, fast, and comes with a powerful standard library.
- Go has concurrency built-in.
- Go uses interfaces as the building blocks of code reuse.

Go quick-start

In this chapter

- Reviewing a comprehensive Go program
- Declaring types, variables, functions, and methods
- Launching and synchronizing goroutines
- Writing generic code using interfaces
- Handling errors as normal program logic

Go has its own elegance and programming idioms that make the language productive and fun to code in. The language designers set out to create a language that would let them be productive without losing access to the lower-level programming constructs they needed. This balance is achieved through a minimized set of keywords, built-in functions, and syntax. Go also provides a comprehensive standard library. The standard library provides all the core packages programmers need to build real-world web- and network-based programs.

To see this in action, we'll review a complete Go program that implements functionality that can be found in many Go programs being developed today. The program pulls different data feeds from the web and compares the content against a search term. The content that matches is then displayed in the terminal window.

The program reads text files, makes web calls, and decodes both XML and JSON into struct type values, and it does all of this using Go concurrency to make things fast.

You can download and review the code in your favorite editor by navigating to the book repository for this chapter:

```
https://github.com/goinaction/code/tree/master/chapter2/sample
```

Don't feel that you need to understand everything you read and review in this chapter the first, second, or even the third time. Though many of the programming concepts you know today can be applied when learning Go, Go also has its unique idioms and style. If you can liberate yourself from your current programming language and look at Go with a fresh set of eyes and a clear mind, you'll find it easier to understand and appreciate, and you'll see Go's elegance.

2.1 Program architecture

Before we dive into the code, let's review the architecture behind the program (shown in figure 2.1) and see how searching all the different feeds is accomplished.

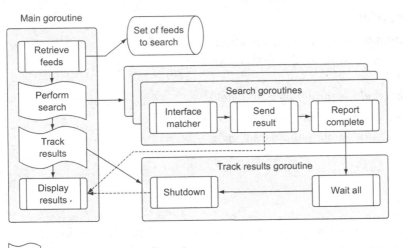

Figure 2.1 **The flow of the program architecture**

The program is broken into several distinct steps that run across many different goroutines. We'll explore the code as it flows from the main goroutine into the searching and tracking goroutines and then back to the main goroutine. To start, here's the structure of the project.

Listing 2.1   Project structure for the application

```
cd $GOPATH/src/github.com/goinaction/code/chapter2

- sample
    - data
        data.json     -- Contains a list of data feeds
    - matchers
```

```
      rss.go        -- Matcher for searching rss feeds
   - search
      default.go   -- Default matcher for searching data
      feed.go      -- Support for reading the json data file
      match.go     -- Interface support for using different matchers
      search.go    -- Main program logic for performing search
   main.go          -- Programs entry point
```

The code is organized into these four folders, which are listed in alphabetical order. The data folder contains a JSON document of data feeds the program will retrieve and process to match the search term. The matchers folder contains the code for the different types of feeds the program supports. Currently the program only supports one matcher that processes RSS type feeds. The search folder contains the business logic for using the different matchers to search content. Finally we have the parent folder, sample, which contains the main.go code file, which is the entry point for the program.

Now that you've seen where all the code for the program is, you can begin to explore and understand how the program works. Let's start with the entry point for the program.

2.2 Main package

The program's entry point can be found in the main.go code file. Even though there are only 21 lines of code, there are a few things going on that we have to mention.

Listing 2.2 main.go

```
01 package main
02
03 import (
04     "log"
05     "os"
06
07     _ "github.com/goinaction/code/chapter2/sample/matchers"
08     "github.com/goinaction/code/chapter2/sample/search"
09 )
10
11 // init is called prior to main.
12 func init() {
13     // Change the device for logging to stdout.
14     log.SetOutput(os.Stdout)
15 }
16
17 // main is the entry point for the program.
18 func main() {
19     // Perform the search for the specified term.
20     search.Run("president")
21 }
```

Every Go program that produces an executable has two distinct features. One of those features can be found on line 18. There you can see the function main declared. For the build tools to produce an executable, the function main must be declared, and it becomes the entry point for the program. The second feature can be found on line 01 of program.

Listing 2.3   main.go: line 01

```
01 package main
```

You can see the function main is located in a package called main. If your main function doesn't exist in package main, the build tools won't produce an executable.

Every code file in Go belongs to a package, and main.go is no exception. We'll go into much more detail about packages in chapter 3, because packages are an important feature of Go. For now, understand that packages define a unit of compiled code and their names help provide a level of indirection to the identifiers that are declared inside of them, just like a namespace. This makes it possible to distinguish identifiers that are declared with exactly the same name in the different packages you import.

Now turn your attention to lines 03 through 09 of the main.go code file, which declares imports.

Listing 2.4   main.go: lines 03–09

```
03 import (
04    "log"
05    "os"
06
07    _ "github.com/goinaction/code/chapter2/sample/matchers"
08    "github.com/goinaction/code/chapter2/sample/search"
09 )
```

Imports are just that: they import code and give you access to identifiers such as types, functions, constants, and interfaces. In our case, the code in the main.go code file can now reference the Run function from the search package, thanks to the import on line 08. On lines 04 and 05, we import code from the standard library for the log and os packages.

All code files in a folder must use the same package name, and it's common practice to name the package after the folder. As stated before, a package defines a unit of compiled code, and each unit of code represents a package. If you quickly look back at listing 2.1, you'll see how we have a folder in this project called search that matches the import path on line 08.

You may have noticed that on line 07 we import the matchers package and use the blank identifier before listing out the import path.

Listing 2.5   main.go: line 07

```
07    _ "github.com/goinaction/code/chapter2/sample/matchers"
```

This is a technique in Go to allow initialization from a package to occur, even if you don't directly use any identifiers from the package. To make your programs more readable, the Go compiler won't let you declare a package to be imported if it's not used. The blank identifier allows the compiler to accept the import and call any `init` functions that can be found in the different code files within that package. For our program, this is required because the rss.go code file in the `matchers` package contains an `init` function to register the RSS matcher for use. We'll come back to how all this works later.

The main.go code file also has an `init` function that's declared on lines 12 through 15.

> **Listing 2.6   main.go: lines 11–15**

```
11 // init is called prior to main.
12 func init() {
13     // Change the device for logging to stdout.
14     log.SetOutput(os.Stdout)
15 }
```

All `init` functions in any code file that are part of the program will get called before the `main` function. This init function sets the logger from the standard library to write to the `stdout` device. By default, the logger is set to write to the `stderr` device. In chapter 7 we'll talk more about the `log` package and other important packages from the standard library.

Finally, let's look at the one statement that the `main` function performs on line 20.

> **Listing 2.7   main.go: lines 19–20**

```
19     // Perform the search for the specified term.
20     search.Run("president")
```

Here you see a call to the `Run` function that belongs to the `search` package. This function contains the core business logic for the program, which requires a string for the search term. Once the `Run` function returns, the program will terminate.

Now we can look at the code that belongs to the `search` package.

2.3   Search package

The `search` package contains the framework and business logic for the program. The package is organized into four different code files, each with a unique responsibility. As we continue to follow the logic of the program, we'll explore each of these different code files.

Let's briefly talk about what a matcher is, since the entire program revolves around the execution of matchers. A matcher in our program is a value that contains specific intelligence for processing a feed type. In our program we have two matchers. The framework implements a default matcher that has no intelligence, and in the `matchers`

✳ package we have an implementation of an RSS matcher. The RSS matcher knows how to get, read, and search RSS feeds. Later on we could extend the program to use matchers that could read JSON documents or CSV files. We'll talk more about how to implement matchers later.

2.3.1   *search.go*

Following are the first nine lines of code that can be found inside the search.go code file. This is the code file where the Run function is located.

Listing 2.8   search/search.go: lines 01–09

```
01 package search
02
03 import (
04     "log"
05     "sync"
06 )
07
08 // A map of registered matchers for searching.
09 var matchers = make(map[string]Matcher)       // package level var
```

As you'll see, each code file will contain the keyword package at the top with a name for the package. Each code file in the search folder will contain search for the package name. The lines from 03 through 06 import the log and sync packages from the standard library.

When you import code from the standard library, you only need to reference the name of the package, unlike when you import code from outside of the standard ✳ library. The compiler will always look for the packages you import at the locations referenced by the GOROOT and GOPATH environment variables.   at or relative to

---

Listing 2.9   GOROOT and GOPATH environmental variables

```
GOROOT="/Users/me/go"
GOPATH="/Users/me/spaces/go/projects"
```

The log package provides support for logging messages to the stdout, stderr, or even custom devices. The sync package provides support for synchronizing goroutines, which is required by our program. On line 09 you'll see our first variable declaration.

Listing 2.10   search/search.go: lines 08–09

```
08 // A map of registered matchers for searching.
09 var matchers = make(map[string]Matcher)
```
keyword type   value type

@ 15 This variable is located outside the scope of any function and so is considered a package-level variable. The variable is declared using the keyword var and is declared as a map of Matcher type values with a key of type string. The declaration for the

Matcher type can be found in the match.go code file, and we'll describe the purpose of this type later. There's another important aspect of this variable declaration: the name of the variable matchers starts with a lowercase letter.

In Go, identifiers are either exported or unexported from a package. An exported identifier can be directly accessed by code in other packages when the respective package is imported. These identifiers start with a capital letter. Unexported identifiers start with a lowercase letter and can't be directly accessed by code in other packages. But just because an identifier is unexported, it doesn't mean other packages can't indirectly access these identifiers. As an example, a function can return a value of an unexported type and this value is accessible by any calling function, even if the calling function has been declared in a different package.

This variable declaration also contains an initialization of the variable via the assignment operator and a special built-in function called make.

Listing 2.11 Making a map

```
make(map[string]Matcher)
```

A map is a reference type that you're required to make in Go. If you don't make the map first and assign it to your variable, you'll receive errors when you try to use the map variable. This is because the zero value for a map variable is nil. In chapter 4 we'll go into greater detail about maps.

In Go, all variables are initialized to their zero value. For numeric types, that value is 0; for strings it's an empty string; for Booleans it's false; and for pointers, the zero value is nil. When it comes to reference types, there are underlying data structures that are initialized to their zero values. But variables declared as a reference type set to their zero value will return the value of nil.

Now let's walk through the Run function that's called by the main function, which you saw earlier.

Listing 2.12 search/search.go: lines 11–57

```
11  // Run performs the search logic.
12  func Run(searchTerm string) {
13      // Retrieve the list of feeds to search through.
14      feeds, err := RetrieveFeeds()
15      if err != nil {
16          log.Fatal(err)
17      }
18
19      // Create a unbuffered channel to receive match results.
20      results := make(chan *Result)
21
22      // Setup a wait group so we can process all the feeds.
23      var waitGroup sync.WaitGroup
24
25      // Set the number of goroutines we need to wait for while
```

```
26      // they process the individual feeds.
27      waitGroup.Add(len(feeds))
28
29      // Launch a goroutine for each feed to find the results.
30      for _, feed := range feeds {
31          // Retrieve a matcher for the search.
32          matcher, exists := matchers[feed.Type]
33          if !exists {
34              matcher = matchers["default"]
35          }
36
37          // Launch the goroutine to perform the search.
38          go func(matcher Matcher, feed *Feed) {
39              Match(matcher, feed, searchTerm, results)
40              waitGroup.Done()
41          }(matcher, feed)
42      }
43
44      // Launch a goroutine to monitor when all the work is done.
45      go func() {
46          // Wait for everything to be processed.
47          waitGroup.Wait()
48
49          // Close the channel to signal to the Display
50          // function that we can exit the program.
51          close(results)
52      }()
53
54      // Start displaying results as they are available and
55      // return after the final result is displayed.
56      Display(results)
57  }
```

The Run function contains the main control logic for the program. It's a good representation of how Go programs can be structured to handle the launching and synchronization of goroutines that run concurrently. Let's walk through the logic section by section, and then explore the other code files that lend their support.

Let's review how the Run function is declared.

Listing 2.13   search/search.go: lines 11–12

```
11  // Run performs the search logic.
12  func Run(searchTerm string) {
```

To declare a function in Go, use the keyword func followed by the function name, any parameters, and then any return values. In the case of Run, you have a single parameter called searchTerm of type string. The term the program will search against is passed into the Run function, and if you look at the main function again, you can see that exchange.

Listing 2.14   main.go: lines 17–21

```
17 // main is the entry point for the program.
18 func main() {
19     // Perform the search for the specified term.
20     search.Run("president")
21 }
```

The first thing that the Run function does is retrieve a list of data feeds. These feeds are used to pull content from the internet that is then matched against the specified search term.

Listing 2.15   search/search.go: lines 13–17

```
13     // Retrieve the list of feeds to search through.
14     feeds, err := RetrieveFeeds()
15     if err != nil {
16         log.Fatal(err)
17     }
```

There are a few important concepts here that we need to go through. You can see on line 14 that we make a function call to the function RetrieveFeeds. This function belongs to the search package and returns two values. The first return value is a slice of Feed type values. A slice is a reference type that implements a dynamic array. You use slices in Go to work with lists of data. Chapter 4 goes into greater detail about slices.

The second return value is an error. On line 15, the error value is evaluated for errors, and if an error did occur, the function Fatal from the log package is called. The Fatal function accepts an error value and will log to the terminal window before terminating the program.

Though not unique to Go, you can see that our functions can have multiple return values. It's common to declare functions that return a value and an error value just like the RetrieveFeeds function. If an error occurs, never trust the other values being returned from the function. They should always be ignored, or else you run the risk of the code generating more errors or panics.

Let's take a closer look at how the values being returned from the function are being assigned to variables.

Listing 2.16   search/search.go: lines 13–14

```
13     // Retrieve the list of feeds to search through.
14     feeds, err := RetrieveFeeds()
```

Here you see the use of the short variable declaration operator (:=). This operator is used to both declare and initialize variables at the same time. The type of each value being returned is used by the compiler to determine the type for each variable, respectively. The short variable declaration operator is just a shortcut to streamline your code and make the code more readable. The variable it declares is no different than any other variable you may declare when using the keyword var.

Now that we have our list of data feeds, we can move on to the next line of code.

Listing 2.17   search/search.go: lines 19–20

```
19    // Create a unbuffered channel to receive match results.
20    results := make(chan *Result)
```

On line 20, we use the built-in function make to create an unbuffered channel. We use the short variable declaration operator to declare and initialize the channel variable with the call to make. A good rule of thumb when declaring variables is to use the keyword var when declaring variables that will be initialized to their zero value, and to use the short variable declaration operator when you're providing extra initialization or making a function call.

Channels are also a reference type in Go like maps and slices, but channels implement a queue of typed values that are used to communicate data between goroutines. Channels provide inherent synchronization mechanisms to make communication safe. In chapter 6 we'll go into more details about channels and goroutines.

The next two lines of code are used later to prevent the program from terminating before all the search processing is complete.

Listing 2.18   search/search.go: lines 22–27

```
22    // Setup a wait group so we can process all the feeds.
23    var waitGroup sync.WaitGroup
24
25    // Set the number of goroutines we need to wait for while
26    // they process the individual feeds.
27    waitGroup.Add(len(feeds))
```

In Go, once the main function returns, the program terminates. Any goroutines that were launched and are still running at this time will also be terminated by the Go runtime. When you write concurrent programs, it's best to cleanly terminate any goroutines that were launched prior to letting the main function return. Writing programs that can cleanly start and shut down helps reduce bugs and prevents resources from corruption.

Our program is using a WaitGroup from the sync package to track all the goroutines we're going to launch. A WaitGroup is a great way to track when a goroutine is finished performing its work. A WaitGroup is a counting semaphore, and we'll use it to count off goroutines as they finish their work.

On line 23 we declare a variable of type WaitGroup from the sync package. Then on line 27 we set the value of the WaitGroup variable to match the number of goroutines we're going to launch. As you'll soon see, we'll process each feed concurrently with its own goroutine. As each goroutine completes its work, it will decrement the count of the WaitGroup variable, and once the variable gets to zero, we'll know all the work is done.

Next let's look at the code that launches these goroutines for each feed.

Listing 2.19 search/search.go: lines 29–42

```
29      // Launch a goroutine for each feed to find the results.
30      for _, feed := range feeds {
31          // Retrieve a matcher for the search.
32          matcher, exists := matchers[feed.Type]
33          if !exists {
34              matcher = matchers["default"]
35          }
36
37          // Launch the goroutine to perform the search.
38          go func(matcher Matcher, feed *Feed) {
39              Match(matcher, feed, searchTerm, results)
40              waitGroup.Done()
41          }(matcher, feed)
42      }
```

The code for lines 30 through 42 iterate through the list of data feeds we retrieved earlier and launch a goroutine for each one. To iterate over the slice of feeds, we use the keywords for range. The keyword range can be used with arrays, strings, slices, maps, and channels. When we use for range to iterate over a slice, we get two values back on each iteration. The first is the index position of the element we're iterating over, and the second is a copy of the value in that element.

If you look closer at the for range statement on line 30, you'll see the use of the blank identifier again.

Listing 2.20   search/search.go: lines 29–30

```
29      // Launch a goroutine for each feed to find the results.
30      for _, feed := range feeds {
```

This is the second time you see the blank identifier being used. You first saw it in main.go when we imported the matchers package. Now it's being used as a substitution for the variable that would be assigned to the index value for the range call. When you have a function that returns multiple values, and you don't have a need for one, you can use the blank identifier to ignore those values. In our case with this range, we won't be using the index value, so the blank identifier allows us to ignore it.

The first thing we do in the loop is check the map for a Matcher value that can be used to process a feed of the specific feed type.

Listing 2.21   search/search.go: lines 31–35

```
31      // Retrieve a matcher for the search.
32      matcher, exists := matchers[feed.Type]
```

```
33              if !exists {
34                  matcher = matchers["default"]
35              }
```

We haven't talked about how this map gets its values yet. You'll see later on how the program initializes itself and populates this map. On line 32 we check the map for a key that matches the feed type. When looking up a key in a map, you have two options: you can assign a single variable or two variables for the lookup call. The first variable is always the value returned for the key lookup, and the second value, if specified, is a Boolean flag that reports whether the key exists or not. When a key doesn't exist, the map will return the zero value for the type of value being stored in the map. When the key does exist, the map will return a copy of the value for that key.

On line 33 we check whether the key was located in the map, and if it's not, we assign the default matcher to be used. This allows the program to function without causing any issues or interruption for feeds that the program currently doesn't support. Then we launch a goroutine to perform the search.

Listing 2.22   search/search.go: lines 37–41

```
37              // Launch the goroutine to perform the search.
38              go func(matcher Matcher, feed *Feed) {
39                  Match(matcher, feed, searchTerm, results)
40                  waitGroup.Done()              channel where results
41              }(matcher, feed)                  are written
```

In chapter 6 we'll go into more detail about goroutines, but for now a *goroutine* is a function that's launched to run independently from other functions in the program. Use the keyword go to launch and schedule goroutines to run concurrently. On line 38 we use the keyword go to launch an anonymous function as a goroutine. An *anonymous function* is a function that's declared without a name. In our for range loop, we launch an anonymous function as a goroutine for each feed. This allows each feed to be processed independently in a concurrent fashion.

Anonymous functions can take parameters, which we declare for this anonymous function. On line 38 we declare the anonymous function to accept a value of type Matcher and the address of a value of type Feed. This means the variable feed is a *pointer variable*. Pointer variables are great for sharing variables between functions. They allow functions to access and change the state of a variable that was declared within the scope of a different function and possibly a different goroutine.

On line 41 the values of the matcher and feed variables are being passed into the anonymous function. In Go, all variables are passed by value. Since the value of a pointer variable is the address to the memory being pointed to, passing pointer variables between functions is still considered a pass by value.

On lines 39 and 40 you see the work each goroutine is performing.

Listing 2.23   search/search.go: lines 39–40

```
39              Match(matcher, feed, searchTerm, results)
40              waitGroup.Done()    // decrement the WaitGroup counting semaphore
```

The first thing the goroutine does is call a function called `Match`, which can be found in the match.go code file. The `Match` function takes a value of type `Matcher`, a pointer to a value of type `Feed`, the search term, and the channel where the results are written to. We'll look at the internals of this function later, but for now it's enough to know that `Match` will search the feed and output matches to the `results` channel.

Once the function call to `Match` completes, we execute the code on line 40, which is to decrement the `WaitGroup` count. Once every goroutine finishes calling the `Match` function and the `Done` method, the program will know every feed has been processed. There's something else interesting about the method call to `Done`: the `WaitGroup` value was never passed into the anonymous function as a parameter, yet the anonymous function has access to it.

Go supports closures and you're seeing this in action. In fact, the `searchTerm` and `results` variables are also being accessed by the anonymous function via closures. Thanks to closures, the function can access those variables directly without the need to pass them in as parameters. The anonymous function isn't given a copy of these variables; it has direct access to the same variables declared in the scope of the outer function. This is the reason why we don't use closures for the matcher and feed variables.

Listing 2.24   search/search.go: lines 29–32

```
29      // Launch a goroutine for each feed to find the results.
30      for _, feed := range feeds {
31          // Retrieve a matcher for the search.
32          matcher, exists := matchers[feed.Type]
```

The values of the `feed` and `matcher` variables are changing with each iteration of the loop, as you can see on lines 30 and 32. If we used closures for these variables, as the values of these variables changed in the outer function, those changes would be reflected in the anonymous function. All the goroutines would be sharing the same variables as the outer function thanks to closures. Unless we passed these values in as function parameters, most of the goroutines would end up processing the same feed using the same matcher—most likely the last one in the `feeds` slice.

With all the search goroutines working, sending results on the `results` channel and decrementing the `waitGroup` counter, we need a way to display those results and keep the `main` function alive until all the processing is done.

Listing 2.25   search/search.go: lines 44–57

```
44      // Launch a goroutine to monitor when all the work is done.
45      go func() {
46          // Wait for everything to be processed.
```

```
47       waitGroup.Wait()
48
49       // Close the channel to signal to the Display
50       // function that we can exit the program.
51       close(results)
52   }()
53
54   // Start displaying results as they are available and
55   // return after the final result is displayed.
56   Display(results)
57 }
```

The code between lines 45 and 56 is tricky to explain until we dive deeper into some of the other code in the search package. For now let's describe what we see and come back to it later to understand the mechanics. On lines 45 through 52 we launch yet another anonymous function as a goroutine. This anonymous function takes no parameters and uses closures to access both the WaitGroup and results variables. This goroutine calls the method Wait on the WaitGroup value, which is causing the goroutine to block until the count for the WaitGroup hits zero. Once that happens, the goroutine calls the built-in function close on the channel, which as you'll see causes the program to terminate.

The final piece of code in the Run function is on line 56. This is a call to the Display function, which can be found in the match.go code file. Once this function returns, the program terminates. This doesn't happen until all the results in the channel are processed.

2.3.2   *feed.go*

Now that you've seen the Run function, let's look at the code behind the function call to RetrieveFeeds on line 14 of the search.go code file. This function reads the data.json file and returns the slice of data feeds. These feeds drive the content that will be searched by the different matchers. Here are the first eight lines of code that can be found inside the feed.go code file.

Listing 2.26   feed.go: lines 01–08

```
01 package search
02
03 import (
04     "encoding/json"
05     "os"
06 )
07
08 const dataFile = "data/data.json"
```

This code file exists in the search folder, and on line 01 the code file is declared to be in package search. You can see that on lines 03 through 06 we import two packages from the standard library. The json package provides support for encoding and decoding JSON and the os package provides support for accessing operating system functionality like reading files.

You may have noticed that to import the json package, we needed to specify a path that includes the encoding folder. Regardless of the path we specify, the name of the package is json. The physical location of the package from within the standard library doesn't change this fact. As we access functionality from the json package, we'll use just the name json.

On line 08 we declare a constant named dataFile, which is assigned a string that specifies the relative path to the data file on disk. Since the Go compiler can deduce the type from the value on the right side of the assignment operator, specifying the type when declaring the constant is unnecessary. We also use a lowercase letter for the name of the constant, which means this constant is unexported and can only be directly accessed by code within the search package.

Next let's look at a portion of the data.json data file.

Listing 2.27 data.json

```
[                                        // array of json objects
    {
        "site" : "npr",
        "link" : "http://www.npr.org/rss/rss.php?id=1001",
        "type" : "rss"
    },
    {
        "site" : "cnn",
        "link" . "http://rss.cnn.com/rss/cnn_world.rss",
        "type" : "rss"
    },
    {
        "site" : "foxnews",
        "link" : "http://feeds.foxnews.com/foxnews/world?format=xml",
        "type" : "rss"
    },
    {
        "site" : "nbcnews",
        "link" : "http://feeds.nbcnews.com/feeds/topstories",
        "type" : "rss"
    }
]
```

The actual data file contains more than four data feeds, but listing 2.27 shows a valid version of the data file. The data file contains an array of JSON documents. Each document in the data file provides a name of the site we're getting the data from, a link to the data, and the type of data we expect to receive.

These documents need to be decoded into a slice of struct types so we can use this data in our program. Let's look at the struct type that will be used to decode this data file.

Listing 2.28 feed.go: lines 10–15

```
10 // Feed contains information we need to process a feed.
11 type Feed struct {
12     Name string `json:"site"`
```

```
13     URI  string `json:"link"`
14     Type string `json:"type"`
15 }
```

On lines 11 through 15 we declare a struct type named Feed, which is an exported type. This type is declared with three fields, each of which are strings that match the fields for each document in the data file. If you look at each field declaration, tags have been included to provide the metadata that the JSON decoding function needs to create the slice of Feed type values. Each tag maps a field name in the struct type to a field name in the document.

Now we can review the RetrieveFeeds function that we called on line 14 in the search.go code file. This is the function that reads the data file and decodes every document into a slice of Feed type values.

Listing 2.29 feed.go: lines 17–36

```
17 // RetrieveFeeds reads and unmarshals the feed data file.
18 func RetrieveFeeds() ([]*Feed, error) {
19     // Open the file.
20     file, err := os.Open(dataFile)
21     if err != nil {
22         return nil, err
23     }
24
25     // Schedule the file to be closed once
26     // the function returns.
27     defer file.Close()
28
29     // Decode the file into a slice of pointers
30     // to Feed values.
31     var feeds []*Feed
32     err = json.NewDecoder(file).Decode(&feeds)
33
34     // We don't need to check for errors, the caller can do this.
35     return feeds, err
36 }
```

Let's start with the declaration of the function on line 18. The function takes no parameters and returns two values. The first return value is a slice of pointers to Feed type values. The second return value is an error value that reports back if the function call was successful. As you'll continue to see, returning error values is common practice in this code example and throughout the standard library.

Now let's look at lines 20 through 23, where we use the os package to open the data file. The call to the Open method takes the relative path to our data file and returns two values. The first return value is a pointer to a value of type File, and the second return value is an error to check if the call to Open was successful. Immediately on line 21 we check the error value and return the error if we did have a problem opening the file.

If we're successful in opening the file, we then move to line 27. Here you see the use of the keyword `defer`.

Listing 2.30   feed.go: lines 25–27

```
25    // Schedule the file to be closed once
26    // the function returns.
27    defer file.Close()
```

The keyword `defer` is used to schedule a function call to be executed right after a function returns. It's our responsibility to close the file once we're done with it. By using the keyword `defer` to schedule the call to the `close` method, we can guarantee that the method will be called. This will happen even if the function panics and terminates unexpectedly. The keyword `defer` lets us write this statement close to where the opening of the file occurs, which helps with readability and reducing bugs.

Now we can review the final lines of code in the function. Let's look at lines 31 through 35.

Listing 2.31   feed.go: lines 29–36

```
29    // Decode the file into a slice of pointers
30    // to Feed values.
31    var feeds []*Feed
32    err = json.NewDecoder(file).Decode(&feeds)
33
34    // We don't need to check for errors, the caller can do this.
35    return feeds, err
36 }
```

On line 31 we declare a `nil` slice named feeds that contains pointers to `Feed` type values. Then on line 32 we make a call to the `Decode` method off the value returned by the `NewDecoder` function from the `json` package. The `NewDecoder` function takes the file handle we created from the method call to `Open` and returns a pointer to a value of type `Decoder`. From that value we call the `Decode` method, passing the address to the slice. The `Decode` method then decodes the data file and populates our slice with a set of `Feed` type values.

The `Decode` method can accept any type of value thanks to its declaration.

Listing 2.32   Using the empty interface

```
func (dec *Decoder) Decode(v interface{}) error
```

The parameter for the `Decode` method accepts a value of type `interface{}`. This is a special type in Go and works with the reflection support that can be found in the `reflect` package. In chapter 9 we'll go into more detail about reflection and how this method works.

The last line of code on line 35 returns the slice and error values back to the calling function. In this case there's no need for the function to check the error value after the call to Decode. The function is complete and the calling function can check the error value and determine what to do next.

Now it's time to see how the search code supports different types of feed implementations by reviewing the matcher code.

2.3.3 *match.go/default.go*

The match.go code file contains the support for creating different types of matchers that can be used by the search Run function. Let's go back and look at the code from the Run function that executes the search using the different types of matchers.

Listing 2.33   search/search.go : lines 29 - 42

```
29      // Launch a goroutine for each feed to find the results.
30      for _, feed := range feeds {
31          // Retrieve a matcher for the search.
32          matcher, exists := matchers[feed.Type]
33          if !exists {
34              matcher = matchers["default"]
35          }
36
37          // Launch the goroutine to perform the search.
38          go func(matcher Matcher, feed *Feed) {
39              Match(matcher, feed, searchTerm, results)
40              waitGroup.Done()
41          }(matcher, feed)
42      }
```

The code on line 32 looks up a matcher value based on the feed type; that value is then used to process a search against that specific feed. Then on line 38 through 41, a goroutine is launched for that matcher and feed value. The key to making this code work is the ability of this framework code to use an interface type to capture and call into the specific implementation for each matcher value. This allows the code to handle different types of matcher values in a consistent and generic way. Let's look at the code in match.go and see how we're able to implement this functionality.

Here are the first 17 lines of code for match.go.

Listing 2.34   search/match.go: lines 01–17

```
01 package search
02
03 import (
04     "log"
05 )
06
07 // Result contains the result of a search.
08 type Result struct {
09     Field   string
10     Content string
11 }
12
```

```
13 // Matcher defines the behavior required by types that want
14 // to implement a new search type.
15 type Matcher interface {
16     Search(feed *Feed, searchTerm string) ([]*Result, error)
17 }
```

Let's jump to lines 15 through 17 and look at the declaration of the interface type named Matcher. Up until now we've only been declaring struct types, but here you see code that's declaring an interface type. We'll get into a lot more detail about interfaces in chapter 5, but for now know that interfaces declare behavior that's required to be implemented by struct or named types to satisfy the interface. The behavior of an interface is defined by the methods that are declared within the interface type.

In the case of the Matcher interface, there's only one method declared, Search, which takes a pointer to a value of type Feed and a search term of type string. The method also returns two values: a slice of pointers to values of type Result and an error value. The Result type is declared on lines 08 through 11.

You follow a naming convention in Go when naming interfaces. If the interface type contains only one method, the name of the interface ends with the *er* suffix. This is the exact case for our interface, so the name of the interface is Matcher. When multiple methods are declared within an interface type, the name of the interface should relate to its general behavior.

For a user-defined type to implement an interface, the type in question needs to implement all the methods that are declared within that interface type. Let's switch to the default.go code file and see how the default matcher implements the Matcher interface.

Listing 2.35   search/default.go: lines 01–15

```
01 package search
02
03 // defaultMatcher implements the default matcher.
04 type defaultMatcher struct{}
05
06 // init registers the default matcher with the program.
07 func init() {
08     var matcher defaultMatcher
09     Register("default", matcher)
10 }
11
12 // Search implements the behavior for the default matcher.
13 func (m defaultMatcher) Search(feed *Feed, searchTerm string)
                                           ([]*Result, error) {
14     return nil, nil
15 }
```

On line 04 we declare a struct type named defaultMatcher using an empty struct. An empty struct allocates zero bytes when values of this type are created. They're great when you need a type but not any state. For the default matcher, we don't need to maintain any state; we only need to implement the interface.

On lines 13 through 15 you see the implementation of the `Matcher` interface by the `defaultMatcher` type. The implementation of the interface method `Search` just returns `nil` for both return values. Other implementations, such as the implementation for the RSS matcher, will implement the specific business rules for processing searches in their version of this method.

The declaration of the `Search` method is declared with a value receiver of type `defaultMatcher`.

Listing 2.36   search/default.go: line 13

```
13 func (m defaultMatcher) Search
```

The use of a receiver with any function declaration declares a method that's bound to the specified receiver type. In our case, the declaration of the `Search` method is now bound to values of type `defaultMatcher`. This means we can call the method `Search` from values and pointers of type `defaultMatcher`. Whether we use a value or pointer of the receiver type to make the method call, the compiler will reference or dereference the value if necessary to support the call.

Listing 2.37   Example of method calls

```
// Method declared with a value receiver of type defaultMatcher
func (m defaultMatcher) Search(feed *Feed, searchTerm string)

// Declare a pointer of type defaultMatch
dm := new(defaultMatch)

// The compiler will dereference the dm pointer to make the call
dm.Search(feed, "test")

// Method declared with a pointer receiver of type defaultMatcher
func (m *defaultMatcher) Search(feed *Feed, searchTerm string)

// Declare a value of type defaultMatch
var dm defaultMatch

// The compiler will reference the dm value to make the call
dm.Search(feed, "test")
```

It's best practice to declare methods using pointer receivers, since many of the methods you implement need to manipulate the state of the value being used to make the method call. In the case of the `defaultMatcher` type, we want to use a value receiver because creating values of type `defaultMatcher` result in values of zero allocation. Using a pointer makes no sense since there's no state to be manipulated.

Unlike when you call methods directly from values and pointers, when you call a method via an interface type value, the rules are different. Methods declared with pointer receivers can only be called by interface type values that contain pointers. Methods declared with value receivers can be called by interface type values that contain both values and pointers.

Listing 2.38 Example of interface method call restrictions

```
// Method declared with a pointer receiver of type defaultMatcher
func (m *defaultMatcher) Search(feed *Feed, searchTerm string)

// Call the method via an interface type value
var dm defaultMatcher
var matcher Matcher = dm       // Assign value to interface type
matcher.Search(feed, "test") // Call interface method with value

> go build
cannot use dm (type defaultMatcher) as type Matcher in assignment

// Method declared with a value receiver of type defaultMatcher
func (m defaultMatcher) Search(feed *Feed, searchTerm string)

// Call the method via an interface type value
var dm defaultMatcher
var matcher Matcher = &dm       // Assign pointer to interface type
matcher.Search(feed, "test") // Call interface method with pointer

> go build
Build Successful
```

There's nothing else that the defaultMatcher type needs to do to implement the interface. From this point forward, values and pointers of type defaultMatcher satisfy the interface and can be used as values of type Matcher. That's the key to making this work. Values and pointers of type defaultMatcher are now also values of type Matcher and can be assigned or passed to functions accepting values of type Matcher.

Let's look at the implementation of the Match function declared in the match go code file. This is the function called by the Run function on line 39 in the search.go code file.

Listing 2.39 search/match.go: lines 19–33

```
19 // Match is launched as a goroutine for each individual feed to run
20 // searches concurrently.
21 func Match(matcher Matcher, feed *Feed, searchTerm string,
                                   results chan<- *Result) {
22     // Perform the search against the specified matcher.
23     searchResults, err := matcher.Search(feed, searchTerm)
24     if err != nil {
25         log.Println(err)
26         return
27     }
28
29     // Write the results to the channel.
30     for _, result := range searchResults {
31         results <- result
32     }
33 }
```

This is the function that performs the actual search using values or pointers that implement the Matcher interface. This function accepts values of type Matcher as the first parameter. Only values or pointers that implement the `Matcher` interface will be accepted for this parameter. Since the `defaultMatcher` type now implements the interface declared with a value receiver, values or pointers of type `defaultMatcher` can be passed into this function.

On line 23, the `Search` method is called from the `Matcher` type value that was passed into the function. Here the specific implementation of the `Search` method for the value assigned to the `Matcher` variable is executed. Once the `Search` method returns, the error value on line 24 is checked for an error. If there's an error, the function writes the error to the log and returns. If the search doesn't return an error and there are results, the results are written to the channel so that they can be picked up by the main function that's listening on that channel.

The final piece of code in match.go is the `Display` function that's called by the `main` function on line 56. This is the function preventing the program from terminating until all the results from the search goroutines are received and logged.

> **Listing 2.40   search/match.go: lines 35–43**

```
35 // Display writes results to the terminal window as they
36 // are received by the individual goroutines.
37 func Display(results chan *Result) {
38     // The channel blocks until a result is written to the channel.
39     // Once the channel is closed the for loop terminates.
40     for result := range results {
41         fmt.Printf("%s:\n%s\n\n", result.Field, result.Content)
42     }
43 }
```

A bit of channel magic allows this function to process all of the results before returning. It's based on how channels and the keyword `range` behaves when a channel is closed. Let's briefly look at the code in the `Run` function again that closes the `results` channel and calls the `Display` function.

> **Listing 2.41   search/search.go: lines 44–57**

```
44     // Launch a goroutine to monitor when all the work is done.
45     go func() {
46         // Wait for everything to be processed.
47         waitGroup.Wait()
48
49         // Close the channel to signal to the Display
50         // function that we can exit the program.
51         close(results)
52     }()
53
54     // Start displaying results as they are available and
55     // return after the final result is displayed.
56     Display(results)
57 }
```

The goroutine on lines 45 through 52 waits on the waitGroup for all the search gorou- @ 3 o
tines to call the Done method. Once the last search goroutine calls Done, the Wait
method returns, and then the code on line 51 closes the results channel. Once the
channel is closed, the goroutine terminates and is no more.

You saw on lines 30 through 32 in the match.go code file where the search results
were being written to the channel.

Listing 2.42   search/match.go: lines 29–32

```
29      // Write the results to the channel.
30      for _, result := range searchResults {
31          results <- result
32      }
```

If we look back at the for range loop on lines 40 through 42 of the match.go code file,
we can connect the writing of the results, the closing of the channel, and the processing of results all together.

Listing 2.43   search/match.go: lines 38–42

```
38      // The channel blocks until a result is written to the channel.
39      // Once the channel is closed the for loop terminates.
40      for result := range results {
41          log.Printf("%s:\n%s\n\n", result.Field, result.Content)
42      }
```

The for range loop on line 40 of the match.go code file will block until a result is writ- @
ten to the channel. As each search goroutine writes its results to the channel (as you
see on line 31 of the code file match.go), the for range loop wakes up and is given
those results. The results are then immediately written to the log. It seems this for
range loop is stuck in an endless loop, but it isn't. Once the channel is closed on D 3o
line 51 of the search.go code file, the for range loop is terminated and the Display
function returns.

Before we look at the implementation of the RSS matcher, let's review how the different matchers are initialized when the program starts. To see this we need to look
back at lines 07 through 10 of the default.go code file.

Listing 2.44   search/default.go: lines 06–10

```
06 // init registers the default matcher with the program.
07 func init() {
08     var matcher defaultMatcher
09     Register("default", matcher)
10 }
```

The default.go code file has a special function declared called init. You saw this
function also declared in the main.go code file, and we talked about how all the init

functions in the program would be called before the main function begins. Let's look at the imports again from the main.go code file.

> **Listing 2.45   main.go: lines 07–08**

```
07   _ "github.com/goinaction/code/chapter2/sample/matchers"
08     "github.com/goinaction/code/chapter2/sample/search"
```

The import to the search package on line 08 allows the compiler to find the init function in the default.go code file. Once the compiler sees the init function, it's scheduled to be called prior to the main function being called.

The init function in the default.go code file is performing a special task. It's creating a value of the defaultMatcher type and passing that value to the Register function that can be found in the search.go code file.

> **Listing 2.46   search/search.go: lines 59–67**

```
59 // Register is called to register a matcher for use by the program.
60 func Register(feedType string, matcher Matcher) {
61     if _, exists := matchers[feedType]; exists {
62         log.Fatalln(feedType, "Matcher already registered")
63     }
64
65     log.Println("Register", feedType, "matcher")
66     matchers[feedType] = matcher
67 }
```

This function is responsible for adding the Matcher value to the map of registered matchers. All of this registration needs to happen before the main function gets called. Using init functions is a great way to accomplish this type of initialized registration.

2.4   *RSS matcher*

The last piece of code to review is the implementation of the RSS matcher. Everything we've reviewed up to now was to allow the implementation of different matcher types to run and search content within the program's framework. The structure of the RSS matcher is similar to the structure of the default matcher. It's the implementation of the interface method Search that's different and in the end gives each matcher its uniqueness.

The RSS document in listing 2.47 shows you a sample of what we expect to receive when we use any link in the data feed that's typed as an RSS feed.

> **Listing 2.47   Expected RSS feed document**

```
<rss xmlns:npr="http://www.npr.org/rss/" xmlns:nprml="http://api
    <channel>
        <title>News</title>
        <link>...</link>
        <description>...</description>
```

```
<language>en</language>
<copyright>Copyright 2014 NPR - For Personal Use
<image>...</image>
<item>
    <title>
        Putin Says He'll Respect Ukraine Vote But U.S.
    </title>
    <description>
        The White House and State Department have called on the
    </description>
```

If you take any link from listing 2.47 and put it in a browser, you'll be able to see a complete view of the expected RSS document. The implementation of the RSS matcher pulls down these RSS documents, searches the title and description fields for the search term, and sends the results over the results channel. Let's start by looking at the first 12 lines of code for the rss.go code file.

Listing 2.48 matchers/rss.go: lines 01–12

```
01 package matchers
02
03 import (
04     "encoding/xml"
05     "errors"
06     "fmt"
07     "log"
08     "net/http"
09     "regexp"
10
11     "github.com/goinaction/code/chapter2/sample/search"
12 )
```

As with every code file, we start on line 01 with the name of the package. This code file can be found in a folder called matchers, so the package name is matchers. Next we have six imports from the standard library and one import to the search package. Again, we have some packages from the standard library being imported from subfolders within the standard library, such as xml and http. Just like with the json package, the name of the last folder in the path represents the name of the package.

There are four struct types that are used to decode the RSS document, so we can use the document data in our program.

Listing 2.49 matchers/rss.go: lines 14–58

```
14 type (
15     // item defines the fields associated with the item tag
16     // in the rss document.
17     item struct {
18         XMLName     xml.Name `xml:"item"`
19         PubDate     string   `xml:"pubDate"`
20         Title       string   `xml:"title"`
21         Description string   `xml:"description"`
```

```
22            Link          string    `xml:"link"`
23            GUID          string    `xml:"guid"`
24            GeoRssPoint string      `xml:"georss:point"`
25        }
26
27        // image defines the fields associated with the image tag
28        // in the rss document.
29        image struct {
30            XMLName xml.Name  `xml:"image"`
31            URL       string    `xml:"url"`
32            Title     string    `xml:"title"`
33            Link      string    `xml:"link"`
34        }
35
36        // channel defines the fields associated with the channel tag
37        // in the rss document.
38        channel struct {
39            XMLName          xml.Name  `xml:"channel"`
40            Title            string    `xml:"title"`
41            Description      string    `xml:"description"`
42            Link             string    `xml:"link"`
43            PubDate          string    `xml:"pubDate"`
44            LastBuildDate    string    `xml:"lastBuildDate"`
45            TTL              string    `xml:"ttl"`
46            Language         string    `xml:"language"`
47            ManagingEditor   string    `xml:"managingEditor"`
48            WebMaster        string    `xml:"webMaster"`
49            Image            image     `xml:"image"`
50            Item             []item    `xml:"item"`
51        }
52
53        // rssDocument defines the fields associated with the rss document
54        rssDocument struct {
55            XMLName xml.Name  `xml:"rss"`
56            Channel channel   `xml:"channel"`
57        }
58 )
```

If you match these structures to the RSS document from any of the feed links, you'll see how everything correlates. Decoding XML is identical to how we decoded JSON in the feed.go code file. Next we can look at the declaration of the rssMatcher type.

Listing 2.50   matchers/rss.go: lines 60–61

```
60 // rssMatcher implements the Matcher interface.
61 type rssMatcher struct{}
```

Again, this looks just like how we declared the defaultMatcher type. We use an empty struct since we don't need to maintain any state; we just implement the Matcher interface. Next we have the implementation of the matcher init function.

Listing 2.51   matchers/rss.go: lines 63–67

```
63 // init registers the matcher with the program.
64 func init() {
65     var matcher rssMatcher
66     search.Register("rss", matcher)
67 }
```

Just like you saw with the default matcher, the init function registers a value of the rssMatcher type with the program for use. Let's look at the import in the main.go code file once more.

Listing 2.52   main.go: lines 07–08

```
07   _ "github.com/goinaction/code/chapter2/sample/matchers"
08     "github.com/goinaction/code/chapter2/sample/search"
```

The code in the main.go code file doesn't directly use any identifiers from the matchers package. Yet we need the compiler to schedule the call to the init function in the rss.go code file. On line 07 we accomplish this by using the blank identifier as the alias name for the import. This allows the compiler to not produce an error for declaring the import and to locate the init function. With all of the imports, types, and initialization set, let's look at the two remaining methods that support the implementation of the Matcher interface.

Listing 2.53   matchers/rss.go: lines 114–140

```
114 // retrieve performs a HTTP Get request for the rss feed and decodes
115 func (m rssMatcher) retrieve(feed *search.Feed)
                                              (*rssDocument, error) {
116     if feed.URI == "" {
117         return nil, errors.New("No rss feed URI provided")
118     }
119
120     // Retrieve the rss feed document from the web.
121     resp, err := http.Get(feed.URI)
122     if err != nil {
123         return nil, err
124     }
125
126     // Close the response once we return from the function.
127     defer resp.Body.Close()
128
129     // Check the status code for a 200 so we know we have received a
130     // proper response.
131     if resp.StatusCode != 200 {
132         return nil, fmt.Errorf("HTTP Response Error %d\n",
                                              resp.StatusCode)
133     }
134
135     // Decode the rss feed document into our struct type.
```

```
136     // We don't need to check for errors, the caller can do this.
137     var document rssDocument
138     err = xml.NewDecoder(resp.Body).Decode(&document)
139     return &document, err
140 }
```

The unexported method `retrieve` performs the logic for pulling the RSS document from the web for each individual feed link. On line 121 you can see the use of the `Get` method from the `http` package. In chapter 8 we'll explore this package more, but for now Go makes it really easy to make web requests using the `http` package. When the `Get` method returns, we'll get back a pointer to a value of type `Response`. After checking for errors, we need to schedule the call to the `Close` method, which we do on line 127.

On line 131 we check the `StatusCode` field of the `Response` value to verify we received a 200. Anything other than 200 must be handled as an error and we do just that. If the value isn't 200, we then return a custom error using the `Errorf` function from the `fmt` package. The last three lines of code are similar to how we decoded the JSON data file. This time we use the `xml` package and call the same function named `NewDecoder`, which returns a pointer to a `Decoder` value. With the pointer, we call the `Decode` method passing the address of the local variable named `document` of type `rssDocument`. Then the address to the `rssDocument` type value and the error from the `Decode` method call are returned.

The final method to look at implements the `Matcher` interface.

Listing 2.54 matchers/rss.go: lines 69–112

```
69 // Search looks at the document for the specified search term.
70 func (m rssMatcher) Search(feed *search.Feed, searchTerm string)
                                             ([]*search.Result, error) {
71     var results []*search.Result
72
73     log.Printf("Search Feed Type[%s] Site[%s] For Uri[%s]\n",
                                  feed.Type, feed.Name, feed.URI)
74
75     // Retrieve the data to search.
76     document, err := m.retrieve(feed)
77     if err != nil {
78         return nil, err
79     }
80
81     for _, channelItem := range document.Channel.Item {
82         // Check the title for the search term.
83         matched, err := regexp.MatchString(searchTerm,
                                             channelItem.Title)
84         if err != nil {
85             return nil, err
86         }
87
88         // If we found a match save the result.
89         if matched {
90             results = append(results, &search.Result{
91                 Field:   "Title",
92                 Content: channelItem.Title,
```

```
 93                })
 94            }
 95
 96            // Check the description for the search term.
 97            matched, err = regexp.MatchString(searchTerm,
                                                  channelItem.Description)
 98            if err != nil {
 99                return nil, err
100            }
101
102            // If we found a match save the result.
103            if matched {
104                results = append(results, &search.Result{
105                    Field:   "Description",
106                    Content: channelItem.Description,
107                })
108            }
109        }
110
111     return results, nil
112 }
```

We start on line 71 with the declaration of the `results` variable, which will be used to store and return any results that may be found.

Listing 2.55 matchers/rss.go: line 71

```
71     var results []*search.Result
```

We use the keyword `var` and declare a nil slice of pointers to `Result` type values. The declaration of the `Result` type can be found again on line 08 of the match.go code file. Next on line 76 we make a web call using the `retrieve` method we just reviewed.

Listing 2.56 matchers/rss.go: lines 75–79

```
75     // Retrieve the data to search.
76     document, err := m.retrieve(feed)
77     if err != nil {
78         return nil, err
79     }
```

The call to the `retrieve` method returns a pointer to a value of type `rssDocument` and an error value. Then, as you've seen throughout the code, we check the error value for errors and return if there was an error. If no error exists, we then iterate through the results performing the match of the search term against the title and description of the retrieved RSS document.

Listing 2.57 matchers/rss.go: lines 81–86

```
81     for _, channelItem := range document.Channel.Item {
82         // Check the title for the search term.
83         matched, err := regexp.MatchString(searchTerm,
                                                channelItem.Title)
```

```
84              if err != nil {
85                  return nil, err
86              }
```

Since the value of `document.Channel.Item` is a slice of `item` type values, we use a `for`
range loop on line 81 to iterate through all the items. On line 83 we use the `Match-
String` function from the `regexp` package to match the search term against the con-
tent in the `Title` field of the `channelItem` value. Then we check for errors on line 84.
If there are no errors, we move to lines 89 through 94 to check the results of the match.

Listing 2.58   matchers/rss.go: lines 88–94

```
88              // If we found a match save the result.
89              if matched {
90                  results = append(results, &search.Result{
91                      Field:    "Title",
92                      Content: channelItem.Title,
93                  })
94              }
```

If the value of `matched` is `true` after the call to the `MatchString` method, we use the
built-in function `append` to add the search results to the `results` slice. The built-in
function `append` will grow the length and capacity of the slice as it needs to. You'll
learn more about the built-in function `append` in chapter 4. The first parameter to
`append` is the value of the slice you want to append to, and the second parameter is the
value you want to append. In our case, we use a struct literal to declare and initialize a
value of type `Result`, and then we use the ampersand (`&`) operator to get the address
of this new value, which is stored in the slice.

After the title is checked for matches, lines 97 through 108 perform the same logic
again for the description field. Finally, on line 111, the method returns the results to
the calling function.

2.5   Summary

- Every code file belongs to a package, and that package name should be the
  same as the folder the code file exists in.
- Go provides several ways to declare and initialize variables. If the value of a
  variable isn't explicitly initialized, the compiler will initialize the variable to its
  zero value.
- Pointers are a way of sharing data across functions and goroutines.
- Concurrency and synchronization are accomplished by launching goroutines
  and using channels.
- Go provides built-in functions to support using Go's internal data structures.
- The standard library contains many packages that will let you do some powerful
  things.
- Interfaces in Go allow you to write generic code and frameworks.

Packaging and tooling

In this chapter

- Understanding how Go code is organized
- Using the Go command
- Going farther with other Go developer tools
- Collaborating with other Go developers

In chapter 2 you got an overview of the syntax and language structure of Go. Now you'll dive deeper into how code is organized into packages and how you interact with those packages. Packages are a critical concept in Go. The idea is to separate semantic units of functionality into different packages. When you do this, you enable code reuse and control the use of the data inside each package.

Before we get into the particulars, you should already be familiar with the command prompt or system shell, and you should have Go installed according to the guidelines in the preface of this book. If you're ready, let's start by understanding what a package is and why it's important in the Go ecosystem.

3.1   Packages

All Go programs are organized into groups of files called *packages*, so that code has the ability to be included into other projects as smaller reusable pieces. Let's look at the packages that make up Go's http functionality in the standard library:

```
net/http/
    cgi/
    cookiejar/
        testdata/
    fcgi/
    httptest/
    httputil/
    pprof/
    testdata/
```

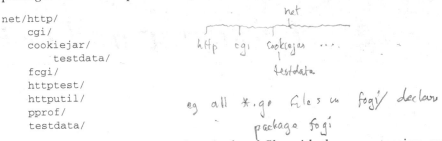

These directories contain a series of related files with the .go extension, and provide clear separation of smaller units of code relating to the implementation of HTTP servers, clients, and utilities to test and profile them. For example, the cookiejar package contains code related to storing and retrieving cookies from a web session. Each package can be imported and used individually so that developers can import only the specific functionality that they need. If you're implementing an HTTP client, you only need to import the http package.

All .go files must declare the package that they belong to as the first line of the file excluding whitespace and comments. Packages are contained in a single directory. You may not have multiple packages in the same directory, nor may you split a package across multiple directories. This means that all .go files in a single directory must declare the same package name.

3.1.1   Package-naming conventions

The convention for naming your package is to use the name of the directory containing it. This has the benefit of making it clear what the package name is when you import it. If we continue with our example from the net/http package, all the files contained within the http directory are a part of the http package. When naming your packages and their directories, you should use short, concise, lowercase names, because they will be typed often while you're developing. The packages under net/http are great examples of concise names such as cgi, httputil, and pprof.

Keep in mind that a unique name is not required, because you import the package using its full path. Your package name is used as the default name when your package is imported, but it can be overridden. This is beneficial when you need to import multiple packages with the same name. We'll discuss how this is done in section 3.2.

3.1.2   Package main

The package name main has special meaning in Go. It designates to the Go command that this package is intended to be compiled into a binary executable. All of the executable programs you build in Go must have a package called main.

1   except for package "main"

When the main package is encountered by the compiler, it must also find a function called main(); otherwise a binary executable won't be created. The main() function is the entry point for the program, so without one, the program has no starting point. The name of the final binary will take the name of the directory the main package is declared in.

COMMANDS AND PACKAGES The Go documentation uses the term *command* frequently to refer to an executable program—like a command-line application. This can be confusing for new Go developers who are reading the documentation. Remember that in Go, a command is any executable program, in contrast to a package, which generally means an importable semantic unit of functionality.

Go ahead and try it out. First start by creating a file called hello.go inside GOPATH/ src/hello/, and type the contents of listing 3.1 into it. This is the traditional Hello World! application again, but as you look at it, pay attention to the package declaration and import statements.

Listing 3.1 Traditional Hello World! application

```
01 package main
02
03 import "fmt"        ◄──────  The fmt package provides methods
04                              for performing formatted printing.
05 func main(){
06     fmt.Println("Hello World!")
07 }
```

GETTING PACKAGE DOCUMENTATION Don't forget that you can get more details on a package by visiting http://golang.org/pkg/fmt/ or running godoc fmt from your terminal.

Once you've saved the file, you can run the command go build from within the GOPATH/src/hello/ directory. When it completes, you should see a binary file. On Unix, Linux, and Mac OS X this file will be named hello, whereas on Windows it will be called hello.exe. You can now run this application and see Hello World! printed to your console.

Had you named the package something other than main, like hello for instance,[1] you'd have been telling the compiler this is just a package, not a command.

Listing 3.2 Invalid Go program with main function

```
01 package hello
02
03 import "fmt"
04
05 func main(){
06     fmt.Println("Hello, World!")
07 }
```

3.2   *Imports*

Now that we've looked at the organization of code into packages, we'll take a look at how to import these individual packages so that you can access the code contained within them. The `import` statement tells the compiler where to look on disk to find the package you want to import. You import packages by using the keyword `import`, which tells the compiler that you want to reference the code contained within the package at that file location. If you need to import more than one package, the idiomatic way of doing so is to wrap the import statements in an import block, as demonstrated here.

Listing 3.3   Import statement blocks

```
import (
    "fmt"
    "strings"
)
```

The strings package provides many methods for searching, replacing, and transforming strings. You can get more details at http://golang.org/pkg/strings/ or by running "godoc strings" from your terminal.

Packages are found on disk based on their relative path to the directories referenced by the Go environment. Packages in the standard library are found under where Go is installed on your computer. Packages that are created by you or other Go developers live inside the GOPATH, which is your own personal workspace for packages.

Let's take a look at an example. If Go was installed under /usr/local/go and your GOPATH was set to /home/myproject:/home/mylibraries, the compiler would look for the net/http package in the following order:

```
/usr/local/go/src/pkg/net/http
/home/myproject/src/net/http
/home/mylibraries/src/net/http
```

This is where the standard library source code is contained.

The compiler will stop searching once it finds a package that satisfies the import statement. The important thing to remember is that the Go installation directory is the first place the compiler looks and then each directory listed in your GOPATH in the order that they're listed.

If the compiler searches your GOPATH and never finds the package that you've referenced, you'll get an error when you try to run or build your program. You'll see how to use the go get command to fix those problems later in this chapter.

3.2.1   *Remote imports*

There's a huge trend toward sharing code via distributed version control systems (DVCS) such as sharing sites like GitHub, Launchpad, and Bitbucket. The Go tooling has built-in support for fetching source code from these sites and others. The import path can be used by the Go tooling to determine where the code you need fetched is on the network.

For example:

```
import "github.com/spf13/viper"
```

[handwritten: // go build : finds import in GOPATH dir]
[handwritten: fetches code from github]
[handwritten: places it in dirl/src/github.com/...]

When you try to build a program with this import path, the go build command will search the GOPATH for this package location on disk. The fact that it represents a URL to a repository on GitHub is irrelevant as far as the go build command is concerned. When an import path contains a URL, the Go tooling can be used to fetch the package from the DVCS and place the code inside the GOPATH at the location that matches the URL. This fetching is done using the go get command. go get will fetch any specified URL or can be used to fetch the dependencies a package is importing that are go-gettable. Since go get is recursive, it can walk down the source tree for a package and fetch all the dependencies it finds.

[handwritten: go get]

3.2.2   *Named imports*

What happens when you need to import multiple packages with the same name? For example, you could need a network/convert package for converting data that's read from a network and a file/convert package for converting data read from text files. When this is the case, both of these packages can be imported by using *named imports*. This is performed by giving one of the packages a new name to the left of the import statement.

[handwritten: (a)]

As an example, let's say you were already using the fmt package that comes as part of the standard library. Now you need to import a package named fmt that you had created as part of your own project. You can import your own fmt package by renaming the import, as demonstrated in the next listing.

[handwritten: (2)]

Listing 3.4   Renaming imports

```
01 package main
02
03 import (
04     "fmt"
05     myfmt "mylib/fmt"
06 )
07
08 func main() {
09     fmt.Println("Standard Library")
10     myfmt.Println("mylib/fmt")
11 }
```

[handwritten: (a) // named import]
[handwritten: p45   for use of]
[handwritten: " " for an "anonymous" import]
[handwritten: to register a DB driver]

The Go compiler will fail the build and output an error whenever you import a package that you don't use. The Go team considers this a feature to eliminate code bloat from packages that are imported but not used. Although this feature is occasionally annoying, the Go team has put a great deal of effort into making decisions to prevent some of the problems that you encounter in other languages. You don't want to have an unnecessarily large binary, filled with unused libraries, and they feel that if it's worth the compiler telling you about, it's worth failing the build. Anyone who has

[handwritten: ʃ]

compiled a large C program knows just how hard it can be to pinpoint the things that matter in a sea of compiler warnings.

Sometimes you may need to import a package that you don't need to reference identifiers from. You'll see why this might be useful in the next section. When this is the case, you can use the blank identifier _ to rename an import.

> **BLANK IDENTIFIER**   The _ (underscore character) is known as the *blank identifier* and has many uses within Go. It's used when you want to throw away the assignment of a value, including the assignment of an import to its package name, or ignore return values from a function when you're only interested in the others.

3.3   init

Each package has the ability to provide as many init functions as necessary to be invoked at the beginning of execution time. All the init functions that are discovered by the compiler are scheduled to be executed prior to the main function being executed. The init functions are great for setting up packages, initializing variables, or performing any other bootstrapping you may need prior to the program running.

An example of this is database drivers. They register themselves with the sql package when their init function is executed at startup because the sql package can't know about the drivers that exist when it's compiled. Let's look at an example of what an init function might do.

Listing 3.5   init function usage

```
01 package postgres
02
03 import (
04     "database/sql"
05 )
06
07 func init() {
08     sql.Register("postgres", new(PostgresDriver))
09 }
```

Creates new instance of the postgres driver. We've intentionally left out its definition to focus on init().

This code lives inside your pretend database driver for the PostgreSQL database. When a program imports this package, the init function will be called, causing the database driver to be registered with Go's sql package as an available driver.

In the program that we write using this new database driver, we'll use the blank identifier to import the package so the new driver is included with the sql package. As stated earlier, you can't import a package that you aren't using, so renaming the import with the blank identifier allows the init function to be discovered and scheduled to run without the compiler issuing an error about unused imports.

Now we can tell the sql.Open method to use this driver.

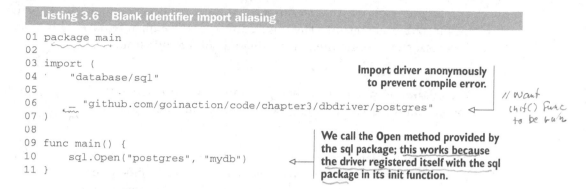

Listing 3.6   Blank identifier import aliasing

```
01 package main
02
03 import (
04     "database/sql"
05
06     _ "github.com/goinaction/code/chapter3/dbdriver/postgres"
07 )
08
09 func main() {
10     sql.Open("postgres", "mydb")
11 }
```

Import driver anonymously to prevent compile error.

// want (init() func to be run

We call the Open method provided by the sql package; this works because the driver registered itself with the sql package in its init function.

3.4   Using Go tools

We've been working with the go tool for a few chapters now, but we haven't explored all it can do. Let's dive a little deeper into this diminutively named powerhouse and explore more of its capabilities. From a shell prompt, type the go command with no arguments:

```
$ go        // See go commands
```

As you can see in figure 3.1, there are a lot of features buried in the go tooling.

```
The commands are:

        build       compile packages and dependencies        41,46
        clean       remove object files                      45
        doc         show documentation for package or symbol 48,49   42
        env         print Go environment information
        fix         run go tool fix on packages
        fmt         run gofmt on package sources             48
        generate    generate Go files by processing source
        get         download and install packages and dependencies  43  51
        install     compile and install packages and dependencies
        list        list packages
        run         compile and run Go program               47
        test        test packages
        tool        run specified go tool
        version     print Go version
        vet         run go tool vet on packages              47

Use "go help [command]" for more information about a command.

Additional help topics:

        c           calling between Go and C
        buildmode   description of build modes
        filetype    file types
        gopath      GOPATH environment variable
        importpath  import path syntax
        packages    description of package lists
        testflag    description of testing flags
        testfunc    description of testing functions

Use "go help [topic]" for more information about that topic.
```

Figure 3.1   Output of go command help text

cd .../dir   // dir contains file.go containing {package main, func main
Then can
go build
go run file.go
go install   // Requires that GOBIN is in env

Looking through the list, you can see that there really is a compiler in there; it's used by the `build` command. The `build` and `clean` commands do exactly what you'd expect them to do. Try them now using the source code from listing 3.2:

```
go build hello.go
```

You might not want that file hanging around when it's time to check your code into source control. To get rid of it, use the `clean` command:

```
go clean hello.go
```

After calling `clean`, the executable program is gone. Let's take a closer look at some of the features of the go tool, and ways that you can save time when you're using it. For the next examples, we'll use the sample code in the following listing.

Listing 3.7 Working with the `io` package

```
01 package main
02
03 import (
04     "fmt"
05     "io/ioutil"
06     "os"
07
08     "github.com/goinaction/code/chapter3/words"
09 )
10
11 // main is the entry point for the application.
12 func main() {
13     filename := os.Args[1]
14
15     contents, err := ioutil.ReadFile(filename)
16     if err != nil {
17         fmt.Println(err)
18         return
19     }
20
21     text := string(contents)
22
23     count := words.CountWords(text)
24     fmt.Printf("There are %d words in your text. \n", count)
25 }
```

If you've downloaded the source code for the book, this package should be at GOPATH/src/github.com/goinaction/code/chapter3/words. Make sure you have it there to follow along.

Most of the commands that are part of the Go tooling take a package specifier as an argument. Look closer at the commands we've just used, and you'll see one of the shortcuts built into the tooling. You can omit the filename of the source code file that you want to build, and the go tool will default to *the current package*.

```
go build
```

Building a package is a common practice, and the package can also be specified directly:

```
go build github.com/goinaction/code/chapter3/wordcount
```

You can also specify wildcards in your package specifiers. Three periods in your package specifier indicate a pattern matching any string. For example, the following command will build every package under the chapter3 directory:

```
go build github.com/goinaction/code/chapter3/...
```

Instead of a package specifier, you can also use a path shortcut as an argument to most of the Go commands. For example, you could achieve the same effect with these two commands:

```
go build wordcount.go

go build .
```

To execute this program, you need to run the wordcount or wordcount.exe program that was created after the build. But there's a different command that can perform both operations in a single call:

```
go run wordcount.go                // build and execute                     go run
```

The go run command both builds and executes the program contained in wordcount .go, which saves a lot on typing.

You'll use the go build and go run commands the most when you're developing. Let's take a look at a few of the other available commands and see what they can do.

3.5 Going farther with Go developer tools

You've seen how to compile and run your Go programs using the convenient go tool. But that handy little developer tool has a lot of other tricks hidden inside.

3.5.1 go vet

It won't write code for you, but once you've written some code, the vet command will   go vet
check your code for common errors. Let's look at the types of errors vet can catch:

- Bad parameters in Printf-style function calls
- Method signature errors for common method definitions
- Bad struct tags
- Unkeyed composite literals

Let's look at a mistake many new Go developers make. The fmt.Printf function is a great way to produce formatted output, but the function requires you to remember all the different format specifiers. The following listing is an example.

Listing 3.8 Working with go vet

```
01 package main
02
03 import "fmt"
04
05 func main() {
06     fmt.Printf("The quick brown fox jumped over lazy dogs", 3.14)
07 }
```

This program inserts the floating-point number 3.14, but there's no placeholder in the formatted string. If you run go vet against this source code, you get the following message:

```
go vet main.go
main.go:6: no formatting directive in Printf call
```

The go vet tool won't keep you from making huge errors in logic, or from creating buggy code. However, as you can see from the last example, it does catch some common errors quite nicely. It's a great idea to get in the habit of running go vet on your code base before you commit it to a source repository.

3.5.2 Go format

go fmt ⟨srcfile⟩

The fmt command is a favorite in the Go community. Instead of arguing about where curly braces should go, or whether to use tabs or spaces when you indent, the fmt tool makes these decisions moot by applying a predetermined layout to Go source code. To invoke this code formatter, type go fmt followed by a file or package specification. The fmt command will automatically format the source code files you specify and save them. Here's a before-and-after snapshot of a few lines of code run through go fmt:

```
if err != nil { return err }
```

After running go fmt on this code, you'll get the following:

```
if err != nil {
    return err
}
```

Many Go developers configure their development environment to perform a go fmt on save or before committing to a code repository. Do yourself a favor and configure this right now.

3.5.3 Go documentation

go doc ⟨pkg⟩

There's another tool that will make your Go development process easier. Go has two ways to deliver documentation to developers. If you're working at a command prompt, you can use the go doc command to print documentation directly to your terminal session. You can view a quick reference for a command or package without leaving your terminal. But if a browsable interface is more your speed, you can use the

eg go doc math   for pkg documentation

godoc program to start a web server with a clickable index of Go packages. The godoc web server gives you a fully navigable web version of the documentation for all the Go source code installed in your system.

GETTING DOCUMENTATION AT THE COMMAND LINE

If you're the kind of developer who has a text editor open and a terminal session open right next to it (or a text editor open in your terminal session), then go doc is going to be your tool of choice. The first time you need to read a Unix tar file from your Go application, you'll be happy that you can access the documentation for the archive/tar package by simply typing this:

```
go doc tar
```

Running this command produces the following output, directly to the terminal:

```
PACKAGE DOCUMENTATION

package tar // import "archive/tar"

Package tar implements access to tar archives. It aims to cover most of the
variations, including those produced by GNU and BSD tars.

References:

    http://www.freebsd.org/cgi/man.cgi?query=tar&sektion=5
    http://www.gnu.org/software/tar/manual/html_node/Standard.html
    http://pubs.opengroup.org/onlinepubs/9699919799/utilities/pax.html
var ErrWriteTooLong = errors.New("archive/tar: write too long") ...
var ErrHeader = errors.New("archive/tar: invalid tar header")
func FileInfoHeader(fi os.FileInfo, link string) (*Header, error)
func NewReader(r io.Reader) *Reader
func NewWriter(w io.Writer) *Writer
type Header struct { ... }
type Reader struct { ... }
type Writer struct { ... }
```

You can skim through the documentation and find the information you need without breaking your workflow.

BROWSING THE DOCUMENTATION

The Go documentation is also available in a browsable format. Sometimes it's easier to get the whole picture of a package or function when you can click around and see all the related details. For those cases, you'll want to use godoc as a web server. If you prefer to get your documentation from a web browser in a clickable format, then this will be your favorite way to get to the documentation.

To start your own documentation server, type the following command into a terminal session:

```
godoc -http=:6060
```

This command instructs godoc to start a web server on port 6060. If you open your web browser and navigate to http://localhost:6060, you'll see a web page with documentation for both the Go standard libraries and any Go source that lives in your GOPATH.

At localhost:6060

after
godoc -http=:6060

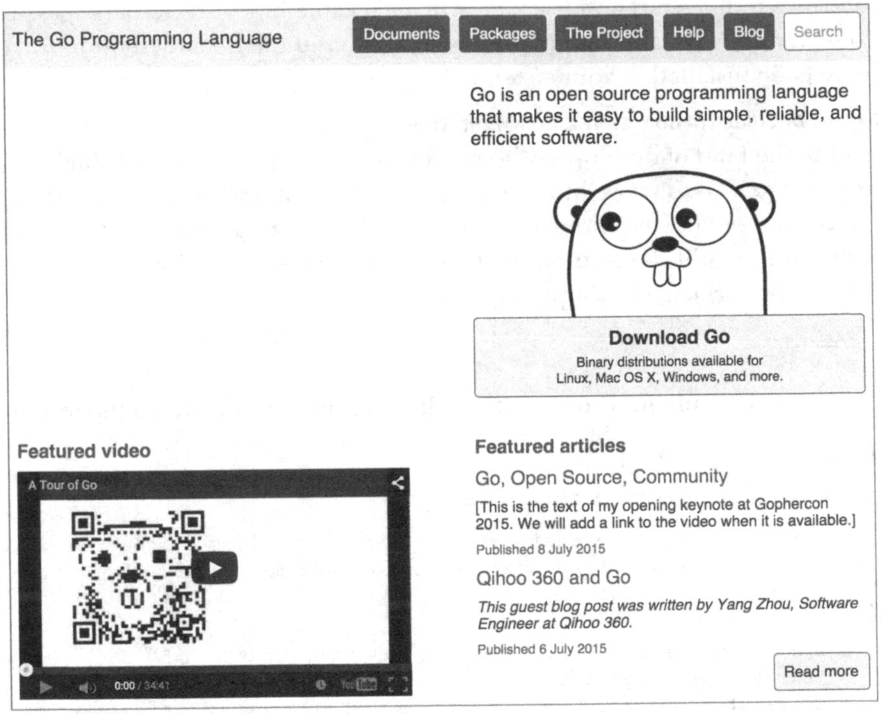

Figure 3.2   Local Go documentation

If the documentation in figure 3.2 looks familiar to you, it's because a slightly modified version of godoc is serving up the documentation for the Go website. To navigate to the documentation for a specific package, just click the Packages link at the top of the page.

The best part of Go's documentation tool is that it works for your code, too. If you follow simple conventions while writing your code, it will automatically include your comments in the Go documentation generated by godoc.

To be included in the godoc generated documentation, your code needs to be documented by adding comments that follow a specific convention. We won't go through the whole convention in this chapter, but we'll hit the highlights.

Start by adding comments directly above the identifiers you want to document. This works for packages, functions, types, and global variables. Comments can be started using either two slashes, or using the slash-asterisk style.

```
// Retrieve connects to the configuration repository and gathers
// various connection settings, usernames, passwords. It returns a
// config struct on success, or an error.
func Retrieve() (config, error) {
    // ... omitted
}
```

In this example, we show the idiomatic way to document a function in Go. The documentation for the function immediately precedes the function and is written in complete sentences. If you want to add a large body of text to document your package, include a file called doc.go that declares the same package as your project, and put your package introduction as a comment before the package declaration:

Sample doc.go
for package usb

```
/*
    Package usb provides types and functions for working with USB
    devices.  To connect to a USB device start by creating a new USB
    connection with NewConnection
    ...
*/
package usb
```

This package documentation will be shown before any type or function documentation is displayed for your package. It also demonstrates using the slash-asterisk type of comment. You can read more about creating good documentation for your code by searching for *golang documentation* in Google.

3.6 *Collaborating with other Go developers*

Modern developers don't code in a vacuum, and the Go tooling recognizes and embraces this fact. The concept of packages extends beyond your local development environment, thanks to the go tool. Let's look at a few conventions to follow in order to be a good citizen in a distributed development environment.

3.6.1 *Creating repositories for sharing*

Once you start cranking out awesome Go code, you're probably going to want to share that code with the rest of the Go community. It's really easy as long as you follow a few simple steps.

PACKAGE SHOULD LIVE AT THE ROOT OF THE REPOSITORY

go get

When you're using go get, you specify the full path to the package that should be imported. This means that when you create a repository that you intend to share, the package name should be the repository name, and the package's source should be in the root of the repository's directory structure.[1]

A common mistake that new Go developers make is to create a code or src directory in their public repository. Doing so will make the package's public import longer. Instead, just put the package source files at the root of the public repository.

PACKAGES CAN BE SMALL

It's common in Go to see packages that are relatively small by the standards of other programming languages. Don't be afraid to make a package that has a small API or performs only a single task. That's normal and expected.

RUN GO FMT ON THE CODE

Just like any other open source repository, people will look at your code to gauge the quality of it before they try it out. You need to be running go fmt before checking

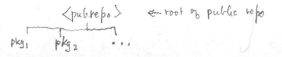
⟨pubrepo⟩ ← root of public repo
pkg₁ pkg₂ . . .

anything in. It makes your code readable and puts everyone on the same page when reading source code.

DOCUMENT THE CODE

Go developers use godoc to read documentation, and http://godoc.org to read documentation for open source packages. If you've followed go doc best practices in documenting your code, your packages will appear well documented when viewed locally or online, and people will find it easier to use.

3.7   Dependency management

The community has been hard at work since the release of Go 1.0 to provide Go tooling that makes life easier for developers. Many of these tools focus on helping with dependency management. The most popular tools today are *godep* by Keith Rarick, *vendor* by Daniel Theophanes, and a tool by Gustavo Niemeyer called *gopkg.in*, which helps package authors publish different versions of their packages.

As a call to action, with version 1.5 the Go language team started to experiment with new build options and features to provide better internal tooling support for dependency management. While we wait today to see where these experiments lead, there are existing tools that provide the ability to manage, build, and test Go code in a reproducible way.

3.7.1   Vendoring dependencies

Community tools such as godep and vendor have solved the dependency problem by using a technique called *vendoring* and import path rewriting. The idea is to copy all the dependencies into a directory inside the project repo, and then rewrite any import paths that reference those dependencies by providing the location inside the project itself.

Listing 3.9   Project using godep

```
$GOPATH/src/github.com/ardanstudios/myproject
    |-- Godeps
    |    |-- Godeps.json
    |    |-- Readme
    |    |-- _workspace
    |        |-- src
    |            |-- bitbucket.org
    |            |-- ww
    |            |    |-- goautoneg
    |            |    |    |-- Makefile
    |            |    |    |-- README.txt
    |            |    |    |-- autoneg.go
    |            |    |    |-- autoneg_test.go
    |            |-- github.com
    |                |-- beorn7
    |                    |-- perks
    |                        |-- README.md
    |                        |-- quantile
```

```
    |                                         |-- bench_test.go
    |                                         |-- example_test.go
    |                                         |-- exampledata.txt
    |                                         |-- stream.go
    |
    |-- examples
    |-- model
    |-- README.md
    |-- main.go
```

Listing 3.9 shows a typical source tree when using godep to vendor the dependencies
for a project. You can see how godep created a directory called Godeps. The source
code for the dependencies that the tooling vendored is located inside another set of
directories called _workspace/src.

Next, if you look at the import statements that are declared inside of main.go for
these dependencies, you'll see that some things needed to change.

Listing 3.10   Before vendoring

```
01 package main
02
03 import (
04     "bitbucket.org/ww/goautoneg"
05     "github.com/bcorn7/perks"
06 )
```

Listing 3.11   After vendoring

```
01 package main
02
03 import (
04     "github.ardanstudios.com/myproject/Godeps/_workspace/src/
                                           bitbucket.org/ww/goautoneg"
05     "github.ardanstudios.com/myproject/Godeps/_workspace/src/
                                           github.com/bcorn7/perks"
06 )
```

Before the dependencies were vendored, the import statements used the canonical
path for the package. The code was physically located on disk within the scope of
GOPATH. After vendoring, import path rewriting became necessary to reference the
packages, which are now physically located on disk inside the project itself. You can
see these imports are very large and tedious to use.

With vendoring, you have the ability to create reproducible builds, since all the
source code required to build the binary is housed inside the single project repo. One
other benefit of vendoring and import path rewriting is that the project repo is still
go-gettable. When go get is called against the project repo, the tooling can find each
package and store the package exactly where it needs to be inside the project itself.

3.7.2 *Introducing gb*

Gb is a whole new class of build tool being developed by members of the Go community. Gb takes a different approach to solving the reproducible-build problem, which starts with the understanding that wrapping the Go tooling is not an option.

The philosophy behind gb stems from the idea that Go doesn't have reproducible builds because of the import statement. The import statement drives go get, but import doesn't contain sufficient information to identify which revision of a package should be fetched any time go get is called. The possibility that go get can fetch a different version of code for any given package at any time makes supporting the Go tooling in any reproducible solution complicated and tedious at best. You saw some of this tediousness with the large import paths when using godep.

This understanding resulted in the creation of the gb build tool. Gb doesn't wrap the Go tooling, nor does it use GOPATH. Gb replaces the Go tooling workspace metaphor with a project-based approach. This has natively allowed vendoring without the need for rewriting import paths, which is mandated by go get and a GOPATH workspace.

Let's look at how the last project could be converted into a gb project.

Listing 3.12 Example of a gb project

```
/home/bill/devel/myproject ($PROJECT)
|-- src
|   |-- cmd
|   |   |-- myproject
|   |   |   |-- main.go
|   |-- examples
|   |-- model
|   |-- README.md
|-- vendor
    |-- src
        |-- bitbucket.org
        |   |-- ww
        |       |-- goautoneg
        |       |-- Makefile
        |       |-- README.txt
        |       |-- autoneg.go
        |       |-- autoneg_test.go
        |-- github.com
            |-- beorn7
                |-- perks
                |-- README.md
                |-- quantile
                |-- bench_test.go
        |-- example_test.go
        |-- exampledata.txt
        |-- stream.go
```

A gb project is simply a directory on disk that contains a subdirectory named src/. The symbol $PROJECT refers to the root directory on disk where the src/ directory is located and is only used as a shortcut for describing the location on disk for the project.

$PROJECT is *not* an environmental variable that needs to be set. In fact, gb requires no environmental variables to be set at all.

Gb projects differentiate between the code you write and the code your code depends on. The code your code depends on is called *vendored code*. A gb project makes a clear distinction between your code and vendored code.

Listing 3.13   The location for the code you write for the project

```
$PROJECT/src/
```

Listing 3.14   The location of vendored code

```
$PROJECT/vendor/src/
```

One of the best things about gb is that there's no need for import path rewriting. Look at the `import` statements that are declared inside of main.go—nothing needs to change to reference the vendored dependencies.

Listing 3.15   Import paths for gb projects

```
01 package main
02
03 import (
04     "bitbucket.org/ww/goautoneg"
05     "github.com/beorn7/perks"
06 )
```

The gb tool will look inside the $PROJECT/vendor/src/ directory for these imports if they can't be located inside the $PROJECT/src/ directory first. The entire source code for the project is located within a single repo and directory on disk, split between the src/ and vendor/src/ subdirectories. This, in conjunction with no need to rewrite import paths and the freedom to place your project anywhere you wish on disk, makes gb a popular tool in the community to develop projects that require reproducible builds.

One thing to note: a gb project is not compatible with the Go tooling, including go get. Since there's no need for GOPATH, and the Go tooling doesn't understand the structure of a gb project, it can't be used to build, test, or get. Building and testing a gb project requires navigating to the $PROJECT directory and using the gb tool.

Listing 3.16   Building a gb project

```
gb build all
```

Many of the same features that are supported by the Go tooling are supported in gb. Gb also has a plugin system to allow the community to extend support. One such plugin is called vendor, which provides conveniences to manage the dependencies in the `$PROJECT/vendor/src/` directory, something the Go tooling does not have today. To learn more about gb, check out the website: getgb.io.

3.8   Summary

- Packages are the basic unit of code organization in Go.
- Your GOPATH determines on disk where Go source code is saved, compiled, and installed.
- You can set your GOPATH for each different project, keeping all of your source and dependencies separate.
- The go tool is your best friend when working from the command line.
- You can use packages created by other people by using go get to fetch and install them in your GOPATH.
- It's easy to create packages for others to use if you host them on a public source code repository and follow a few simple rules.
- Go was designed with code sharing as a central driving feature of the language.
- It's recommended that you use vendoring to manage dependencies.
- There are several community-developed tools for dependency management such as godep, vendor, and gb.

Arrays, slices, and maps

4

In this chapter

- Array internals and fundamentals
- Managing collections of data with slices
- Working with key/value pairs using maps

It's difficult to write programs that don't need to store and read collections of data. If you use databases or files, or access the web, you need a way to handle the data you receive and send. Go has three different data structures that allow you to manage collections of data: arrays, slices, and maps. These data structures are baked into the language and used throughout the standard library. Once you learn how these data structures work, programming in Go will become fun, fast, and flexible.

4.1 Array internals and fundamentals

It makes sense to start with arrays because they form the base data structure for both slices and maps. Understanding how arrays work will help you appreciate the elegance and power that slices and maps provide.

4.1.1 *Internals*

An array in Go is a fixed-length data type that contains a contiguous block of elements of the same type. This could be a built-in type such as integers and strings, or it can be a struct type.

In figure 4.1 you can see the representation of an array. The elements of the array are marked as a grey box and are connected in series to each other. Each element contains the same type, in this case an integer, and can be accessed through a unique index position.

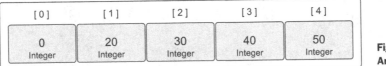

Figure 4.1
Array internals

Arrays are valuable data structures because the memory is allocated sequentially. Having memory in a contiguous form can help to keep the memory you use stay loaded within CPU caches longer. Using index arithmetic, you can iterate through all the elements of an array quickly. The type information for the array provides the distance in memory you have to move to find each element. Since each element is of the same type and follows each other sequentially, moving through the array is consistent and fast.

4.1.2 *Declaring and initializing*

An array is declared by specifying the type of data to be stored and the total number of elements required, also known as the array's length.

Listing 4.1   Declaring an array set to its zero value

```
// Declare an integer array of five elements.
var array [5]int
         ⌐ variable
```

Once an array is declared, neither the type of data being stored nor its length can be changed. If you need more elements, you need to create a new array with the length needed and then copy the values from one array to the other.

When variables in Go are declared, they're always initialized to their zero value for their respective type, and arrays are no different. When an array is initialized, each individual element that belongs to the array is initialized to its zero value. In figure 4.2, you can see an array of integers with each element in the array initialized to 0, the zero value for integers.

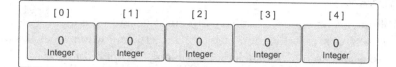

Figure 4.2 **Values of the array after the declaration of the array variable**

A fast and easy way to create and initialize arrays is to use an array literal. Array literals allow you to declare the number of elements you need and specify values for those elements.

Listing 4.2   Declaring an array using an array literal

```
// Declare an integer array of five elements.
// Initialize each element with a specific value.
array := [5]int{10, 20, 30, 40, 50}
```

If the length is given as . . . , Go will identify the length of the array based on the number of elements that are initialized.

Listing 4.3   Declaring an array with Go calculating size

```
// Declare an integer array.
// Initialize each element with a specific value.
// Capacity is determined based on the number of values initialized.
array := [...]int{10, 20, 30, 40, 50}
```

If you know the length of the array you need, but are only ready to initialize specific elements, you can use this syntax.

Listing 4.4   Declaring an array initializing specific elements

```
// Declare an integer array of five elements.
// Initialize index 1 and 2 with specific values.
// The rest of the elements contain their zero value.
array := [5]int{1: 10, 2: 20}
```

The values for the array declared in listing 4.4 will look like figure 4.3 after the array is declared and initialized.

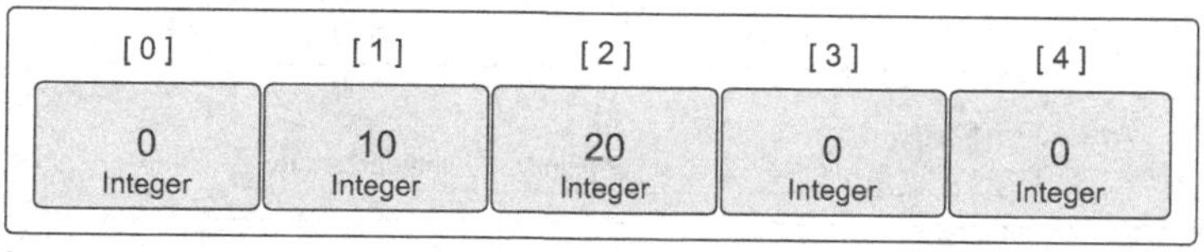

[0]	[1]	[2]	[3]	[4]
0 Integer	10 Integer	20 Integer	0 Integer	0 Integer

Figure 4.3   Values of the array after the declaration of the array variable

4.1.3   *Working with arrays*

As we talked about, arrays are efficient data structures because the memory is laid out in sequence. This gives arrays the advantage of being efficient when accessing individual elements. To access an individual element, use the [ ] operator.

Listing 4.5   Accessing array elements

```
// Declare an integer array of five elements.
// Initialize each element with a specific value.
array := [5]int{10, 20, 30, 40, 50}

// Change the value at index 2.
array[2] = 35
```

The values for the array declared in listing 4.5 will look like figure 4.4 after the array operations are complete.

[0]	[1]	[2]	[3]	[4]
10	20	35	40	50
Integer	Integer	Integer	Integer	Integer

Figure 4.4   Values of the array after changing the value of index 2

You can have an array of pointers. Like in chapter 2, you use the * operator to access the value that each element pointer points to.

Listing 4.6   Accessing array pointer elements

```
// Declare an integer pointer array of five elements.
// Initialize index 0 and 1 of the array with integer pointers.
array := [5]*int{0: new(int), 1: new(int)}

// Assign values to index 0 and 1.
*array[0] = 10
*array[1] = 20
```

The values for the array declared in listing 4.6 will look like figure 4.5 after the array operations are complete.

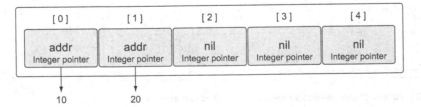

Figure 4.5   An array of pointers that point to integers

An array is a value in Go. This means you can use it in an assignment operation. The variable name denotes the entire array and, therefore, an array can be assigned to other arrays of the same type.

Listing 4.7   Assigning one array to another of the same type

```
// Declare a string array of five elements.
var array1 [5]string

// Declare a second string array of five elements.
// Initialize the array with colors.
array2 := [5]string{"Red", "Blue", "Green", "Yellow", "Pink"}

// Copy the values from array2 into array1.
array1 = array2
```

After the copy, you have two arrays with identical values, as shown in figure 4.6.

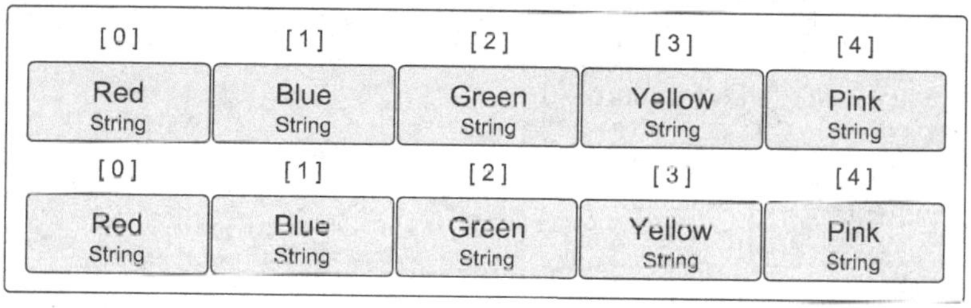

Figure 4.6   Both arrays after the copy

The type of an array variable includes both the length and the type of data that can be stored in each element. Only arrays of the same type can be assigned.

Listing 4.8   Compiler error assigning arrays of different types

```
// Declare a string array of four elements.
var array1 [4]string

// Declare a second string array of five elements.
// Initialize the array with colors.
array2 := [5]string{"Red", "Blue", "Green", "Yellow", "Pink"}

// Copy the values from array2 into array1.
array1 = array2

Compiler Error:
cannot use array2 (type [5]string) as type [4]string in assignment
```

Copying an array of pointers copies the pointer values and not the values that the pointers are pointing to.

Listing 4.9 Assigning one array of pointers to another

```
// Declare a string pointer array of three elements.
var array1 [3]*string

// Declare a second string pointer array of three elements.
// Initialize the array with string pointers.
array2 := [3]*string{new(string), new(string), new(string)}

// Add colors to each element
*array2[0] = "Red"
*array2[1] = "Blue"
*array2[2] = "Green"

// Copy the values from array2 into array1.
array1 = array2
```

After the copy, you have two arrays pointing to the same strings, as shown in figure 4.7.

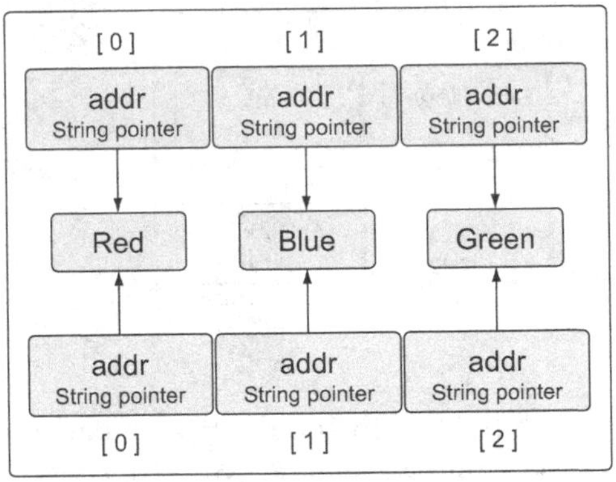

Figure 4.7 **Two arrays of pointers that point to the same strings**

4.1.4 *Multidimensional arrays*

Arrays are always one-dimensional, but they can be composed to create multidimensional arrays. Multidimensional arrays come in handy when you need to manage data that may have parent/child relationships or is associated with a coordinate system.

Listing 4.10 Declaring two-dimensional arrays

```
// Declare a two dimensional integer array of four elements
// by two elements.
var array [4][2]int

// Use an array literal to declare and initialize a two
// dimensional integer array.
array := [4][2]int{{10, 11}, {20, 21}, {30, 31}, {40, 41}}

// Declare and initialize index 1 and 3 of the outer array.
array := [4][2]int{1: {20, 21}, 3: {40, 41}}

// Declare and initialize individual elements of the outer
// and inner array.
array := [4][2]int{1: {0: 20}, 3: {1: 41}}
```

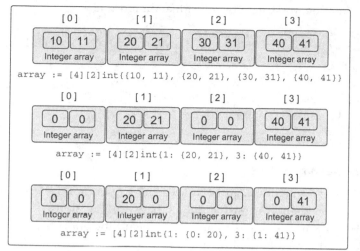

array := [4][2]int{{10, 11}, {20, 21}, {30, 31}, {40, 41}}

array := [4][2]int{1: {20, 21}, 3: {40, 41}}

array := [4][2]int{1: {0: 20}, 3: {1: 41}}

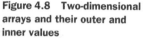

Figure 4.8 Two-dimensional arrays and their outer and inner values

Figure 4.8 shows the values each array contains after declaring and initializing these arrays.

To access an individual element, use the [ ] operator again and a bit of composition.

Listing 4.11 Accessing elements of a two-dimensional array

```
// Declare a two dimensional integer array of two elements.
var array [2][2]int

// Set integer values to each individual element.
array[0][0] = 10
array[0][1] = 20
array[1][0] = 30
array[1][1] = 40
```

You can copy multidimensional arrays into each other as long as they have the same type. The type of a multidimensional array is based on the length of each dimension and the type of data that can be stored in each element.

Listing 4.12 Assigning multidimensional arrays of the same type

```
// Declare two different two dimensional integer arrays.
var array1 [2][2]int
var array2 [2][2]int

// Add integer values to each individual element.
array2[0][0] = 10
array2[0][1] = 20
array2[1][0] = 30
array2[1][1] = 40

// Copy the values from array2 into array1.
array1 = array2
```

Because an array is a value, you can copy individual dimensions.

```
// Copy index 1 of array1 into a new array of the same type.
var array3 [2]int = array1[1]

// Copy the integer found in index 1 of the outer array
// and index 0 of the interior array into a new variable of
// type integer.
var value int = array1[1][0]
```

4.1.5   *Passing arrays between functions*

Passing an array between functions can be an expensive operation in terms of memory and performance. When you pass variables between functions, they're always passed by value. When your variable is an array, this means the entire array, regardless of its size, is copied and passed to the function.

To see this in action, let's create an array of one million elements of type int. On a 64-bit architecture, this would require eight million bytes, or eight megabytes, of memory. What happens when you declare an array of that size and pass it to a function?

```
// Declare an array of 8 megabytes.
var array [1e6]int

// Pass the array to the function foo.
foo(array)

// Function foo accepts an array of one million integers.
func foo(array [1e6]int) {
    ...
}
```

Every time the function foo is called, eight megabytes of memory has to be allocated on the stack. Then the value of the array, all eight megabytes of memory, has to be copied into that allocation. Go can handle this copy operation, but there's a better and more efficient way of doing this. You can pass a pointer to the array and only copy eight bytes, instead of eight megabytes of memory on the stack.

Compare p80
passing slices

```
// Allocate an array of 8 megabytes.
var array [1e6]int

// Pass the address of the array to the function foo.
foo(&array)

// Function foo accepts a pointer to an array of one million integers.
func foo(array *[1e6]int) {
    ...
}
```

Note   *foo (* array))*
            func foo (array &[1e6]int) { ...   // No
            }

This time the function foo takes a pointer to an array of one million elements of type integer. The function call now passes the address of the array, which only requires eight bytes of memory to be allocated on the stack for the pointer variable.

This operation is much more efficient with memory and could yield better performance. You just need to be aware that because you're now using a pointer, changing the value that the pointer points to will change the memory being shared. What is really awesome is that slices inherently take care of dealing with these types of issues, as you'll see.

4.2 Slice internals and fundamentals

A *slice* is a data structure that provides a way for you to work with and manage collections of data. Slices are built around the concept of dynamic arrays that can grow and shrink as you see fit. They're flexible in terms of growth because they have their own built-in function called append, which can grow a slice quickly with efficiency. You can also reduce the size of a slice by slicing out a part of the underlying memory. Slices give you all the benefits of indexing, iteration, and garbage collection optimizations because the underlying memory is allocated in contiguous blocks.

4.2.1 Internals

Slices are tiny objects that abstract and manipulate an underlying array. They're three-field data structures that contain the metadata Go needs to manipulate the underlying arrays (see figure 4.9).

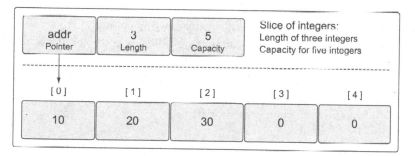

Figure 4.9 Slice internals with underlying array

The three fields are a pointer to the underlying array, the length or the number of elements the slice has access to, and the capacity or the number of elements the slice has available for growth. The difference between length and capacity will make more sense in a bit.

4.2.2 Creating and initializing

There are several ways to create and initialize slices in Go. Knowing the capacity you need ahead of time will usually determine how you go about creating your slice.

MAKE AND SLICE LITERALS

One way to create a slice is to use the built-in function make. When you use make, one option you have is to specify the length of the slice.

Listing 4.16   Declaring a slice of strings by length

```
// Create a slice of strings.
// Contains a length and capacity of 5 elements.
slice := make([]string, 5)
```

When you just specify the length, the capacity of the slice is the same. You can also specify the length and capacity separately.

Listing 4.17   Declaring a slice of integers by length and capacity

```
// Create a slice of integers.
// Contains a length of 3 and has a capacity of 5 elements.
slice := make([]int, 3, 5)
```

When you specify the length and capacity separately, you can create a slice with available capacity in the underlying array that you don't have access to initially. Figure 4.9 depicts what the slice of integers declared in listing 4.17 could look like after it's initialized with some values.

The slice in listing 4.17 has access to three elements, but the underlying array has five elements. The two elements not associated with the length of the slice can be incorporated so the slice can use those elements as well. New slices can also be created to share this same underlying array and use any existing capacity.

Trying to create a slice with a capacity that's smaller than the length is not allowed.

Listing 4.18   Compiler error setting capacity less than length

```
// Create a slice of integers.
// Make the length larger than the capacity.
slice := make([]int, 5, 3)

Compiler Error:
len larger than cap in make([]int)
```

An idiomatic way of creating a slice is to use a slice literal. It's similar to creating an array, except you don't specify a value inside of the [ ] operator. The initial length and capacity will be based on the number of elements you initialize.

Listing 4.19   Declaring a slice with a slice literal

```
// Create a slice of strings.
// Contains a length and capacity of 5 elements.
slice := []string{"Red", "Blue", "Green", "Yellow", "Pink"}
```

```
// Create a slice of integers.
// Contains a length and capacity of 3 elements.
slice := []int{10, 20, 30}
```

When using a slice literal, you can set the initial length and capacity. All you need to do is initialize the index that represents the length and capacity you need. The following syntax will create a slice with a length and capacity of 100 elements.

Listing 4.20 Declaring a slice with index positions

```
// Create a slice of strings.
// Initialize the 100th element with an empty string.
slice := []string{99: ""}              // len = cap = 100 ;  slice[99] == ""
```

Remember, if you specify a value inside the [ ] operator, you're creating an array. If you don't specify a value, you're creating a slice.

Listing 4.21 Declaration differences between arrays and slices

```
// Create an array of three integers.
array := [3]int{10, 20, 30}            // array

// Create a slice of integers with a length and capacity of three.
slice := []int{10, 20, 30}             // slice
```

arrays vs slices

NIL AND EMPTY SLICES

Sometimes in your programs you may need to declare a nil slice. A nil slice is created by declaring a slice without any initialization.

Listing 4.22 Declaring a nil slice

```
// Create a nil slice of integers.
var slice []int                        X
```

A nil slice is the most common way you create slices in Go. They can be used with many of the standard library and built-in functions that work with slices. They're useful when you want to represent a slice that doesn't exist, such as when an exception occurs in a function that returns a slice (see figure 4.10).

Nil slice
Takes 3×8 bytes

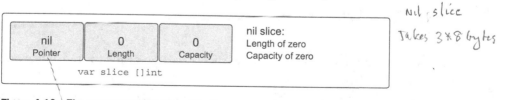

Figure 4.10 The representation of a nil slice

Compare @ 68

nil slice   var x   [] int
empty slice [var y   [] int {}
             [var y := make ([]int, 0)

You can also create an empty slice by declaring a slice with initialization.

Listing 4.23 Declaring an empty slice

```
// Use make to create an empty slice of integers.
slice := make([]int, 0)

// Use a slice literal to create an empty slice of integers.
slice := []int{}
```

An empty slice contains a zero-element underlying array that allocates no storage. Empty slices are useful when you want to represent an empty collection, such as when a database query returns zero results (see figure 4.11).

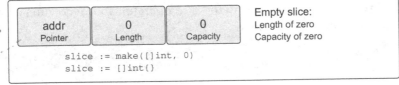

Figure 4.11 The representation of an empty slice

Regardless of whether you're using a `nil` slice or an empty slice, the built-in functions append, `len`, and `cap` work the same.

4.2.3 Working with slices

Now that you know what a slice is and how to create them, you can learn how to use them in your programs.

ASSIGNING AND SLICING

Assigning a value to any specific index within a slice is identical to how you do this with arrays. To change the value of an individual element, use the [ ] operator.

Listing 4.24 Declaring an array using an array literal

```
// Create a slice of integers.
// Contains a length and capacity of 5 elements.
slice := []int{10, 20, 30, 40, 50}

// Change the value of index 1.
slice[1] = 25
```

Slices are called such because you can slice a portion of the underlying array to create a new slice.

Listing 4.25 Taking the slice of a slice

```
// Create a slice of integers.
// Contains a length and capacity of 5 elements.
slice := []int{10, 20, 30, 40, 50}
```

```
// Create a new slice.
// Contains a length of 2 and capacity of 4 elements.
newSlice := slice[1:3]
```
// slice of a slice :

After the slicing operation performed in listing 4.25, we have two slices that are sharing the same underlying array. However, each slice views the underlying array in a different way (see figure 4.12).

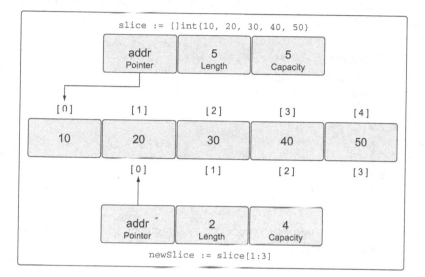

Figure 4.12 Two slices sharing the same underlying array

The original slice views the underlying array as having a capacity of five elements, but the view of newSlice is different. For newSlice, the underlying array has a capacity of four elements. newSlice can't access the elements of the underlying array that are prior to its pointer. As far as newSlice is concerned, those elements don't even exist.

Calculating the length and capacity for any new slice is performed using the following formula.

Listing 4.26 How length and capacity are calculated

```
For slice[i:j] with an underlying array of capacity k

Length:    j - i
Capacity:  k - i
```

If you apply this formula to newSlice you get the following.

Listing 4.27 Calculating the new length and capacity

```
For slice[1:3] with an underlying array of capacity 5

Length:    3 - 1 = 2
Capacity:  5 - 1 = 4
```

Another way to look at this is that the first value represents the starting index position of the element the new slice will start with—in this case, 1. The second value represents the starting index position (1) plus the number of elements you want to include (2); 1 plus 2 is 3, so the second value is 3. Capacity will be the total number of elements associated with the slice.

You need to remember that you now have two slices sharing the same underlying array. Changes made to the shared section of the underlying array by one slice can be seen by the other slice.

Listing 4.28   Potential consequence of making changes to a slice

```
// Create a slice of integers.
// Contains a length and capacity of 5 elements.
slice := []int{10, 20, 30, 40, 50}

// Create a new slice.
// Contains a length of 2 and capacity of 4 elements.
newSlice := slice[1:3]

// Change index 1 of newSlice.
// Change index 2 of the original slice.
newSlice[1] = 35
```

After the number 35 is assigned to the second element of newSlice, that change can also be seen by the original slice in element 3 (see figure 4.13).

A slice can only access indexes up to its length. Trying to access an element outside of its length will cause a runtime exception. The elements associated with a slice's capacity are only available for growth. They must be incorporated into the slice's length before they can be used.

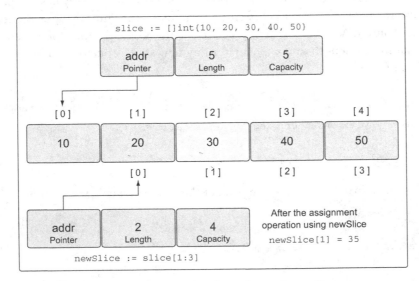

Figure 4.13   The underlying array after the assignment operation

Listing 4.29   Runtime error showing index out of range

```
// Create a slice of integers.
// Contains a length and capacity of 5 elements.
slice := []int{10, 20, 30, 40, 50}

// Create a new slice.
// Contains a length of 2 and capacity of 4 elements.
newSlice := slice[1:3]

// Change index 3 of newSlice.
// This element does not exist for newSlice.
newSlice[3] = 45

Runtime Exception:
panic: runtime error: index out of range
```

Having capacity is great, but useless if you can't incorporate it into your slice's length. Luckily, Go makes this easy when you use the built-in function append.

GROWING SLICES

One of the advantages of using a slice over using an array is that you can grow the capacity of your slice as needed. Go takes care of all the operational details when you use the built-in function append.

To use append, you need a source slice and a value that is to be appended. When your append call returns, it provides you a new slice with the changes. The append function will always increase the length of the new slice. The capacity, on the other hand, may or may not be affected, depending on the available capacity of the source slice.

Listing 4.30   Using append to add an element to a slice

```
// Create a slice of integers.
// Contains a length and capacity of 5 elements.
slice := []int{10, 20, 30, 40, 50}

// Create a new slice.
// Contains a length of 2 and capacity of 4 elements.
newSlice := slice[1:3]

// Allocate a new element from capacity.
// Assign the value of 60 to the new element.
newSlice = append(newSlice, 60)
```

After the append operation in listing 4.30, the slices and the underlying array will look like figure 4.14.

Because there was available capacity in the underlying array for newSlice, the append operation incorporated the available element into the slice's length and assigned the value. Since the original slice is sharing the underlying array, slice also sees the changes in index 3.

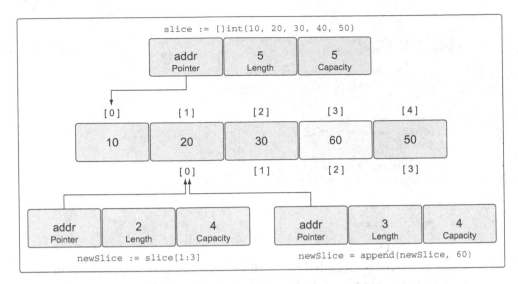

Figure 4.14   The underlying array after the append operation

When there's no available capacity in the underlying array for a slice, the append function will create a new underlying array, copy the existing values that are being referenced, and assign the new value.

Listing 4.31   Using append to increase the length and capacity of a slice

```
// Create a slice of integers.
// Contains a length and capacity of 4 elements.
slice := []int{10, 20, 30, 40}

// Append a new value to the slice.
// Assign the value of 50 to the new element.
newSlice := append(slice, 50)
```

After this append operation, newSlice is given its own underlying array, and the capacity of the array is doubled from its original size (see figure 4.15).

The append operation is clever when growing the capacity of the underlying array. Capacity is always doubled when the existing capacity of the slice is under 1,000 elements. Once the number of elements goes over 1,000, the capacity is grown by a factor of 1.25, or 25%. This growth algorithm may change in the language over time.

THREE INDEX SLICES

There's a third index option we haven't mentioned yet that you can use when you're slicing. This third index gives you control over the capacity of the new slice. The purpose is not to increase capacity, but to restrict the capacity. As you'll see, being able to restrict the capacity of a new slice provides a level of protection to the underlying array and gives you more control over append operations.

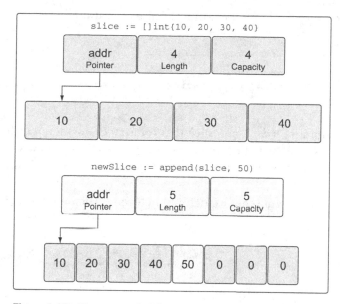

Figure 4.15 The new underlying array after the append operation

Let's start with a slice of five strings that contain fruit you can find in your local super-market.

```
// Create a slice of strings.
// Contains a length and capacity of 5 elements.
source := []string{"Apple", "Orange", "Plum", "Banana", "Grape"}
```

If you inspect the values for this slice of fruit, it will look something like figure 4.16.

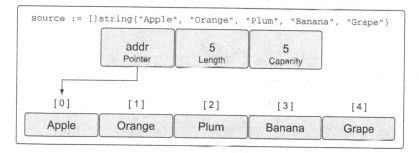

Figure 4.16   A representation of the slice of strings

Now let's use the third index option to perform a slicing operation.

Listing 4.33　Performing a three-index slice

```
// Slice the third element and restrict the capacity.
// Contains a length of 1 element and capacity of 2 elements.
slice := source[2:3:4]          len 3-2 , cap 4-2
```

After this slicing operation, we have a new slice that references one element from the underlying array and has a capacity of two elements. Specifically, the new slice references the `Plum` element and has capacity up to the `Banana` element, as shown in figure 4.17.

We can apply the same formula that we defined before to calculate the new slice's length and capacity.

Listing 4.34　How length and capacity are calculated

```
For slice[i:j:k]   or   [2:3:4]

Length:   j - i   or   3 - 2 = 1
Capacity: k - i   or   4 - 2 = 2
```

Again, the first value represents the starting index position of the element the new slice will start with—in this case, 2. The second value represents the starting index position (2) plus the number of elements you want to include (1); 2 plus 1 is 3, so the second value is 3. For setting capacity, you take the starting index position of 2, plus the number of elements you want to include in the capacity (2), and you get the value of 4.

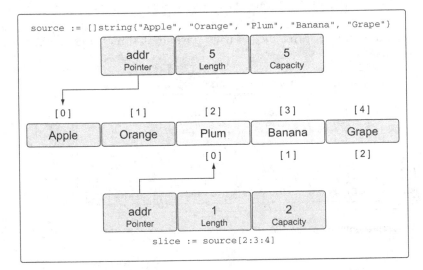

Figure 4.17　A representation of the new slice after the operation

of the underlying slice

If you attempt to set a capacity that's larger than the available capacity, you'll get a runtime error.

Listing 4.35   Runtime error setting capacity larger than existing capacity

```
// This slicing operation attempts to set the capacity to 4.
// This is greater than what is available.
slice := source[2:3:6]

Runtime Error:
panic: runtime error: slice bounds out of range
```

As we've discussed, the built-in function append will use any available capacity first.
Once that capacity is reached, it will allocate a new underlying array. It's easy to forget
which slices are sharing the same underlying array. When this happens, making
changes to a slice can result in random and odd-looking bugs. Suddenly changes
appear on multiple slices out of nowhere.

By having the option to set the capacity of a new slice to be the same as the length,
you can force the first append operation to detach the new slice from the underlying
array. Detaching the new slice from its original source array makes it safe to change.

Listing 4.36   Benefits of setting length and capacity to be the same

```
// Create a slice of strings.
// Contains a length and capacity of 5 elements.
source := []string{"Apple", "Orange", "Plum", "Banana", "Grape"}

// Slice the third element and restrict the capacity.
// Contains a length and capacity of 1 element.
slice := source[2:3:3]

// Append a new string to the slice.
slice = append(slice, "Kiwi")
```

Without this third index, appending Kiwi to our slice would've changed the value of
Banana in index 3 of the underlying array, because all of the remaining capacity would
still belong to the slice. But in listing 4.36, we restricted the capacity of the slice to 1.
When we call append for the first time on the slice, it will create a new underlying
array of two elements, copy the fruit Plum, add the new fruit Kiwi, and return a new
slice that references this underlying array, as in figure 4.18.

With the new slice now having its own underlying array, we've avoided potential
problems. We can now continue to append fruit to our new slice without worrying if
we're changing fruit to other slices inappropriately. Also, allocating the new underlying array for the slice was easy and clean.

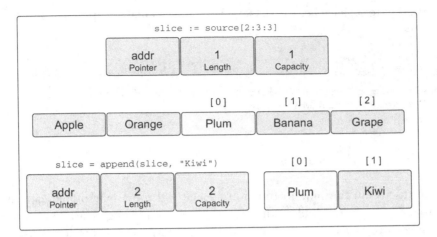

Figure 4.18   A representation of the new slice after the append operation

The built-in function append is also a variadic function. This means you can pass multiple values to be appended in a single slice call. If you use the . . . operator, you can append all the elements of one slice into another.

Listing 4.37   Appending to a slice from another slice

```
// Create two slices each initialized with two integers.
s1 := []int{1, 2}
s2 := []int{3, 4}

// Append the two slices together and display the results.
fmt.Printf("%v\n", append(s1, s2...))

Output:
[1 2 3 4]
```

↑ append all values of s2 to s1

As you can see by the output, all the values of slice s2 have been appended to slice s1. The value of the new slice returned by the append function is then displayed by the call to Printf.

ITERATING OVER SLICES

Since a slice is a collection, you can iterate over the elements. Go has a special keyword called range that you use in conjunction with the keyword for to iterate over slices.

Listing 4.38   Iterating over a slice using `for range`

```
// Create a slice of integers.
// Contains a length and capacity of 4 elements.
slice := []int{10, 20, 30, 40}

// Iterate over each element and display each value.
for index, value := range slice {
    fmt.Printf("Index: %d  Value: %d\n", index, value)
}
```

compare @ 85
(map iteration)

```
Output:
Index: 0  Value: 10
Index: 1  Value: 20
Index: 2  Value: 30
Index: 3  Value: 40
```

The keyword range, when iterating over a slice, will return two values. The first value is the index position and the second value is a copy of the value in that index position (see figure 4.19).

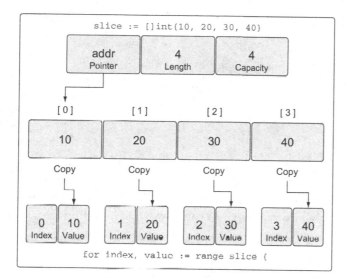

Figure 4.19 Using `range` to iterate over a slice creates a copy of each element.

It's important to know that range is making a copy of the value, not returning a reference. If you use the address of the value variable as a pointer to each element, you'll be making a mistake. Let's see why.

Listing 4.39   range provides a copy of each element

```
// Create a slice of integers.
// Contains a length and capacity of 4 elements.
slice := []int{10, 20, 30, 40}

// Iterate over each element and display the value and addresses.
for index, value := range slice {
    fmt.Printf("Value: %d  Value-Addr: %X  ElemAddr: %X\n",
        value, &value, &slice[index])
}

Output:
Value: 10  Value-Addr: 10500168  ElemAddr: 1052E100
Value: 20  Value-Addr: 10500168  ElemAddr: 1052E104
Value: 30  Value-Addr: 10500168  ElemAddr: 1052E108
Value: 40  Value-Addr: 10500168  ElemAddr: 1052E10C
```

The address for the `value` variable is always the same because it's a variable that contains a copy. The address of each individual element can be captured using the slice variable and the index value.

If you don't need the index value, you can use the underscore character to discard the value.

Listing 4.40   Using the blank identifier to ignore the index value

```
// Create a slice of integers.
// Contains a length and capacity of 4 elements.
slice := []int{10, 20, 30, 40}

// Iterate over each element and display each value.
for _, value := range slice {
    fmt.Printf("Value: %d\n", value)
}


Output:
Value: 10
Value: 20
Value: 30
Value: 40
```

The keyword range will always start iterating over a slice from the beginning. If you need more control iterating over a slice, you can always use a traditional for loop.

Listing 4.41   Iterating over a slice using a traditional `for` loop

```
// Create a slice of integers.
// Contains a length and capacity of 4 elements.
slice := []int{10, 20, 30, 40}

// Iterate over each element starting at element 3.
for index := 2; index < len(slice); index++ {
    fmt.Printf("Index: %d  Value: %d\n", index, slice[index])
}


Output:
Index: 2  Value: 30
Index: 3  Value: 40
```

There are two special built-in functions called `len` and `cap` that work with arrays, slices, and channels. For slices, the `len` function returns the length of the slice, and the `cap` function returns the capacity. In listing 4.41, we used the `len` function to determine when to stop iterating over the slice.

Now that you know how to create and work with slices, you can use them to compose and iterate over multidimensional slices.

4.2.4 Multidimensional slices

Like arrays, slices are one-dimensional, but they can be composed to create multidimensional slices for the same reasons we discussed earlier.

Listing 4.42 Declaring a multidimensional slice

```
// Create a slice of a slice of integers.
slice := [][]int{{10}, {100, 200}}          // inner slices of len 1, 2
                                 outer slice has 2 members
```

We now have an outer slice of two elements that contain an inner slice of integers. The values for our slice of a slice of integers will look like figure 4.20.

In figure 4.20 you can see how composition is working to embed slices into slices. The outer slice contains two elements, each of which are slices. The slice in the first element is initialized with the single integer 10 and the slice in the second element contains two integers, 100 and 200.

Composition allows you to create very complex and powerful data structures. All of the rules you learned about the built-in function append still apply.

Listing 4.43 Composing slices of slices

```
// Create a slice of a slice of integers.
slice := [][]int{{10}, {100, 200}}

// Append the value of 20 to the first slice of integers.
slice[0] = append(slice[0], 20)
```

The append function and Go are elegant in how they handle growing and assigning the new slice of integers back into the first element of the outer slice. When the operation

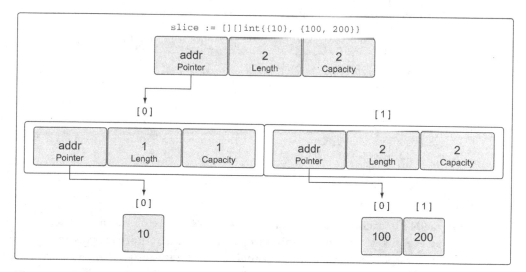

Figure 4.20   Values for our slice of a slice of integers

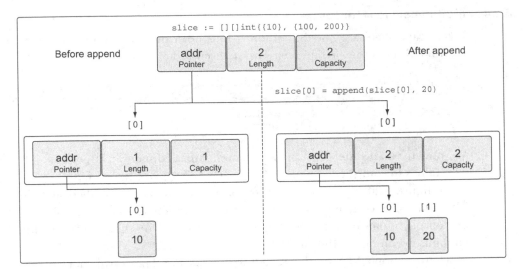

Figure 4.21   What index 0 of the outer slice looks like after the append operation

in listing 4.43 is complete, an entire new slice of integers and a new underlying array is allocated and then copied back into index 0 of the outer slice, as shown in figure 4.21.

Even with this simple multidimensional slice, there are a lot of layers and values involved. Passing a data structure like this between functions could seem complicated. But slices are cheap and passing them between functions is trivial.

4.2.5 *Passing slices between functions*

Compare
p64:
passing arrays

Passing a slice between two functions requires nothing more than passing the slice by value. Since the size of a slice is small, it's cheap to copy and pass between functions. Let's create a large slice and pass that slice by value to our function called foo.

Listing 4.44   Passing slices between functions

```
// Allocate a slice of 1 million integers.
slice := make([]int, 1e6)

// Pass the slice to the function foo.
slice = foo(slice)

// Function foo accepts a slice of integers and returns the slice back.
func foo(slice []int) []int {
    ...
    return slice
}
```

3×8 bytes

On a 64-bit architecture, a slice requires 24 bytes of memory. The pointer field requires 8 bytes, and the length and capacity fields require 8 bytes respectively. Since the data associated with a slice is contained in the underlying array, there are no problems passing a copy of a slice to any function. Only the slice is being copied, not the underlying array (see figure 4.22).

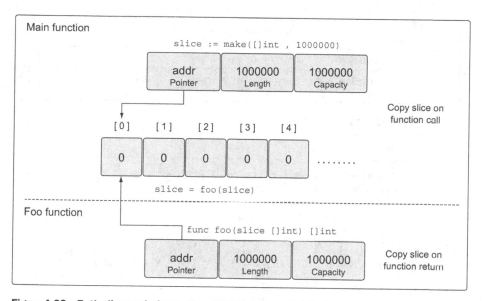

Figure 4.22   Both slices pointing to the underlying array after the function call

Passing the 24 bytes between functions is fast and easy. This is the beauty of slices. You don't need to pass pointers around and deal with complicated syntax. You just create copies of your slices, make the changes you need, and then pass a new copy back.

4.3   *Map internals and fundamentals*

A map is a data structure that provides you with an unordered collection of key/value pairs.

You store values into the map based on a key. Figure 4.23 shows an example of a key/value pair you may store in your maps. The strength of a map is its ability to retrieve data quickly based on the key. A key works like an index, pointing to the value you associate with that key.

Figure 4.23   Relationship of key/value pairs

4.3.1   *Internals*

Maps are collections, and you can iterate over them just like you do with arrays and slices. But maps are *unordered* collections, and there's no way to predict the order in which the key/value pairs will be returned. Even if you store your key/value pairs in the same order, every iteration over a map could return a different order. This is because a map is implemented using a hash table, as shown in figure 4.24.

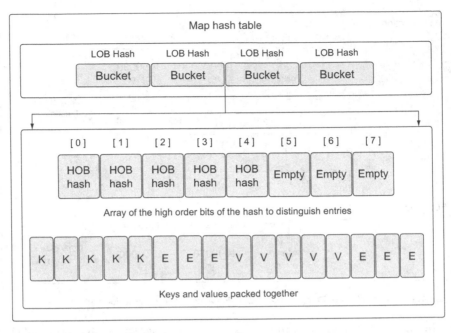

K = Key   V = Value   E = Empty

Figure 4.24 Simple representation of the internal structure of a map

The map's hash table contains a collection of buckets. When you're storing, removing, or looking up a key/value pair, everything starts with selecting a bucket. This is performed by passing the key—specified in your map operation—to the map's hash function. The purpose of the hash function is to generate an index that evenly distributes key/value pairs across all available buckets.

The better the distribution, the quicker you can find your key/value pairs as the map grows. If you store 10,000 items in your map, you don't want to ever look at 10,000 key/value pairs to find the one you want. You want to look at the least number of key/value pairs possible. Looking at only 8 key/value pairs in a map of 10,000 items is a good and balanced map. A balanced list of key/value pairs across the right number of buckets makes this possible.

The hash key that's generated for a Go map is a bit longer than what you see in figure 4.25, but it works the same way. In our example, the keys are strings that represents a color. Those strings are converted into a numeric value within the scope of the number of buckets we have available for storage. The numeric value is then used to select a bucket for storing or finding the specific key/value pair. In the case of a Go map, a portion of the generated hash key, specifically the *low order bits* (LOB), is used to select the bucket.

If you look at figure 4.24 again, you can see what the internals of a bucket look like. There are two data structures that contain the data for the map. First, there's an array

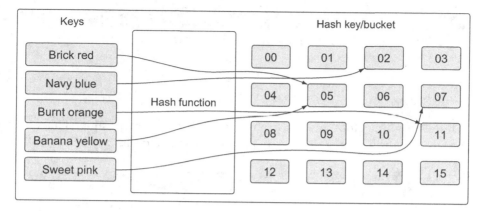

Figure 4.25 Simple view of how hash functions work

bit $n \in \{0,1,2,...,7\}$ select nth k and V in bucket

with the top eight *high order bits* (HOB) from the same hash key that was used to select the bucket. This array distinguishes each individual key/value pair stored in the respective bucket. Second, there's an array of bytes that stores the key/value pairs. The byte array packs all the keys and then all the values together for the respective bucket. The packing of the key/value pairs is implemented to minimize the memory required for each bucket.

There are a lot of other low-level implementation details about maps that are outside the scope of this chapter. You don't need to understand all the internals to learn how to create and use maps. Just remember one thing: a map is an unordered collection of key/value pairs.

4.3.2 Creating and initializing

There are several ways you can create and initialize maps in Go. You can use the built-in function make, or you can use a map literal.   *✗*

Listing 4.45   Declaring a map using make

```
// Create a map with a key of type string and a value of type int.
dict := make(map[string]int)        // Use make
```
nil map? ←

```
// Create a map with a key and value of type string.
// Initialize the map with 2 key/value pairs.
dict := map[string]string{"Red": "#da1337", "Orange": "#e95a22"}
```
// Use map literal
compare struct init , p 90

Using a map literal is the idiomatic way of creating a map. The initial length will be based on the number of key/value pairs you specify during initialization.

The map key can be a value from any built-in or struct type as long as the value can   *✗* be used in an expression with the == operator. Slices, functions, and struct types that contain slices can't be used as map keys. This will produce a compiler error.

Listing 4.46   Declaring an empty map using a map literal

```
// Create a map using a slice of strings as the key.
dict := map[[]string]int{}

Compiler Exception:
invalid map key type []string
```

There's nothing stopping you from using a slice as a map value. This can come in handy when you need a single map key to be associated with a collection of data.

Listing 4.47   Declaring a map that stores slices of strings

```
// Create a map using a slice of strings as the value.
dict := map[int][]string{}
```

4.3.3   *Working with maps*

Assigning a key/value pair to a map is performed by specifying a key of the proper type and assigning a value to that key.

Listing 4.48   Assigning values to a map

```
// Create an empty map to store colors and their color codes.
colors := map[string]string{}

// Add the Red color code to the map.
colors["Red"] = "#da1337"
```

You can create a nil map by declaring a map without any initialization. A nil map can't be used to store key/value pairs. Trying will produce a runtime error.

Listing 4.49   Runtime error assigned to a `nil` **map**

```
// Create a nil map by just declaring the map.
var colors map[string]string

// Add the Red color code to the map.
colors["Red"] = "#da1337"

Runtime Error:
panic: runtime error: assignment to entry in nil map
```

Testing if a map key exists is an important part of working with maps. It allows you to write logic that can determine if you've performed an operation or if you've cached some particular data in the map. It can also be used to compare two maps to identify what key/value pairs match or are missing.

When retrieving a value from a map, you have two choices. You can retrieve the value and a flag that explicitly lets you know if the key exists.

[handwritten notes:]
empty map   x := make(map[int]bool{})
  nil map   y := make(map[int]bool)

Listing 4.50 Retrieving a value from a map and testing existence.

```
// Retrieve the value for the key "Blue".
value, exists := colors["Blue"]

// Did this key exist?
if exists {
    fmt.Println(value)
}
```

The other option is to just return the value and test for the zero value to determine if the key exists. This will only work if the zero value is not a valid value for the map.

Listing 4.51 Retrieving a value from a map testing the value for existence

```
// Retrieve the value for the key "Blue".
value := colors["Blue"]

// Did this key exist?
if value != "" {
    fmt.Println(value)
}
```

When you index a map in Go, it will always return a value, even when the key doesn't exist. In this case, the zero value for the value's type is returned.

Iterating over a map is identical to iterating over an array or slice. You use the keyword range; but when it comes to maps, you don't get back the index/value, you get back the key/value pairs.

Listing 4.52 Iterating over a map using `for range`

```
// Create a map of colors and color hex codes.
colors := map[string]string{
    "AliceBlue":   "#f0f8ff",
    "Coral":       "#ff7F50",
    "DarkGray":    "#a9a9a9",
    "ForestGreen": "#228b22",
}

// Display all the colors in the map.
for key, value := range colors {
    fmt.Printf("Key: %s  Value: %s\n", key, value)
}
```

compare @ 76 [slice ituation]

If you want to remove a key/value pair from the map, you use the built-in function delete.

Listing 4.53 Removing an item from a map

```
// Remove the key/value pair for the key "Coral".
delete(colors, "Coral")

// Display all the colors in the map.
```

what if try to delete an element not in map?

```
for key, value := range colors {
    fmt.Printf("Key: %s  Value: %s\n", key, value)
}
```

This time when you iterate through the map, the color Coral would not be displayed on the screen.

4.3.4   *Passing maps between functions*

Passing a map between two functions doesn't make a copy of the map. In fact, you can pass a map to a function and make changes to the map, and the changes will be reflected by all references to the map.

Listing 4.54   Passing maps between functions

```
func main() {
    // Create a map of colors and color hex codes.
    colors := map[string]string{
        "AliceBlue":   "#f0f8ff",
        "Coral":       "#ff7F50",
        "DarkGray":    "#a9a9a9",
        "ForestGreen": "#228b22",
    }

    // Display all the colors in the map.
    for key, value := range colors {
        fmt.Printf("Key: %s  Value: %s\n", key, value)
    }

    // Call the function to remove the specified key.
    removeColor(colors, "Coral")

    // Display all the colors in the map.
    for key, value := range colors {
        fmt.Printf("Key: %s  Value: %s\n", key, value)
    }
}

// removeColor removes keys from the specified map.
func removeColor(colors map[string]string, key string) {
    delete(colors, key)
}
```

If you run this program, you'll get the following output.

Listing 4.55   Output for listing 4.54

```
Key: AliceBlue Value: #F0F8FF
Key: Coral Value: #FF7F50
Key: DarkGray Value: #A9A9A9
Key: ForestGreen Value: #228B22

Key: AliceBlue Value: #F0F8FF
Key: DarkGray Value: #A9A9A9
Key: ForestGreen Value: #228B22
```

You can see that after the call to `removeColor` is complete, the color Coral is no longer present in the map referenced by `main`. Maps are designed to be cheap, similar to slices.

4.4 Summary

- Arrays are the building blocks for both slices and maps.
- Slices are the idiomatic way in Go you work with collections of data. Maps are the way you work with key/value pairs of data.   66, 68   83
- The built-in function `make` allows you to create slices and maps with initial length and capacity. Slice and map literals can be used as well and support setting initial values for use.
- Slices have a capacity restriction, but can be extended using the built-in function `append`.
- Maps don't have a capacity or any restriction on growth.
- The built-in function `len` can be used to retrieve the length of a slice or map.
- The built-in function `cap` only works on slices.
- Through the use of composition, you can create multidimensional arrays and slices. You can also create maps with values that are slices and other maps. A slice can't be used as a map key.
- Passing a slice or map to a function is cheap and doesn't make a copy of the underlying data structure.

Go's type system

In this chapter

- Declaring new user-defined types
- Adding behavior to types with methods
- Knowing when to use pointers and values
- Implementing polymorphism with interfaces
- Extending and changing types through composition
- Exporting and unexporting identifiers

Go is a statically typed programming language. What that means is the compiler always wants to know what the type is for every value in the program. When the compiler knows the type information ahead of time, it can help to make sure that the program is working with values in a safe way. This helps to reduce potential memory corruption and bugs, and provides the compiler the opportunity to produce more performant code.

A value's type provides the compiler with two pieces of information: first, how much memory to allocate—the *size of the value*—and second, what that memory represents. In the case of many of the built-in types, size and representation are part of the type's name. A value of type int64 requires 8 bytes of memory (64 bits) and represents an integer value. A `float32` requires 4 bytes of memory (32 bits) and represents an IEEE-754 binary floating-point number. A bool requires 1 byte of memory (8 bits) and represents a Boolean value of `true` or `false`.

Some types get their representation based on the architecture of the machine the code is built for. A value of type `int`, for example, can either have a size of 8 bytes (64 bits) or 4 bytes (32 bits), depending on the architecture. There are other architecture-specific types as well, such as all the reference types in Go. Luckily, you don't need to know this information to create or work with values. But if the compiler doesn't know this information, it can't protect you from doing things that could cause harm inside your programs and the machines they run on.

5.1   User-defined types

Go allows you the ability to declare your own types. When you declare a new type, the declaration is constructed to provide the compiler with size and representation information, similar to how the built-in types work. There are two ways to declare a user-defined type in Go. The most common way is to use the keyword `struct`, which allows you to create a composite type.

Struct types are declared by composing a fixed set of unique fields. Each field in a struct is declared with a known type, which could be a built-in type or another user-defined type.

> **Listing 5.1   Declaration of a struct type**

```
01 // user defines a user in the program.
02 type user struct {
03     name       string
04     email      string
05     ext        int
06     privileged bool
07 }
```

In listing 5.1 you see the declaration of a struct type. The declaration starts with the keyword `type`, then a name for the new type, and finally the keyword `struct`. This struct type contains four fields, each based on a different built-in type. You can see how the fields come together to compose a structure of data. Once you have a type declared, you can create values from the type.

> **Listing 5.2   Declaration of a variable of the struct type set to its zero value**

```
09 // Declare a variable of type user.
10 var bill user
```

On line 10 in listing 5.2, the keyword `var` creates a variable named `bill` of type `user`. When you declare variables, the value that the variable represents is always initialized. The value can be initialized with a specific value or it can be initialized to its zero value, which is the default value for that variable's type. For numeric types, the zero value would be 0; for strings it would be empty; and for Booleans it would be `false`. In the case of a struct, the zero value would apply to all the different fields in the struct.

Any time a variable is created and initialized to its zero value, it's idiomatic to use the keyword `var`. Reserve the use of the keyword `var` as a way to indicate that a variable is being set to its zero value. If the variable will be initialized to something other than its zero value, then use the short variable declaration operator with a struct literal.

Listing 5.3   Declaration of a variable of the struct type using a struct literal

```
12 // Declare a variable of type user and initialize all the fields.
13 lisa := user{
14     name:       "Lisa",
15     email:      "lisa@email.com",
16     ext:        123,
17     privileged: true,
18 }
```

*compare map init: p 83
slice init: 68
array init: 59*

Listing 5.3 shows how to declare a variable of type user and initialize the value to something other than its zero value. On line 13, we provide a variable name followed by the short variable declaration operator. This operator is the colon with the equals sign (`:=`). The short variable declaration operator serves two purposes in one operation: it both declares and initializes a variable. Based on the type information on the right side of the operator, the short variable declaration operator can determine the type for the variable.

Since we're creating and initializing a struct type, we use a struct literal to perform the initialization. The struct literal takes the form of curly brackets with the initialization declared within them.

Listing 5.4   Creating a struct type value using a struct literal

```
13 user{
14     name:       "Lisa",
15     email:      "lisa@email.com",
16     ext:        123,
17     privileged: true,       // trailing comma , req
18 }
```

The struct literal can take on two forms for a struct type. Listing 5.4 shows the first form, which is to declare each field and value from the struct to be initialized on a separate line. A colon is used to separate the two, and it requires a trailing comma. The order of the fields doesn't matter. The second form is without the field names and just declares the values.

Listing 5.5   Creating a struct type value without declaring the field names

```
12 // Declare a variable of type user.
13 lisa := user{"Lisa", "lisa@email.com", 123, true}
```

no trailing comma

The values can also be placed on separate lines, but traditionally values are placed on the same line with no trailing comma when using this form. The order of the values does matter in this case and needs to match the order of the fields in the struct declaration. When declaring a struct type, you're not limited to just the built-in types. You can also declare fields using other user-defined types.

Listing 5.6   Declaring fields based on other struct types

```
20 // admin represents an admin user with privileges.
21 type admin struct {
22     person user          // sub type
23     level  string
24 }
```

Listing 5.6 shows a new struct type named admin. This struct type has a field named person of type user, and then declares a second field named level of type string. When creating a variable of a struct type that has a field like person, initializing the type with a struct literal changes a little.

Listing 5.7   Using struct literals to create values for fields

```
26 // Declare a variable of type admin.
27 fred := admin{
28     person: user{
29         name:       "Lisa",
30         email:      "lisa@email.com",
31         ext:        123,
32         privileged: true,
33     },
34     level: "super",
35 }
```

In order to initialize the person field, we need to create a value of type user. This is exactly what we do on line 28 in listing 5.7. Using the struct literal form, a value of type user is created and assigned to the person field.

A second way to declare a user-defined type is by taking an existing type and using it as the type specification for the new type. These types are great when you need a new type that can be represented by an existing type. The standard library uses this type declaration to create high-level functionality from the built-in types.

Listing 5.8   Declaration of a new type based on an int64

```
type Duration int64
```
existing type

Listing 5.8 shows the declaration of a type from the time package of the standard library. Duration is a type that represents the duration of time down to the nanosecond. The type takes its representation from the built-in type int64. In the declaration of Duration, we say that int64 is the base type of Duration. Even though int64 is acting at the base type, it doesn't mean Go considered them to be the same. Duration and int64 are two distinct and different types.

To better clarify what this means, look at this small program that doesn't compile.

Listing 5.9   Compiler error assigning value of different types

```
01 package main
02
03 type Duration int64
04
05 func main() {
06     var dur Duration
07     dur = int64(1000)
08 }
```

[handwritten marginalia: ? , X, Instead: dur := Duration{1000}]

The program in listing 5.9 declares a type on line 03 called Duration. Then on line 06, a variable named dur of type Duration is declared and set to its zero value. Then on line 07, we write code that produces the following compiler error when the program is built.

Listing 5.10   Actual compiler error

```
prog.go:7: cannot use int64(1000) (type int64) as type Duration
           in assignment
```

The compiler is clear as to what the problem is. Values of type int64 can't be used as values of type Duration. In other words, even though type int64 is the base type for Duration, Duration is still its own unique type. Values of two different types can't be assigned to each other, even if they're compatible. The compiler doesn't implicitly convert values of different types.

5.2   Methods

Methods provide a way to add behavior to user-defined types. Methods are really functions that contain an extra parameter that's declared between the keyword func and the function name.

Listing 5.11   listing11.go

```
01 // Sample program to show how to declare methods and how the Go
02 // compiler supports them.
03 package main
04
05 import (
06     "fmt"
07 )
08
09 // user defines a user in the program.
10 type user struct {
11     name   string
```

```
 12     email string
 13 }
 14
 15 // notify implements a method with a value receiver.
 16 func (u user) notify() {          // u of type user is the receiver
 17     fmt.Printf("Sending User Email To %s<%s>\n",
 18         u.name,
 19         u.email)
 20 }
 21
 22 // changeEmail implements a method with a pointer receiver.
 23 func (u *user) changeEmail(email string) {
 24     u.email = email
 25 }
 26
 27 // main is the entry point for the application.
 28 func main() {
 29     // Values of type user can be used to call methods
 30     // declared with a value receiver.
 31     bill := user{"Bill", "bill@email.com"}      // bill is of type user
 32     bill.notify()
 33
 34     // Pointers of type user can also be used to call methods
 35     // declared with a value receiver.
 36     lisa := &user{"Lisa", "lisa@email.com"}     // lisa is of type ptr to user
 37     lisa.notify()
 38
 39     // Values of type user can be used to call methods
 40     // declared with a pointer receiver.
 41     bill.changeEmail("bill@newdomain.com")
 42     bill.notify()
 43
 44     // Pointers of type user can be used to call methods
 45     // declared with a pointer receiver.
 46     lisa.changeEmail("lisa@comcast.com")        // email field being changed
 47     lisa.notify()
 48 }
```

Lines 16 and 23 of listing 5.11 show two different methods. The parameter between the keyword func and the function name is called a *receiver* and binds the function to the specified type. When a function has a receiver, that function is called a *method*. When you run the program, you get the following output.

Listing 5.12   Output for listing11.go

```
Sending User Email To Bill<bill@email.com>
Sending User Email To Lisa<lisa@email.com>
Sending User Email To Bill<bill@newdomain.com>
Sending User Email To Lisa<lisa@comcast.com>
```

Let's examine what the program is doing. On line 10, the program declares a struct type named user and then declares a method named notify.

Listing 5.13   listing11.go: lines 09–20

```
09 // user defines a user in the program.
10 type user struct {
11     name  string
12     email string
13 }
14
15 // notify implements a method with a value receiver.
16 func (u user) notify() {
17     fmt.Printf("Sending User Email To %s<%s>\n",
18         u.name,
19         u.email)
20 }
```

There are two types of receivers in Go: *value* receivers and *pointer* receivers. In listing 5.13 on line 16, the notify method is declared with a value receiver.

Listing 5.14   Declaration of a method with a value receiver

```
func (u user) notify() {
```

The receiver for notify is declared as a value of type user. When you declare a method using a value receiver, the method will always be operating against a copy of the value used to make the method call. Let's skip to line 32 of the program in listing 5.11 to see a method call on notify.

Listing 5.15   listing11.go: lines 29–32

```
29     // Values of type user can be used to call methods
30     // declared with a value receiver.
31     bill := user{"Bill", "bill@email.com"}
32     bill.notify()
```

Listing 5.15 shows a call to the notify method using a value of type user. On line 31, a variable named bill of type user is declared and initialized with a name and email address. Then on line 32, the notify method is called using the variable bill.

Listing 5.16   Calling a method from a variable

```
bill.notify()
```

The syntax looks similar to when you call a function from a package. In this case however, bill is not a package name but a variable name. When we call the notify method in this case, the value of bill is the receiver value for the call and the notify method is operating on a copy of this value.

You can also call methods that are declared with a value receiver using a pointer.

Listing 5.17   listing11.go: lines 34–37

```
34    // Pointers of type user can also be used to call methods
35    // declared with a value receiver.
36    lisa := &user{"Lisa", "lisa@email.com"}
37    lisa.notify()
```

Listing 5.17 shows a call to the notify method using a pointer of type user. On line 36, a variable named lisa of pointer type user is declared and initialized with a name and email address. Then on line 37, the notify method is called using the pointer variable. To support the method call, Go adjusts the pointer value to comply with the method's receiver. You can imagine that Go is performing the following operation.

Listing 5.18   What Go is doing underneath the code

```
(*lisa).notify()
```

Listing 5.18 shows essentially what the Go compiler is doing to support the method call. The pointer value is dereferenced so the method call is in compliance with the value receiver. Once again, notify is operating against a copy, but this time a copy of the value that the lisa pointer points to.

You can also declare methods with pointer receivers.

Listing 5.19   listing11.go: lines 22–25

```
22 // changeEmail implements a method with a pointer receiver.
23 func (u *user) changeEmail(email string) {
24     u.email = email
25 }
```

Listing 5.19 shows the declaration of the changeEmail method, which is declared with a pointer receiver. This time, the receiver is not a value of type user but a pointer of type user. When you call a method declared with a pointer receiver, the value used to make the call is shared with the method.

Listing 5.20   listing11.go: lines 36, 44–46

```
36    lisa := &user{"Lisa", "lisa@email.com"}

44    // Pointers of type user can be used to call methods
45    // declared with a pointer receiver.
46    lisa.changeEmail("lisa@newdomain.com")
```

In listing 5.20 you see the declaration of the lisa pointer variable followed by the method call to changeEmail on line 46. Once the call to changeEmail returns, any changes to the value that the lisa pointer points to will be reflected after the call. This is thanks to the pointer receiver. Value receivers operate on a copy of the value used to make the method call and pointer receivers operate on the actual value.

You can also call methods that are declared with a pointer receiver using a value.

Listing 5.21   listing11.go: line 31

```
31      bill := user{"Bill", "bill@email.com"}

39      // Values of type user can be used to call methods
40      // declared with a pointer receiver.
41      bill.changeEmail("bill@newdomain.com")
```

In listing 5.21, you see the declaration of the variable bill and then a call to the changeEmail method, which is declared with a pointer receiver. Once again, Go adjusts the value to comply with the method's receiver to support the call.

Listing 5.22   What Go is doing underneath the code

```
(&bill).notify()
```

Listing 5.22 shows essentially what the Go compiler is doing to support the method call. In this case, the value is referenced so the method call is in compliance with the receiver type. This is a great convenience Go provides, allowing method calls with values and pointers that don't match a method's receiver type natively.

Determining whether to use a value or pointer receiver can sometimes be confusing. There are some basic guidelines you can follow that come directly from the standard library.

5.3   *The nature of types*

After declaring a new type, try to answer this question before declaring methods for the type. Does adding or removing something from a value of this type need to create a new value or mutate the existing one? If the answer is create a new value, then use value receivers for your methods. If the answer is mutate the value, then use pointer receivers. This also applies to how values of this type should be passed to other parts of your program. It's important to be consistent. The idea is to not focus on what the method is doing with the value, but to focus on what the nature of the value is.

5.3.1   *Built-in types*

Built-in types are the set of types that are provided by the language. We know them as the set of numeric, string, and Boolean types. These types have a primitive nature to them. Because of this, when adding or removing something from a value of one of these types, a new value should be created. Based on this, when passing values of these types to functions and methods, a copy of the value should be passed. Let's look at a function from the standard library that works with built-in values.

Listing 5.23 golang.org/src/strings/strings.go: lines 620–625

```
620 func Trim(s string, cutset string) string {
621     if s == "" || cutset == "" {
622         return s
623     }
624     return TrimFunc(s, makeCutsetFunc(cutset))
625 }
```

In listing 5.23, you see the `Trim` function, which comes from the `strings` package in the standard library. The `Trim` function is passed a string value to operate on and a string value with characters to find. It then returns a new string value that's the result of the operation. The function operates on copies of the caller's original string values and returns a copy of the new string value. Strings, just like integers, floats, and Booleans, are primitive data values and should be copied when passed in and out of functions or methods.

Let's look at a second example of how the built-in types are treated as having a primitive nature.

Listing 5.24 golang.org/src/os/env.go: lines 38–44

```
38 func isShellSpecialVar(c uint8) bool {
39     switch c {
40     case '*', '#', '$', '@', '!', '?', '0', '1', '2', '3', '4', '5',
                '6', '7', '8', '9':
41         return true
42     }
43     return false
44 }
```

Listing 5.24 shows the `isShellSpecialVar` function from the `env` package. This function is passed a value of type `uint8` and returns a value of type `bool`. Note how pointers aren't being used to share the value for the parameter or return value. The caller passes a copy of their `uint8` value and receives a value of `true` or `false`.

5.3.2 Reference types

Reference types in Go are the set of slice, map, channel, interface, and function types. When you declare a variable from one of these types, the value that's created is called a *header* value. Technically, a string is also a reference type value. All the different header values from the different reference types contain a pointer to an underlying data structure. Each reference type also contains a set of unique fields that are used to manage the underlying data structure. You never share reference type values because the header value is designed to be copied. The header value contains a pointer; therefore, you can pass a copy of any reference type value and share the underlying data structure intrinsically.

Let's look at a type from the net package.

Listing 5.25   golang.org/src/net/ip.go: line 32

```
32 type IP []byte
```

Listing 5.25 shows a type called IP which is declared as a slice of bytes. Declaring a type like this is useful when you want to declare behavior around a built-in or reference type. The compiler will only let you declare methods for user-defined types that are named.

Listing 5.26   golang.org/src/net/ip.go: lines 329–337

```
329 func (ip IP) MarshalText() ([]byte, error) {
330     if len(ip) == 0 {
331         return []byte(""), nil
332     }
333     if len(ip) != IPv4len && len(ip) != IPv6len {
334         return nil, errors.New("invalid IP address")
335     }
336     return []byte(ip.String()), nil
337 }
```

The MarshalText method in listing 5.26 has been declared using a value receiver of type IP. A value receiver is exactly what you expect to see since you don't share reference type values. This also applies to passing reference type values as parameters to functions and methods.

Listing 5.27   golang.org/src/net/ip.go: lines 318–325

```
318 // ipEmptyString is like ip.String except that it returns
319 // an empty string when ip is unset.
320 func ipEmptyString(ip IP) string {
321     if len(ip) == 0 {
322         return ""
323     }
324     return ip.String()
325 }
```

In listing 5.27 you see the ipEmptyString function. This function is passed a value of the type IP. Once again, you can see how the caller's reference type value for this parameter is not shared with the function. The function is passed a copy of the caller's reference type value. This also applies to return values. In the end, reference type values are treated like primitive data values.

5.3.3   *Struct types*

Struct types can represent data values that could have either a primitive or nonprimitive nature. When the decision is made that a struct type value should not be mutated when something needs to be added or removed from the value, then it should follow the guidelines for the built-in and reference types. Let's start with looking at a struct implemented by the standard library that has a primitive nature.

Listing 5.28   golang.org/src/time/time.go: lines 39–55

```
39 type Time struct {
40     // sec gives the number of seconds elapsed since
41     // January 1, year 1 00:00:00 UTC.
42     sec int64
43
44     // nsec specifies a non-negative nanosecond
45     // offset within the second named by Seconds.
46     // It must be in the range [0, 999999999].
47     nsec int32
48
49     // loc specifies the Location that should be used to
50     // determine the minute, hour, month, day, and year
51     // that correspond to this Time.
52     // Only the zero Time has a nil Location.
53     // In that case it is interpreted to mean UTC.
54     loc *Location
55 }
```

The Time struct in listing 5.28 comes from the time package. When you think about time, you realize that any given point in time is not something that can change. This is exactly how the standard library implements the Time type. Let's look at the Now function that creates values of type Time.

Listing 5.29   golang.org/src/time/time.go: lines 781–784

```
781 func Now() Time {
782     sec, nsec := now()
783     return Time{sec + unixToInternal, nsec, Local}
784 }
```

The code in listing 5.29 shows the implementation of the Now function. This function creates a value of type Time and returns a copy of that Time value back to the caller. A pointer is not used to share the Time value created by the function. Next, let's look at a method declared against the Time type.

Listing 5.30   golang.org/src/time/time.go: lines 610–622

```
610 func (t Time) Add(d Duration) Time {
611     t.sec += int64(d / 1e9)
612     nsec := int32(t.nsec) + int32(d%1e9)
613     if nsec >= 1e9 {
614         t.sec++
615         nsec -= 1e9
616     } else if nsec < 0 {
617         t.sec--
618         nsec += 1e9
619     }
620     t.nsec = nsec
621     return t
622 }
```

d is in nanosecs; a nanosec is $\frac{1}{1e9}$ of a sec

The method Add in listing 5.30 is a great example of how the standard library treats the Time type as having a primitive nature. The method is declared using a value receiver and returns a new Time value. The method is operating on its own copy of the caller's Time value and returns a copy of its local Time value back to the caller. It's up to the caller whether they want to replace their Time value with what's returned or declare a new Time variable to hold the result.

In most cases, struct types don't exhibit a primitive nature, but a nonprimitive one. In these cases, adding or removing something from the value of the type should mutate the value. When this is the case, you want to use a pointer to share the value with the rest of the program that needs it. Let's take a look at a struct type implemented by the standard library that has a nonprimitive nature.

Listing 5.31 golang.org/src/os/file_unix.go: lines 15–29

```
15 // File represents an open file descriptor.
16 type File struct {
17     *file
18 }
19
20 // file is the real representation of *File.
21 // The extra level of indirection ensures that no clients of os
22 // can overwrite this data, which could cause the finalizer
23 // to close the wrong file descriptor.
24 type file struct {
25     fd int
26     name string
27     dirinfo *dirInfo // nil unless directory being read
28     nepipe int32 // number of consecutive EPIPE in Write
29 }
```

In listing 5.31 you see the declaration of the File type from the standard library. The nature of this type is nonprimitive. Values of this type are actually unsafe to be copied. The comments for the unexported type make this clear. Since there's no way to prevent programmers from making copies, the implementation of the File type uses an embedded pointer of an unexported type. We'll talk about embedding types later in this chapter, but this extra level of indirection provides protection from copies. Not every struct type requires or should be implemented with this extra protection. Programmers should respect the nature of each type and use it accordingly.

Let's look at the implementation of the Open function.

Listing 5.32 golang.org/src/os/file.go: lines 238–240

```
238 func Open(name string) (file *File, err error) {
239     return OpenFile(name, O_RDONLY, 0)
240 }
```

The implementation of the Open function in listing 5.32 shows how a pointer is used to share File type values with the caller of the function. Open creates a value of type

File and returns a pointer to that value. When a factory function returns a pointer, it's a good indication that the nature of the value being returned is nonprimitive.

Even if a function or method is never going to directly change the state of a nonprimitive value, it should still be shared.

Listing 5.33 golang.org/src/os/file.go: lines 224–232

```
224 func (f *File) Chdir() error {
225     if f == nil {
226         return ErrInvalid
227     }
228     if e := syscall.Fchdir(f.fd); e != nil {
229         return &PathError{"chdir", f.name, e}
230     }
231     return nil
232 }
```

The Chdir method in listing 5.33 shows how a pointer receiver is declared even though no changes are made to the receiver value. Since values of type File have a nonprimitive nature, they're always shared and never copied.

The decision to use a value or pointer receiver should not be based on whether the method is mutating the receiving value. The decision should be based on the nature of the type. One exception to this guideline is when you need the flexibility that value type receivers provide when working with interface values. In these cases, you may choose to use a value receiver even though the nature of the type is nonprimitive. It's entirely based on the mechanics behind how interface values call methods for the values stored inside of them. In the next section, you'll learn about what interface values are and the mechanics behind using them to call methods.

5.4 *Interfaces*

Polymorphism is the ability to write code that can take on different behavior through the implementation of types. Once a type implements an interface, an entire world of functionality can be opened up to values of that type. The standard library is a great example of this. The io package provides an incredible set of interfaces and functions that make streaming data easy to apply to our code. Just by implementing two interfaces, we can take advantage of all the engineering behind the io package.

But a lot of details go into declaring and implementing interfaces for use in our own programs. Even the implementation of existing interfaces requires an understanding of how interfaces work. Before we get into the details of how interfaces work and how to implement them, let's look at a quick example of the use of interfaces from the standard library.

5.4.1 Standard library

Let's start by looking at a sample program that implements a version of a popular program named curl. *Also, 208*

Listing 5.34   listing34.go

```go
01 // Sample program to show how to write a simple version of curl using
02 // the io.Reader and io.Writer interface support.
03 package main
04
05 import (
06     "fmt"
07     "io"
08     "net/http"
09     "os"
10 )
11
12 // init is called before main.
13 func init() {
14     if len(os.Args) != 2 {
15         fmt.Println("Usage: ./example2 <url>")
16         os.Exit(-1)
17     }
18 }
19
20 // main is the entry point for the application.
21 func main() {
22     // Get a response from the web server.
23     r, err := http.Get(os.Args[1])
24     if err != nil {
25         fmt.Println(err)
26         return
27     }
28
29     // Copies from the Body to Stdout.
30     io.Copy(os.Stdout, r.Body)
31     if err := r.Body.Close(); err != nil {
32         fmt.Println(err)
33     }
34 }
```

*r is *http.Request*

r.body is an i/f of type ReadCloser which implements the io.Reader i/f

os.Stdout implements the io.Writer i/f

io.Copy (dst, src) :: func streams data from src to dst
↑ must impl io.Reader i/f
└ must impl io.Writer i/f

Listing 5.34 shows the power of interfaces and their use in the standard library. In a few lines of code, we have a curl program by leveraging two functions that work with interface values. On line 23, we call the Get function from the http package. The http.Get function returns a pointer of type http.Request after it successfully communicates with the server. The http.Request type contains a field named Body, which is an interface value of type io.ReadCloser. *not http.Response ?*

On line 30, the Body field is passed into the io.Copy function as the second parameter. The io.Copy function accepts values of interface type io.Reader for its second parameter, and this value represents a source of data to stream from. Luckily, the Body field implements the io.Reader interface, so we can pass the Body field into io.Copy and use a web server as our source.

The first parameter for io.Copy represents the destination and must be a value that implements the io.Writer interface. For our destination, we pass a special interface value from the os package called Stdout. This interface value represents the standard out device and already implements the io.Writer interface. When we pass the Body and Stdout values to the io.Copy function, the function streams data from the web server to the terminal window in small chunks. Once the last chunk is read and written, the io.Copy function returns.

The io.Copy function can perform this work flow for many different types that already exist in the standard library.

Listing 5.35   listing35.go

```go
01 // Sample program to show how a bytes.Buffer can also be used
02 // with the io.Copy function.
03 package main
04
05 import (
06     "bytes"
07     "fmt"
08     "io"
09     "os"
10 )
11
12 // main is the entry point for the application.
13 func main() {
14     var b bytes.Buffer
15
16     // Write a string to the buffer.
17     b.Write([]byte("Hello"))           // write bytes obtained by converting a string to []byte
18                                        // to the buffer b
19     // Use Fprintf to concatenate a string to the Buffer.
20     fmt.Fprintf(&b, "World!")          // &b implements the io.Writer i/f
21
22     // Write the content of the Buffer to stdout.
23     io.Copy(os.Stdout, &b)             // &b implements the io.Reader i/f
24 }
```

Listing 5.35 shows a program that uses interfaces to concatenate and then stream data to standard out. On line 14, a variable of type Buffer from the bytes package is created, and then the Write method is used on line 17 to add the string Hello to the buffer. On line 20, the Fprintf function from the fmt package is called to append a second string to the buffer.

The fmt.Fprintf function accepts an interface value of type io.Writer as its first parameter. Since pointers of type bytes.Buffer implement the io.Writer interface, it can be passed in and the fmt.Fprintf function performs the concatenation. Finally, on line 23 the io.Copy function is used once again to write characters to the terminal window. Since pointers of type bytes.Buffer also implement the io.Reader interface, the io.Copy function can be used to display the contents of the buffer to the terminal window.

These two small examples hopefully show you some of the benefits of interfaces and how they're used in the standard library. Next, let's explore in greater detail how interfaces are implemented.

5.4.2 *Implementation*

Interfaces are types that just declare behavior. This behavior is never implemented by the interface type directly but instead by user-defined types via methods. When a user-defined type implements the set of methods declared by an interface type, values of the user-defined type can be assigned to values of the interface type. This assignment stores the value of the user-defined type into the interface value.

If a method call is made against an interface value, the equivalent method for the stored user-defined value is executed. Since any user-defined type can implement any interface, method calls against an interface value are polymorphic in nature. The user-defined type in this relationship is often called a *concrete type*, since interface values have no concrete behavior without the implementation of the stored user-defined value.

There are rules around whether values or pointers of a user-defined type satisfy the implementation of an interface. Not all values are created equal. These rules come from the specification under the section called method sets. Before you begin to investigate the details of method sets, it helps to understand what interface type values look like and how user-defined type values are stored inside them.

In figure 5.1 you see what the value of the interface variable looks like after the assignment of the user type value. Interface values are two-word data structures. The first word contains a pointer to an internal table called an *iTable*, which contains type information about the stored value. The iTable contains the type of value that has been stored and a list of methods associated with the value. The second word is a pointer to the stored value. The combination of type information and pointer binds the relationship between the two values.

Figure 5.2 shows what happens when a pointer is assigned to an interface value. In this case, the type information will reflect that a pointer of the assigned type has been stored, and the address being assigned is stored in the second word of the interface value.

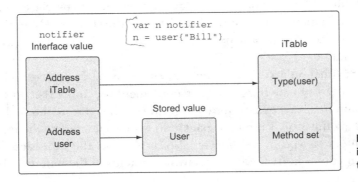

Figure 5.1 **A simple view of an interface value after concrete type value assignment**

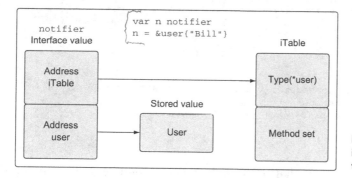

Figure 5.2 A simple view of an interface value after concrete type pointer assignment

5.4.3 *Method sets*

Method sets define the rules around interface compliance. Take a look at the following code to help you understand how method sets play an important role with interfaces.

Listing 5.36 listing36.go

```
01 // Sample program to show how to use an interface in Go.
02 package main
03
04 import (
05     "fmt"
06 )
07
08 // notifier is an interface that defined notification
09 // type behavior.
10 type notifier interface {
11     notify()                    ] method set
12 }
13
14 // user defines a user in the program.
15 type user struct {
16     name  string
17     email string
18 }
19                          on user
20 // notify implements a method with a pointer receiver.
21 func (u *user) notify() {
22     fmt.Printf("Sending user email to %s<%s>\n",
23         u.name,
24         u.email)
25 }
26
27 // main is the entry point for the application.
28 func main() {
29     // Create a value of type User and send a notification.
30     u := user{"Bill", "bill@email.com"}
31
32     sendNotification(u)
33
```

```
34      // ./listing36.go:32: cannot use u (type user) as type
35      //                     notifier in argument to sendNotification:
36      //   user does not implement notifier
37      //                     (notify method has pointer receiver)
38 }
39
40 // sendNotification accepts values that implement the notifier
41 // interface and sends notifications.
42 func sendNotification(n notifier) {
43     n.notify()
44 }
```

In listing 5.36 you see code that you would expect to compile, but it doesn't. On line 10, we declare an interface named notifier with a single method named notify. Then on line 15, we have the declaration of our concrete type named user and the implementation of the notifier interface via the method declaration on line 21. The method is implemented with a pointer receiver of type user.

Listing 5.37   listing36.go: lines 40–44

```
40 // sendNotification accepts values that implement the notifier
41 // interface and sends notifications.
42 func sendNotification(n notifier) {
43     n.notify()
44 }
```

On line 42 in listing 5.37, a function named sendNotification is declared and accepts a single value of the interface type notifier. Then the interface value is used to call the notify method against the stored value. Any value that implements the notifier interface can be passed into the sendNotification function. Now let's look at the main function.

Listing 5.38   listing36.go: lines 28–38

```
28 func main() {
29     // Create a value of type User and send a notification.
30     u := user{"Bill", "bill@email.com"}
31
32     sendNotification(u)
33
34     // ./listing36.go:32: cannot use u (type user) as type
35     //                     notifier in argument to sendNotification:
36     //   user does not implement notifier
37     //                     (notify method has pointer receiver)
38 }
```

In the main function, a value of the concrete type user is created and assigned to the variable u on line 30 in listing 5.38. Then the value of u is passed to the sendNotification function on line 32. But the call to sendNotification results in a compiler error.

Listing 5.39   Compiler error storing a value of type `user` to the interface value

```
./listing36.go:32: cannot use u (type user) as type
                    notifier in argument to sendNotification:
  user does not implement notifier (notify method has pointer receiver)
```

So why do we receive a compiler error when the user type implements the notify method on line 21? Let's take a look at that code again.

Listing 5.40   listing36.go: lines 08–12, 21–25

```
08 // notifier is an interface that defined notification
09 // type behavior.
10 type notifier interface {
11     notify()
12 }

21 func (u *user) notify() {
22     fmt.Printf("Sending user email to %s<%s>\n",
23         u.name,
24         u.email)
25 }
```

(handwritten annotations: "pointer rcvr" pointing to line 12; "// i/f implemented with a pointer recvr" to the right of line 21)

Listing 5.40 shows how the interface has been implemented, yet the compiler tells us that a value of type user doesn't implement the interface. If you look closer at the compiler message, it actually tells us why.

Listing 5.41   Closer look at compiler error

```
(notify method has pointer receiver)
```

To understand why values of type user don't implement the interface when an interface is implemented with a pointer receiver, you need to understand what *method sets* are. Method sets define the set of methods that are associated with values or pointers of a given type. The type of receiver used will determine whether a method is associated with a value, pointer, or both.

Let's start with explaining the rules for method sets as it's documented by the Go specification.

Listing 5.42   Method sets as described by the specification

```
Values                    Methods Receivers
---------------------------------------------------
    T                     (t T)
   *T                     (t T) and (t *T)
```

Listing 5.42 shows how the specification describes method sets. It says that a value of type T only has methods declared that have a value receiver, as part of its method set. But pointers of type T have methods declared with both value and pointer receivers, as part of its method set. Looking at these rules from the perspective of the value is confusing. Let's look at these rules from the perspective of the receiver.

Listing 5.43   Method sets from the perspective of the receiver type

```
Methods Receivers        Values
-------------------------------------------------
   (t T)                 T and *T
   (t *T)                *T
```

Listing 5.43 shows the same rules, but from the perspective of the receiver. It says that if you implement an interface using a pointer receiver, then only pointers of that type implement the interface. If you implement an interface using a value receiver, then both values and pointers of that type implement the interface. If you look at the code in listing 5.36 again, you now have the context to understand the compiler error.

Listing 5.44   listing36.go: lines 28–38

```
28 func main() {
29     // Create a value of type User and send a notification.
30     u := user{"Bill", "bill@email.com"}
31
32     sendNotification(u)
33
34     // ./listing36.go:32: cannot use u (type user) as type
35     //                     notifier in argument to sendNotification:
36     //   user does not implement notifier
37     //                     (notify method has pointer receiver)
38 }
```

We implemented the interface using a pointer receiver and attempted to pass a value of type user to the sendNotification function. Lines 30 and 32 in listing 5.44 show this clearly. But if we pass the address of the user value instead, you'll see that it now compiles and works.

Listing 5.45   listing36.go: lines 28–35

```
28 func main() {
29     // Create a value of type User and send a notification.
30     u := user{"Bill", "bill@email.com"}
31
32     sendNotification(&u)
33
34     // PASSED THE ADDRESS AND NO MORE ERROR.
35 }
```

In listing 5.45, we now have a program that compiles and runs. Only pointers of type user can be passed to the sendNotification function, since a pointer receiver was used to implement the interface.

The question now is why the restriction? The answer comes from the fact that it's not always possible to get the address of a value.

Listing 5.46   listing46.go

```
01 // Sample program to show how you can't always get the
02 // address of a value.
03 package main
04
05 import "fmt"
06
07 // duration is a type with a base type of int.
08 type duration int
09
10 // format pretty-prints the duration value.
11 func (d *duration) pretty() string {
12     return fmt.Sprintf("Duration: %d", *d)
13 }
14
15 // main is the entry point for the application.
16 func main() {
17     duration(42).pretty()
18
19     // ./listing46.go:17: cannot call pointer method on duration(42)
20     // ./listing46.go:17: cannot take the address of duration(42)
21 }
```

The code in listing 5.46 attempts to get the address of a value of type duration and can't. This shows that it's not always possible to get the address of a value. Let's look at the method set rules again.

Listing 5.47   Second look at the method set rules

```
Values                          Methods Receivers
----------------------------    -------------------------

    T                               (t T)
   *T                               (t T) and (t *T)


Methods Receivers               Values
-------------------------------------------------------
   (t T)                            T and *T
   (t *T)                           *T
```

Because it's not always possible to get the address of a value, the method set for a value only includes methods that are implemented with a value receiver.

5.4.4   *Polymorphism*

Now that you understand the mechanics behind interfaces and method sets, let's look at one final example that shows the polymorphic behavior of interfaces.

Listing 5.48   listing48.go

```
01 // Sample program to show how polymorphic behavior with interfaces.
02 package main
03
04 import (
05     "fmt"
06 )
07
08 // notifier is an interface that defines notification
09 // type behavior.
10 type notifier interface {
11     notify()
12 }
13
14 // user defines a user in the program.
15 type user struct {
16     name   string
17     email string
18 }
19
20 // notify implements the notifier interface with a pointer receiver.
21 func (u *user) notify() {
22     fmt.Printf("Sending user email to %s<%s>\n",
23         u.name,
24         u.email)
25 }
26
27 // admin defines a admin in the program.
28 type admin struct {
29     name   string
30     email string
31 }
32
33 // notify implements the notifier interface with a pointer receiver.
34 func (a *admin) notify() {
35     fmt.Printf("Sending admin email to %s<%s>\n",
36         a.name,
37         a.email)
38 }
39
40 // main is the entry point for the application.
41 func main() {
42     // Create a user value and pass it to sendNotification.
43     bill := user{"Bill", "bill@email.com"}
44     sendNotification(&bill)
45
46     // Create an admin value and pass it to sendNotification.
47     lisa := admin{"Lisa", "lisa@email.com"}
48     sendNotification(&lisa)
49 }
50
51 // sendNotification accepts values that implement the notifier
52 // interface and sends notifications.
```

```
53 func sendNotification(n notifier) {
54     n.notify()
55 }
```

In listing 5.48, we have a final example of how interfaces provide polymorphic behavior. On line 10, we have the same `notifier` interface that we declared in previous listings. Then on lines 15 through 25, we have the declaration of a struct named `user` with the implementation of the `notifier` interface using a pointer receiver. On lines 28 through 38, we have the declaration of a struct named `admin` with the implementation of the `notifier` interface as well. We have two concrete types implementing the `notifier` interface.

On line 53, we have our polymorphic `sendNotification` function again that accepts values that implement the `notifier` interface. Since any concrete type value can implement the interface, this function can execute the `notify` method for any concrete type value that's passed in, thus providing polymorphic behavior.

Listing 5.49   listing48.go: lines 40–49

```
40 // main is the entry point for the application.
41 func main() {
42     // Create a user value and pass it to sendNotification.
43     bill := user{"Bill", "bill@email.com"}
44     sendNotification(&bill)
45
46     // Create an admin value and pass it to sendNotification.
47     lisa := admin{"Lisa", "lisa@email.com"}
48     sendNotification(&lisa)
49 }
```

Finally, in listing 5.49 you see it all come together. A value of type `user` is created on line 43 in the main function, and then the address of that value is passed into `sendNotification` on line 44. This causes the `notify` method declared by the `user` type to be executed. Then we do the same with a value of type `admin` on lines 47 and 48. In the end, because `sendNotification` accepts interface values of type `notifier`, the function can execute the behavior implemented by both `user` and `admin`.

5.5   *Type embedding*

Go allows you to take existing types and both extend and change their behavior. This capability is important for code reuse and for changing the behavior of an existing type to suit a new need. This is accomplished through *type embedding*. It works by taking an existing type and declaring that type within the declaration of a new struct type. The type that is embedded is then called an *inner* type of the new *outer* type.

Through inner type promotion, identifiers from the inner type are promoted up to the outer type. These promoted identifiers become part of the outer type as if they were declared explicitly by the type itself. The outer type is then composed of everything the inner type contains, and new fields and methods can be added. The outer type can also declare the same identifiers as the inner type and override any fields or methods it needs to. This is how an existing type can be both extended and changed.

Let's start with a sample program that shows the basics of type embedding.

Listing 5.50   listing50.go

```go
01 // Sample program to show how to embed a type into another type and
02 // the relationship between the inner and outer type.
03 package main
04
05 import (
06     "fmt"
07 )
08
09 // user defines a user in the program.
10 type user struct {
11     name  string
12     email string
13 }
14
15 // notify implements a method that can be called via
16 // a value of type user.
17 func (u *user) notify() {
18     fmt.Printf("Sending user email to %s<%s>\n",
19     u.name,
20     u.email)
21 }
22
23 // admin represents an admin user with privileges.
24 type admin struct {
25     user  // Embedded Type
26     level string
27 }
28
29 // main is the entry point for the application.
30 func main() {
31     // Create an admin user.
32     ad := admin{
33         user: user{
34             name:  "john smith",
35             email: "john@yahoo.com",
36         },
37         level: "super",
38     }
39
40     // We can access the inner type's method directly.
41     ad.user.notify()        // OK
42
43     // The inner type's method is promoted.
44     ad.notify()             // promoted: OK
45 }
```

In listing 5.50, we have a program that shows how to embed a type and access the embedded identifiers. We start with the declaration of two struct types on lines 10 and 24.

Listing 5.51   listing50.go: lines 09–13, 23–27

```
09 // user defines a user in the program.
10 type user struct {
11     name  string
12     email string
13 }

23 // admin represents an admin user with privileges.
24 type admin struct {
25     user  // Embedded Type
26     level string
27 }
```

On line 10 in listing 5.51, we have the declaration of a struct type named user, and then on line 24 we have the declaration of a second struct type named admin. Inside the declaration of the admin type on line 25, we have the embedding of the user type as an inner type of admin. To embed a type, all that needs to happen is for the type name to be declared. One line 26, we have the declaration of a field named level. Notice the difference between declaring a field and embedding a type.

Once we embed the user type inside of admin, we can say that user is an inner type of the outer type admin. The concept of having an inner and outer type makes it easier to understand the relationship between the two.

Listing 5.52   listing50.go: lines 15–21

```
15 // notify implements a method that can be called via
16 // a value of type user.
17 func (u *user) notify() {
18     fmt.Printf("Sending user email to %s<%s>\n",
19     u.name,
20     u.email)
21 }
```

Listing 5.52 shows the declaration of a method named notify using a pointer receiver of type user. The method just displays a friendly message stating an email is being sent to a specific user and email address. Now let's look at the main function.

Listing 5.53   listing50.go: lines 30–45

```
30 func main() {
31     // Create an admin user.
32     ad := admin{
33         user: user{
34             name:  "john smith",
35             email: "john@yahoo.com",
36         },
```

```
37          level: "super",
38      }
39
40      // We can access the inner type's method directly.
41      ad.user.notify()
42
43      // The inner type's method is promoted.
44      ad.notify()
45 }
```

The main function in listing 5.53 shows the mechanics behind type embedding. On line 32, a value of type admin is created. The initialization of the inner type is performed using a struct literal, and to access the inner type we just need to use the type's name. Something special about an inner type is that it always exists in and of itself. This means the inner type never loses its identity and can always be accessed directly.

Listing 5.54   listing50.go: lines 40–41

```
40      // We can access the inner type's method directly.
41      ad.user.notify()
```

On line 41 in listing 5.54, you see a call to the notify method. This call is made by accessing the user inner type directly through the admin outer type variable ad. This shows how the inner type exists in and of itself and is always accessible. But thanks to inner type promotion, the notify method can also be accessed directly from the ad variable.

Listing 5.55   listing50.go: lines 43–45

```
43      // The inner type's method is promoted.
44      ad.notify()
45 }
```

Listing 5.55 on line 44 shows the method call to notify from the outer type variable. Since the identifiers of the inner type are promoted up to the outer type, we can access the inner type's identifiers through values of the outer type. Let's change the sample by adding an interface.

Listing 5.56   listing56.go

```
01 // Sample program to show how embedded types work with interfaces.
02 package main
03
04 import (
05      "fmt"
06 )
07
08 // notifier is an interface that defined notification
09 // type behavior.
10 type notifier interface {
11      notify()
```

```
12 }
13
14 // user defines a user in the program.
15 type user struct {
16     name  string
17     email string
18 }
19
20 // notify implements a method that can be called via
21 // a value of type user.
22 func (u *user) notify() {
23     fmt.Printf("Sending user email to %s<%s>\n",
24     u.name,
25     u.email)
26 }
27
28 // admin represents an admin user with privileges.
29 type admin struct {
30     user
31     level string
32 }
33
34 // main is the entry point for the application.
35 func main() {
36     // Create an admin user.
37     ad := admin{
38         user: user{
39             name:  "john smith",
40             email: "john@yahoo.com",
41         },
42         level: "super",
43     }
44
45     // Send the admin user a notification.
46     // The embedded inner type's implementation of the
47     // interface is "promoted" to the outer type.
48     sendNotification(&ad)
49 }
50
51 // sendNotification accepts values that implement the notifier
52 // interface and sends notifications.
53 func sendNotification(n notifier) {
54     n.notify()
55 }
```

The sample code in listing 5.56 uses the same code from before but with a few changes.

Listing 5.57   listing56.go: lines 08–12, 51–55

```
08 // notifier is an interface that defined notification
09 // type behavior.
10 type notifier interface {
11     notify()
12 }
```

```
51 // sendNotification accepts values that implement the notifier
52 // interface and sends notifications.
53 func sendNotification(n notifier) {
54     n.notify()
55 }
```

On line 08 in listing 5.57, we have the declaration of the notifier interface. Then on line 53, we have the sendNotification function that accepts an interface value of type notifier. We know from the code before that the user type has declared a method named notify that implements the notifier interface with a pointer receiver. Therefore, we can move on to the changes made to the main function.

Listing 5.58   listing56.go: lines 35–49

```
35 func main() {
36     // Create an admin user.
37     ad := admin{
38         user: user{
39             name:  "john smith",
40             email: "john@yahoo.com",
41         },
42         level: "super",
43     }
44
45     // Send the admin user a notification.
46     // The embedded inner type's implementation of the
47     // interface is "promoted" to the outer type.
48     sendNotification(&ad)
49 }
```

This is where things get interesting. On line 37 in listing 5.58, we create the admin outer type variable ad. Then on line 48, we pass the address of the outer type variable to the sendNotification function. The compiler accepts the assignment of the outer type pointer as a value that implements the notifier interface. But if you look at the entire sample program, you won't see the admin type implement the interface.

Thanks to inner type promotion, the implementation of the interface by the inner type has been promoted up to the outer type. That means the outer type now implements the interface, thanks to the inner type's implementation. When we run this sample program, we get the following output.

Listing 5.59   Output for listing56.go

```
Output:
Sending user email to john smith<john@yahoo.com>

20 // notify implements a method that can be called via
21 // a value of type user.
22 func (u *user) notify() {
23     fmt.Printf("Sending user email to %s<%s>\n",
24     u.name,
25     u.email)
26 }
```

You can see in listing 5.59 that the inner type's implementation of the interface was called.

What if the outer type doesn't want to use the inner type's implementation because it needs an implementation of its own? Let's look at another sample program that solves that problem.

Listing 5.60   listing60.go

```
01 // Sample program to show what happens when the outer and inner
02 // types implement the same interface.
03 package main
04
05 import (
06     "fmt"
07 )
08
09 // notifier is an interface that defined notification
10 // type behavior.
11 type notifier interface {
12     notify()
13 }
14
15 // user defines a user in the program.
16 type user struct {
17     name  string
18     email string
19 }
20
21 // notify implements a method that can be called via
22 // a value of type user.
23 func (u *user) notify() {
24     fmt.Printf("Sending user email to %s<%s>\n",
25         u.name,
26         u.email)
27 }
28
29 // admin represents an admin user with privileges.
30 type admin struct {
31     user
32     level string
33 }
34
35 // notify implements a method that can be called via
36 // a value of type admin.
37 func (a *admin) notify() {
38     fmt.Printf("Sending admin email to %s<%s>\n",
39         a.name,
40         a.email)
41 }
42
43 // main is the entry point for the application.
44 func main() {
45     // Create an admin user.
```

```
46    ad := admin{
47        user: user{
48            name:  "john smith",
49            email: "john@yahoo.com",
50        },
51        level: "super",
52    }
53
54    // Send the admin user a notification.
55    // The embedded inner type's implementation of the
56    // interface is NOT "promoted" to the outer type.
57    sendNotification(&ad)
58
59    // We can access the inner type's method directly.
60    ad.user.notify()
61
62    // The inner type's method is NOT promoted.
63    ad.notify()
64 }
65
66 // sendNotification accepts values that implement the notifier
67 // interface and sends notifications.
68 func sendNotification(n notifier) {
69     n.notify()
70 }
```

The sample code in listing 5.60 uses the same code from before, but with a few more changes.

Listing 5.61   listing60.go: lines 35–41

```
35 // notify implements a method that can be called via
36 // a value of type admin.
37 func (a *admin) notify() {
38     fmt.Printf("Sending admin email to %s<%s>\n",
39         a.name,
40         a.email)
41 }
```

This code sample adds an implementation of the notifier interface by the admin type. When the admin type's implementation is called, it will display "Sending admin email" as opposed to the user type's implementation that displays "Sending user email".

There are some more changes to the main function as well.

Listing 5.62   listing60.go: lines 43–64

```
43 // main is the entry point for the application.
44 func main() {
45     // Create an admin user.
46     ad := admin{
47         user: user{
48             name:  "john smith",
49             email: "john@yahoo.com",
```

```
50          },
51          level: "super",
52      }
53
54      // Send the admin user a notification.
55      // The embedded inner type's implementation of the
56      // interface is NOT "promoted" to the outer type.
57      sendNotification(&ad)
58
59      // We can access the inner type's method directly.
60      ad.user.notify()
61
62      // The inner type's method is NOT promoted.
63      ad.notify()
64 }
```

On line 46 in listing 5.62, we have the creation of the outer type ad variable again. On line 57 the address of the ad variable is passed to the sendNotification function, and the value is accepted as implementing the interface. On line 60 the code calls the notify method from accessing the user inner type directly. Finally, on line 63 the notify method is called using the outer type variable ad. When you look at the output of this sample program, you see a different story.

Listing 5.63   Output for listing60.go

```
Sending Admin Email To john smith<john@yahoo.com>
Sending user email to john smith<john@yahoo.com>
Sending admin email to john smith<john@yahoo.com>
```

This time you see how the admin type's implementation of the notifier interface was executed both by the sendNotification function and through the use of the outer type variable ad. This shows how the inner type's implementation was not promoted once the outer type implemented the notify method. But the inner type is always there, in and of itself, so the code is still able to call the inner type's implementation directly.

5.6   *Exporting and unexporting identifiers*

The ability to apply visibility rules to the identifiers you declare is critical for good API design. Go supports the exporting and unexporting of identifiers from a package to provide this functionality. In chapter 3, we talked about packaging and how to import the identifiers from one package into another. Sometimes, you may not want identifiers such as types, functions, or methods to be a part of the public API for a package. In these cases, you need a way to declare those identifiers so they're unknown outside the package. You need to declare them to be unexported.

Let's start with a sample program that shows how to unexport identifiers from a package.

Listing 5.64   listing64/

counters/counters.go

```
----------------------------------------------------------------------
01 // Package counters provides alert counter support.
02 package counters
03
04 // alertCounter is an unexported type that
05 // contains an integer counter for alerts.
06 type alertCounter int
```

listing64.go

```
----------------------------------------------------------------------
01 // Sample program to show how the program can't access an
02 // unexported identifier from another package.
03 package main
04
05 import (
06     "fmt"
07
08     "github.com/goinaction/code/chapter5/listing64/counters"
09 )
10
11 // main is the entry point for the application.
12 func main() {
13     // Create a variable of the unexported type and initialize
14     // the value to 10.
15     counter := counters.alertCounter(10)
16
17     // ./listing64.go:15: cannot refer to unexported name
18     //                                  counters.alertCounter
19     // ./listing64.go:15: undefined: counters.alertCounter
20
21     fmt.Printf("Counter: %d\n", counter)
22 }
```

package name (handwritten annotation)

In this example we have two code files. One is named counters.go and lives inside its own package named counters. The second code file is named listing64.go and is importing the counters package. Let's start with the code inside the counters package.

Listing 5.65   counters/counters.go

```
01 // Package counters provides alert counter support.
02 package counters
03
04 // alertCounter is an unexported type that
05 // contains an integer counter for alerts.
06 type alertCounter int
```

Listing 5.65 isolates the code for just the counters package. The first thing you should notice is on line 02. Up until now, all the code samples have used package main, but here you see package counters. When you're writing code that will live in its own package, it's good practice to name the package the same as the folder the code is in. All the Go tooling expects this convention, so it's a good practice to follow.

In package counters, we've declared a single identifier named alertCounter on line 06. This identifier is a type using int as its base type. An important aspect of this identifier is that it has been unexported.

When an identifier starts with a lowercase letter, the identifier is unexported or unknown to code outside the package. When an identifier starts with an uppercase letter, it's exported or known to code outside the package. Let's look at the code that imports this package.

Listing 5.66   listing64.go

```
01 // Sample program to show how the program can't access an
02 // unexported identifier from another package.
03 package main
04
05 import (
06     "fmt"
07
08     "github.com/goinaction/code/chapter5/listing64/counters"
09 )
10
11 // main is the entry point for the application.
12 func main() {
13     // Create a variable of the unexported type and initialize
14     // the value to 10.
15     counter := counters.alertCounter(10)
16
17     // ./listing64.go:15: cannot refer to unexported name
18     //                                   counters.alertCounter
19     // ./listing64.go:15: undefined: counters.alertCounter
20
21     fmt.Printf("Counter: %d\n", counter)
22 }
```

The code in listing64.go from listing 5.66 is declaring the main package on line 03, and then on line 08 the counters package is imported. With the counters package imported, we move to the main function and line 15.

Listing 5.67   listing64.go: lines 13–19

```
13     // Create a variable of the unexported type and initialize
14     // the value to 10.
15     counter := counters.alertCounter(10)
16
17     // ./listing64.go:15: cannot refer to unexported name
18     //                                   counters.alertCounter
19     // ./listing64.go:15: undefined: counters.alertCounter
```

On line 15 in listing 5.67, the code attempts to create a value of the unexported type alertCounter. But this code produces a compiler error that states that the code at line 15 can't refer to the unexported identifier counters.alertCounter. This identifier is undefined.

Since the alertCounter type from the counters package was declared using a lowercase letter, it was unexported and therefore unknown to the code in listing64.go. If we change the type to start with a capital letter, then the compiler error will go away. Let's look at a new sample program that implements a factory function for the counters package.

Listing 5.68   listing68/

package

```
counters/counters.go
--------------------------------------------------------------------
01 // Package counters provides alert counter support.
02 package counters
03
04 // alertCounter is an unexported type that
05 // contains an integer counter for alerts.
06 type alertCounter int
07
08 // New creates and returns values of the unexported
09 // type alertCounter
10 func New(value int) alertCounter {          // Factory Function
11     return alertCounter(value)
12 }
```

```
listing68.go
--------------------------------------------------------------------
01 // Sample program to show how the program can access a value
02 // of an unexported identifier from another package.
03 package main
04
05 import (
06     "fmt"
07
08     "github.com/goinaction/code/chapter5/listing68/counters"
09 )
10
11 // main is the entry point for the application.
12 func main() {
13     // Create a variable of the unexported type using the exported
14     // New function from the package counters.
15     counter := counters.New(10)
16
17     fmt.Printf("Counter: %d\n", counter)
18 }
```

This example has been changed to use a factory function to create values of the unexported alertCounter type. Let's look at the code in the counters package first.

Listing 5.69 `counters/counters.go`

```
01 // Package counters provides alert counter support.
02 package counters
03
04 // alertCounter is an unexported type that
05 // contains an integer counter for alerts.
06 type alertCounter int
07
08 // New creates and returns values of the unexported
09 // type alertCounter.
10 func New(value int) alertCounter {
11     return alertCounter(value)
12 }
```

Listing 5.69 shows the changes we made to the counters package. The `alertCounter` type is still unexported, but now on line 10 we have a function called `New`. It's a convention in Go to give factory functions the name of `New`. This `New` function does something interesting: it creates a value of the unexported type and returns that value back to the caller. Let's look at the main function from listing68.go.

Listing 5.70 `listing68.go`

```
11 // main is the entry point for the application.
12 func main() {
13     // Create a variable of the unexported type using the exported
14     // New function from the package counters.
15     counter := counters.New(10)
16
17     fmt.Printf("Counter: %d\n", counter)
18 }
```

On line 15 in listing 5.70, you see a call to the `New` function from the counters package. The value returned by the `New` function is then assigned to a variable named `counter`. This program compiles and runs, but why? The `New` function is returning a value of the unexported type `alertCounter`, yet `main` is able to accept that value and create a variable of the unexported type.

This is possible for two reasons. First, identifiers are exported or unexported, not values. Second, the short variable declaration operator is capable of inferring the type and creating a variable of the unexported type. You can never explicitly create a variable of an unexported type, but the short variable declaration operator can.

Let's look at a new sample program that shows how fields from a struct type are affected by these visibility rules.

Listing 5.71 `listing71/`

`entities/entities.go`

```
--------------------------------------------------------------
01 // Package entities contains support for types of
02 // people in the system.
```

```
03 package entities
04
05 // User defines a user in the program.
06 type User struct {
07     Name   string
08     email  string        // unexported
09 }
```

listing71.go

```
------------------------------------------------------------------
01 // Sample program to show how unexported fields from an exported
02 // struct type can't be accessed directly.
03 package main
04
05 import (
06     "fmt"
07
08     "github.com/goinaction/code/chapter5/listing71/entities"
09 )
10
11 // main is the entry point for the application.
12 func main() {
13     // Create a value of type User from the entities package.
14     u := entities.User{
15         Name:  "Bill",
16         email: "bill@email.com",
17     }
18
19     // ./example69.go:16: unknown entities.User field 'email' in
20     //                    struct literal
21
22     fmt.Printf("User: %v\n", u)
23 }
```

The code in listing 5.71 changed things a bit. Now we have a package called entities that declares a struct type named User.

Listing 5.72   entities/entities.go

```
01 // Package entities contains support for types of
02 // people in the system.
03 package entities
04
05 // User defines a user in the program.
06 type User struct {
07     Name   string        // exported
08     email  string        // unexported
09 }
```

The User type on line 06 in listing 5.72 is declared to be exported. Two fields are declared with the User type, an exported field named Name and an unexported field named email. Let's look at the code in listing71.go.

Listing 5.73   listing71.go

```
01 // Sample program to show how unexported fields from an exported
02 // struct type can't be accessed directly.
03 package main
04
05 import (
06     "fmt"
07
08     "github.com/goinaction/code/chapter5/listing71/entities"
09 )
10
11 // main is the entry point for the application.
12 func main() {
13     // Create a value of type User from the entities package.
14     u := entities.User{
15         Name:  "Bill",
16         email: "bill@email.com",
17     }
18
19     // ./example71.go:16: unknown entities.User field 'email' in
20     //                    struct literal
21
22     fmt.Printf("User: %v\n", u)
23 }
```

The entities package is imported on line 08 in listing 5.73. On line 14 a variable named u of the exported type User from the entities package is declared and its fields initialized. But there's a problem. On line 16 the code attempts to initialize the unexported field email, and the compiler complains the field is unknown. That identifier can't be accessed outside the entities package, since it has been unexported.

Let's look at one final example to show how the exporting and unexporting of embedded types work.

Listing 5.74   listing74/

```
entities/entities.go
-------------------------------------    ------------------------
01 // Package entities contains support for types of
02 // people in the system.
03 package entities
04
05 // user defines a user in the program.
06 type user struct {
07     Name   string        // exported
08     Email  string        // exported
09 }
10
11 // Admin defines an admin in the program.
12 type Admin struct {
13     user   // The embedded type is unexported.          ✗
14     Rights int
15 }
```

```
listing74.go
----------------------------------------------------------------------
01 // Sample program to show how unexported fields from an exported
02 // struct type can't be accessed directly.
03 package main
04
05 import (
06     "fmt"
07
08     "github.com/goinaction/code/chapter5/listing74/entities"
09 )
10
11 // main is the entry point for the application.
12 func main() {
13     // Create a value of type Admin from the entities package.
14     a := entities.Admin{
15         Rights: 10,
16     }
17
18     // Set the exported fields from the unexported
19     // inner type.
20     a.Name = "Bill"
21     a.Email = "bill@email.com"
22
23     fmt.Printf("User: %v\n", a)
24 }
```

Now, in listing 5.74 the entities package contains two struct types.

Listing 5.75   entities/entities.go

```
01 // Package entities contains support for types of
02 // people in the system.
03 package entities
04
05 // user defines a user in the program.
06 type user struct {
07     Name   string        // exported
08     Email  string        // exported
09 }
10
11 // Admin defines an admin in the program.
12 type Admin struct {            // Admin is exported
13     user   // The embedded type is unexported... but fields are available
14     Rights int                                    in promoted form
15 }
```

On line 06 in listing 5.75, an unexported struct type named user is declared. It contains two exported fields named Name and Email. On line 12 an exported struct type named Admin is declared. Admin has an exported field named Rights, but it also embeds the unexported user type. Let's look at the code in the main function for listing74.go.

Listing 5.76   listing74.go: lines 11–24

```
11 // main is the entry point for the application.
12 func main() {
13     // Create a value of type Admin from the entities package.
14     a := entities.Admin{
15         Rights: 10,
16     }
17
18     // Set the exported fields from the unexported
19     // inner type.
20     a.Name = "Bill"
21     a.Email = "bill@email.com"
22
23     fmt.Printf("User: %v\n", a)
24 }
```

The main function starts out on line 14 in listing 5.76 by creating a value of type Admin from the entities package. Since the user inner type is unexported, this code can't access the inner type to initialize it inside the struct literal. Even though the inner type is unexported, the fields declared within the inner type are exported. Since the identifiers from the inner type are promoted to the outer type, those exported fields are known through a value of the outer type.

Therefore, on line 20 and 21 the Name and Email fields from the unexported inner type can be accessed and initialized through the outer type variable a. There's no access to the inner type directly, since the user type is unexported.

5.7   Summary

- User-defined types can be declared using the keyword struct or by specifying an existing type.
- Methods provide a way to add behavior to user-defined types.
- Think of types as having one of two natures, primitive or non-primitive.
- Interfaces are types that declare behavior and provide polymorphism.
- Type embedding provides the ability to extend types without the need for inheritance.
- Identifiers are either exported or unexported from packages.

Concurrency

In this chapter
- Running code with goroutines
- Detecting and fixing race conditions
- Sharing data with channels

Often a program can be written as one linear path of code that performs a single task and finishes. When this is possible, always choose this option, because this type of program is usually simple to write and maintain. But there are times when executing multiple tasks concurrently has greater benefit. One example is with a web service that can receive multiple requests for data on individual sockets at the same time. Each socket request is unique and can be independently processed from any other. Having the ability to execute requests concurrently can dramatically improve the performance of this type of system. With this in mind, support for concurrency has been built directly into Go's language and runtime.

Concurrency in Go is the ability for functions to run independent of each other. When a function is created as a goroutine, it's treated as an independent unit of work that gets scheduled and then executed on an available logical processor. The Go runtime scheduler is a sophisticated piece of software that manages all the goroutines that are created and need processor time. The scheduler sits on

128

top of the operating system, binding operating system's threads to logical processors which, in turn, execute goroutines. The scheduler controls everything related to which goroutines are running on which logical processors at any given time.

Concurrency synchronization comes from a paradigm called *communicating sequential processes* or *CSP*. CSP is a message-passing model that works by communicating data between goroutines instead of locking data to synchronize access. The key data type for synchronizing and passing messages between goroutines is called a *channel*. For many developers who have never experienced writing concurrent programs using channels, they invoke an air of awe and excitement, which you hopefully will experience as well. Using channels makes it easier to write concurrent programs and makes them less prone to errors.

6.1   *Concurrency versus parallelism*

Let's start by learning at a high level what operating system *processes* and *threads* are. This will help you understand later on how the Go runtime scheduler works with the operating system to run goroutines concurrently. When you run an application, such as an IDE or editor, the operating system starts a process for the application. You can think of a process like a container that holds all the resources an application uses and maintains as it runs.

Figure 6.1 shows a process that contains common resources that may be allocated by any process. These resources include but are not limited to a memory address space, handles to files, devices, and threads. A *thread* is a path of execution that's scheduled by the operating system to run the code that you write in your functions. Each process contains at least one thread, and the initial thread for each process is called the *main thread*. When the main thread terminates, the application terminates, because this path of the execution is the origin for the application. The operating system schedules threads to run against processors regardless of the process they belong to. The algorithms that different operating systems use to schedule threads are always changing and abstracted from the programmer.

The operating system schedules threads to run against physical processors and the Go runtime schedules goroutines to run against logical processors. Each logical processor is individually bound to a single operating system thread. As of version 1.5, the default is to allocate a logical processor for every physical processor that's available. Prior to version 1.5, the default was to allocate only a single logical processor. These logical processors are used to execute all the goroutines that are created. Even with a single logical processor, hundreds of thousands of goroutines can be scheduled to run concurrently with amazing efficiency and performance.

In figure 6.2, you can see the relationship between an operating system thread, a logical processor, and the local run queue. As goroutines are created and ready to run, they're placed in the scheduler's global run queue. Soon after, they're assigned to a logical processor and placed into a local run queue for that logical processor. From there, a goroutine waits its turn to be given the logical processor for execution.

The process maintains a memory address space, handles to files, and devices and threads for a running application. The OS scheduler decides which threads will receive time on any given CPU.

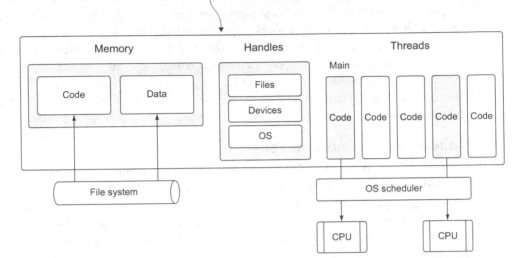

Figure 6.1   A simple view of a process and its threads for a running application

The **Go runtime schedules goroutines to run in a logical processor that is bound to a single operating system thread.** When goroutines are runnable, they are added to a logical processor's run queue.

When a goroutine makes a blocking syscall, the scheduler will detach the thread from the processor and create a new thread to service that processor.

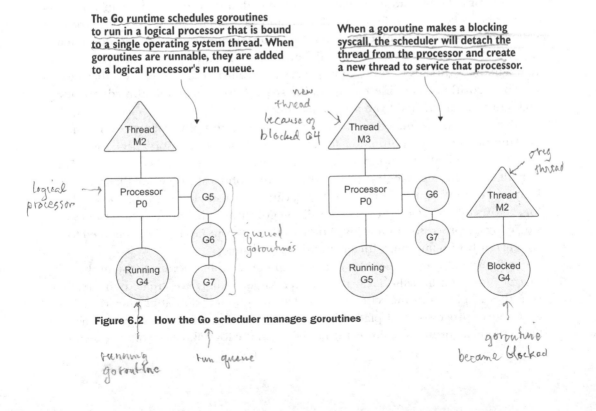

Figure 6.2   How the Go scheduler manages goroutines

Sometimes a running goroutine may need to perform a blocking syscall, such as opening a file. When this happens, the thread and goroutine are detached from the logical processor and the thread continues to block waiting for the syscall to return. In the meantime, there's a logical processor without a thread. So the scheduler creates a new thread and attaches it to the logical processor. Then the scheduler will choose another goroutine from the local run queue for execution. Once the syscall returns, the goroutine is placed back into a local run queue, and the thread is put aside for future use.

If a goroutine needs to make a network I/O call, the process is a bit different. In this case, the goroutine is detached from the logical processor and moved to the runtime integrated network poller. Once the poller indicates a read or write operation is ready, the goroutine is assigned back to a logical processor to handle the operation. There's no restriction built into the scheduler for the number of logical processors that can be created. But the runtime limits each program to a maximum of 10,000 threads by default. This value can be changed by calling the SetMaxThreads function from the runtime/debug package. If any program attempts to use more threads, the program crashes.

Concurrency is not parallelism. Parallelism can only be achieved when multiple pieces of code are executing simultaneously against different physical processors. Parallelism is about doing a lot of things at once. Concurrency is about managing a lot of things at once. In many cases, concurrency can outperform parallelism, because the strain on the operating system and hardware is much less, which allows the system to do more. This less-is-more philosophy is a mantra of the language.

If you want to run goroutines in parallel, you must use more than one logical processor. When there are multiple logical processors, the scheduler will evenly distribute goroutines between the logical processors. This will result in goroutines running on different threads. But to have true parallelism, you still need to run your program on a machine with multiple physical processors. If not, then the goroutines will be running concurrently against a single physical processor, even though the Go runtime is using multiple threads.

Figure 6.3 shows the difference between running goroutines concurrently against a single logical processor and concurrently in parallel against two logical processors. It's not recommended to blindly change the runtime default for a logical processor. The scheduler contains intelligent algorithms that are updated and improved with every release of Go. If you're seeing performance issues that you believe could be resolved by changing the number of logical processors, you have the ability to do so. You'll learn more about this soon.

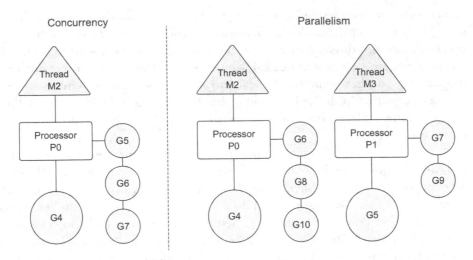

Figure 6.3   Difference between concurrency and parallelism

6.2   *Goroutines*

Let's uncover more about the behavior of the scheduler and how to create goroutines and manage their lifespan. We'll start with samples that run using a single logical processor before discussing how to run goroutines in parallel. Here's a program that creates two goroutines that display the English alphabet with lower and uppercase letters in a concurrent fashion.

> **Listing 6.1   listing01.go**

```
01 // This sample program demonstrates how to create goroutines and
02 // how the scheduler behaves.
03 package main
04
05 import (
06     "fmt"
07     "runtime"
08     "sync"
09 )
10
11 // main is the entry point for all Go programs.
12 func main() {
13     // Allocate 1 logical processor for the scheduler to use.
14     runtime.GOMAXPROCS(1)
15
16     // wg is used to wait for the program to finish.
17     // Add a count of two, one for each goroutine.
18     var wg sync.WaitGroup
19     wg.Add(2)
20
21     fmt.Println("Start Goroutines")
22
```

```
23        // Declare an anonymous function and create a goroutine.
24        go func() {
25            // Schedule the call to Done to tell main we are done.
26            defer wg.Done()
27
28            // Display the alphabet three times
29            for count := 0; count < 3; count++ {
30                for char := 'a'; char < 'a'+26; char++ {
31                    fmt.Printf("%c ", char)
32                }
33            }
34        }()      // immediate execution
35
36        // Declare an anonymous function and create a goroutine.
37        go func() {
38            // Schedule the call to Done to tell main we are done.
39            defer wg.Done()
40
41            // Display the alphabet three times
42            for count := 0; count < 3; count++ {
43                for char := 'A'; char < 'A'+26; char++ {
44                    fmt.Printf("%c ", char)
45                }
46            }
47        }()
48
49        // Wait for the goroutines to finish.
50        fmt.Println("Waiting To Finish")
51        wg.Wait()
52
53        fmt.Println("\nTerminating Program")
54    }
```

In listing 6.1 on line 14, you see a call to the GOMAXPROCS function from the runtime package. This is the function that allows the program to change the number of logical processors to be used by the scheduler. There's also an environmental variable that can be set with the same name if we don't want to make this call specifically in our code. By passing the value of 1, we tell the scheduler to use a single logical processor for this program.

On lines 24 and 37, we declare two anonymous functions that display the English alphabet. The function on line 24 displays the alphabet with lowercase letters and the function on line 37 displays the alphabet with uppercase letters. Both of these functions are created as goroutines by using the keyword go. You can see by the output in listing 6.2 that the code inside each goroutine is running concurrently within a single logical processor.

Listing 6.2   Output for listing01.go

```
Create Goroutines
Waiting To Finish
A B C D E F G H I J K L M N O P Q R S T U V W X Y Z A B C D E F G H I J K L M
N O P Q R S T U V W X Y Z A B C D E F G H I J K L M N O P Q R S T U V W X Y Z
```

```
a b c d e f g h i j k l m n o p q r s t u v w x y z a b c d e f g h i j k l m
n o p q r s t u v w x y z a b c d e f g h i j k l m n o p q r s t u v w x y z
Terminating Program
```

The amount of time it takes the first goroutine to finish displaying the alphabet is so small that it can complete its work before the scheduler swaps it out for the second goroutine. This is why you see the entire alphabet in capital letters first and then in lowercase letters second. The two goroutines we created ran concurrently, one after the other, performing their individual task of displaying the alphabet.

Once the two anonymous functions are created as goroutines, the code in main keeps running. This means that the main function can return before the goroutines complete their work. If this happens, the program will terminate before the goroutines have a chance to run. On line 51, the main function therefore waits for both goroutines to complete their work by using a WaitGroup.

Listing 6.3   listing01.go: lines 17–19, 23–26, 49–51

```
16      // wg is used to wait for the program to finish.
17      // Add a count of two, one for each goroutine.
18      var wg sync.WaitGroup
19      wg.Add(2)

23      // Declare an anonymous function and create a goroutine.
24      go func() {
25          // Schedule the call to Done to tell main we are done.
26          defer wg.Done()

49      // Wait for the goroutines to finish.
50      fmt.Println("Waiting To Finish")
51      wg.Wait()
```

A WaitGroup is a counting semaphore that can be used to maintain a record of running goroutines. When the value of a WaitGroup is greater than zero, the Wait method will block. On line 18 a variable of type WaitGroup is created, and then on line 19 we set the value of the WaitGroup to 2, noting two running goroutines. To decrement the value of the WaitGroup and eventually release the main function, calls to the Done method on lines 26 and 39 are made within the scope of a defer statement.

The keyword defer is used to schedule other functions from inside the executing function to be called when the function returns. In the case of our sample program, we use the keyword defer to guarantee that the method call to Done is made once each goroutine is finished with its work.

Based on the internal algorithms of the scheduler, a running goroutine can be stopped and rescheduled to run again before it finishes its work. The scheduler does this to prevent any single goroutine from holding the logical processor hostage. It will stop the currently running goroutine and give another runnable goroutine a chance to run.

Figure 6.4 shows this scenario from a logical processor point of view. In step 1 the scheduler begins to execute goroutine A while goroutine B waits for its turn in the

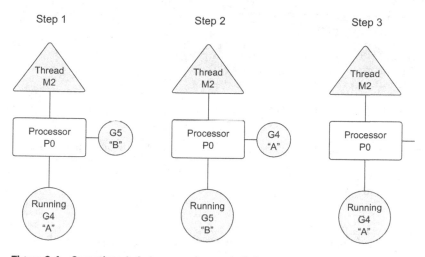

Figure 6.4 Goroutines being swapped on and off the logical processor's thread

run queue. Then, suddenly in step 2, the scheduler swaps out goroutine A for goroutine B. Since goroutine A doesn't finish, it's placed back into the run queue. Then, in step 3 goroutine B completes its work and it's gone. This allows goroutine A to get back to work.

You can see this behavior by creating a goroutine that requires a longer amount of time to complete its work.

Listing 6.4   listing04.go

```
01 // This sample program demonstrates how the goroutine scheduler
02 // will time slice goroutines on a single thread.
03 package main
04
05 import (
06     "fmt"
07     "runtime"
08     "sync"
09 )
10
11 // wg is used to wait for the program to finish.
12 var wg sync.WaitGroup
13
14 // main is the entry point for all Go programs.
15 func main() {
16     // Allocate 1 logical processors for the scheduler to use.
17     runtime.GOMAXPROCS(1)
18
19     // Add a count of two, one for each goroutine.
20     wg.Add(2)
21
22     // Create two goroutines.
23     fmt.Println("Create Goroutines")
```

```
24    go printPrime("A")
25    go printPrime("B")
26
27    // Wait for the goroutines to finish.
28    fmt.Println("Waiting To Finish")
29    wg.Wait()
30
31    fmt.Println("Terminating Program")
32 }
33
34 // printPrime displays prime numbers for the first 5000 numbers.
35 func printPrime(prefix string) {
36    // Schedule the call to Done to tell main we are done.
37    defer wg.Done()
38
39 next:
40    for outer := 2; outer < 5000; outer++ {
41        for inner := 2; inner < outer; inner++ {
42            if outer%inner == 0 {
43                continue next
44            }
45        }
46        fmt.Printf("%s:%d\n", prefix, outer)
47    }
48    fmt.Println("Completed", prefix)
49 }
```

[handwritten annotations: "outer ← 5", "inner ← 2,3,4", "// jump to next; outer incremented"]

The program in listing 6.4 creates two goroutines that print any prime numbers between 1 and 5,000 that can be found. Finding and displaying the prime numbers take a bit of time and will cause the scheduler to time-slice the first running goroutine before it finishes finding all the prime numbers it's looking for.

When the program starts, it declares a WaitGroup variable on line 12 and then sets the value of the WaitGroup to 2 on line 20. Two goroutines are created on lines 24 and 25 by specifying the name of the function printPrime after the keyword go. The first goroutine is given the prefix A and the second goroutine is given the prefix B. Like any calling function, parameters can be passed into the function being created as a goroutine. Return parameters aren't available when the goroutine terminates. When you look at the output in listing 6.5, you can see the swapping of the first goroutine by the scheduler.

> **Listing 6.5   Output for listing04.go**

```
Create Goroutines
Waiting To Finish
B:2
B:3
...
B:4583
B:4591
A:3               ** Goroutines Swapped
A:5
...
```

```
A:4561
A:4567
B:4603              ** Goroutines Swapped
B:4621
...
Completed B
A:4457              ** Goroutines Swapped
A:4463
...
A:4993
A:4999
Completed A
Terminating Program
```

Goroutine B begins to display prime numbers first. Once goroutine B prints prime number 4591, the scheduler swaps out the goroutine for goroutine A. Goroutine A is then given some time on the thread and swapped out for the B goroutine once again. The B goroutine is allowed to finish all its work. Once goroutine B returns, you see that goroutine A is given back the thread to finish its work. Every time you run this program, the scheduler will slightly change the point where the time slice occurs.

Both example programs in listings 6.1 and 6.4 have shown how the scheduler runs goroutines concurrently within a single logical processor. As stated earlier, the Go standard library has a function called GOMAXPROCS in the runtime package that allows you to specify the number of logical processors to be used by the scheduler. This is how you can change the runtime to allocate a logical processor for every available physical processor. The next listing will have our goroutines running in parallel.

Listing 6.6 How to change the number of logical processors

```
import "runtime"

// Allocate a logical processor for every available core.
runtime.GOMAXPROCS(runtime.NumCPU())
```

Compare @ 132

The runtime package provides support for changing Go runtime configuration parameters. In listing 6.6, we use two runtime functions to change the number of logical processors for the scheduler to use. The NumCPU function returns the number of physical processors that are available; therefore, the function call to GOMAXPROCS creates a logical processor for each available physical processor. It's important to note that using more than one logical processor doesn't necessarily mean better performance. Benchmarking is required to understand how your program performs when changing any runtime configuration parameters.

If we give the scheduler more than one logical processor to use, we'll see different behavior in the output of our example programs. Let's change the number of logical processors to 2 and rerun the first example that printed the English alphabet.

Listing 6.7   listing07.go

```go
01 // This sample program demonstrates how to create goroutines and
02 // how the goroutine scheduler behaves with two logical processors.
03 package main
04
05 import (
06     "fmt"
07     "runtime"
08     "sync"
09 )
10
11 // main is the entry point for all Go programs.
12 func main() {
13     // Allocate two logical processors for the scheduler to use.
14     runtime.GOMAXPROCS(2)
15
16     // wg is used to wait for the program to finish.
17     // Add a count of two, one for each goroutine.
18     var wg sync.WaitGroup
19     wg.Add(2)
20
21     fmt.Println("Start Goroutines")
22
23     // Declare an anonymous function and create a goroutine.
24     go func() {
25         // Schedule the call to Done to tell main we are done.
26         defer wg.Done()
27
28         // Display the alphabet three times.
29         for count := 0; count < 3; count++ {
30             for char := 'a'; char < 'a'+26; char++ {
31                 fmt.Printf("%c ", char)
32             }
33         }
34     }()
35
36     // Declare an anonymous function and create a goroutine.
37     go func() {
38         // Schedule the call to Done to tell main we are done.
39         defer wg.Done()
40
41         // Display the alphabet three times.
42         for count := 0; count < 3; count++ {
43             for char := 'A'; char < 'A'+26; char++ {
44                 fmt.Printf("%c ", char)
45             }
46         }
47     }()
48
49     // Wait for the goroutines to finish.
50     fmt.Println("Waiting To Finish")
51     wg.Wait()
52
53     fmt.Println("\nTerminating Program")
54 }
```

The example in listing 6.7 creates two logical processors with the call to the GOMAX-PROCS function on line 14. This will allow the goroutines to be run in parallel.

```
Create Goroutines
Waiting To Finish
A B C a D E b F c G d H e I f J g K h L i M j N k O l P m Q n R o S p T
q U r V s W t X u Y v Z w A x B y C z D a E b F c G d H e I f J g K h L
i M j N k O l P m Q n R o S p T q U r V s W t X u Y v Z w A x B y C z D
a E b F c G d H e I f J g K h L i M j N k O l P m Q n R o S p T q U r V
s W t X u Y v Z w x y z
Terminating Program
```

If you look closely at the output in listing 6.8, you'll see that the goroutines are running in parallel. Almost immediately, both goroutines start running, and the letters in the display are mixed. The output is based on running the program on an eight-core machine, so each goroutine is running on its own core. Remember that goroutines can only run in parallel if there's more than one logical processor and there's a physical processor available to run each goroutine simultaneously.

You now know how to create goroutines and understand what's happening under the hood. Next you need to understand the potential dangers and the things to look out for when writing concurrent programs.

6.3   *Race conditions*

When two or more goroutines have unsynchronized access to a shared resource and attempt to read and write to that resource at the same time, you have what's called a *race condition*. Race conditions are the reason concurrent programming is complicated and has a greater potential for bugs. Read and write operations against a shared resource must always be atomic, or in other words, done by only one goroutine at a time.

Here's an example program that contains a race condition.

```
01 // This sample program demonstrates how to create race
02 // conditions in our programs. We don't want to do this.
03 package main
04
05 import (
06     "fmt"
07     "runtime"
08     "sync"
09 )
10
11 var (
12     // counter is a variable incremented by all goroutines.
13     counter int          // "resource" accessed by 2 goroutines
14
15     // wg is used to wait for the program to finish.
```

```
16      wg sync.WaitGroup
17 )
18
19 // main is the entry point for all Go programs.
20 func main() {
21      // Add a count of two, one for each goroutine.
22      wg.Add(2)
23
24      // Create two goroutines.
25      go incCounter(1)
26      go incCounter(2)
27                      ⌐ ids
28      // Wait for the goroutines to finish.
29      wg.Wait()
30      fmt.Println("Final Counter:", counter)
31 }
32
33 // incCounter increments the package level counter variable.
34 func incCounter(id int) {
35      // Schedule the call to Done to tell main we are done.
36      defer wg.Done()
37
38      for count := 0; count < 2; count++ {
39          // Capture the value of Counter.
40          value := counter        // read counter value
41
42          // Yield the thread and be placed back in queue.
43          runtime.Gosched()  // yield thread  @141
44
45          // Increment our local value of Counter.
46          value++              // increment counter value prev. read
47
48          // Store the value back into Counter.
49          counter = value
50      }
51 }
```

(handwritten annotations: arrows pointing to lines 25, 26, 40, 49; "problem code" bracketing lines 42–46)

Listing 6.10   Output for listing09.go

```
Final Counter: 2
```

The counter variable is read and written to four times, twice by each goroutine, but the value of the counter variable when the program terminates is 2. Figure 6.5 provides a clue as to why this is happening.

Each goroutine overwrites the work of the other. This happens when the goroutine swap is taking place. Each goroutine makes its own copy of the counter variable and then is swapped out for the other goroutine. When the goroutine is given time to execute again, the value of the counter variable has changed, but the goroutine doesn't update its copy. Instead it continues to increment the copy it has and set the value back to the counter variable, replacing the work the other goroutine performed.

Let's walk through the code to understand what it's doing. Two goroutines are created from the function incCounter, which can be seen on lines 25 and 26. The

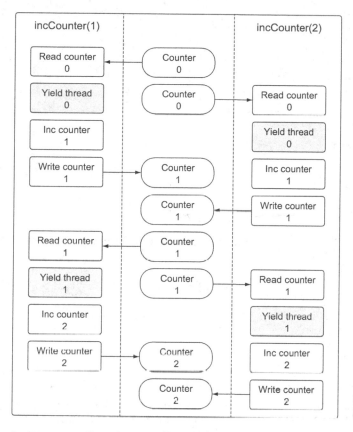

Figure 6.5 Visual of the race condition in action

incCounter function on line 34 reads and writes to the package variable counter, which is our shared resource in this example. Both goroutines start reading and storing a copy of the counter variable into a local variable called value on line 40. Then, on line 46 they increment their copy of value by one and finally assign the new value back into the counter variable on line 49. The function contains a call to the Gosched @ 140 function from the runtime package on line 43 to yield the thread and give the other goroutine a chance to run. This is being done in the middle of the operation to force the scheduler to swap between the two goroutines to exaggerate the effects of the race condition.

Go has a special tool that can detect race conditions in your code. It's extremely ✗ useful to find these types of bugs, especially when they're not as obvious as our example. Let's run the race detector against our example code.

Listing 6.11 Building and running listing09 with the race detector

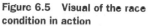

```
go build -race    // Build the code using the race detector flag      ✱
./example         // Run the code

====================
WARNING: DATA RACE
Write by goroutine 5:
```

```
    main.incCounter()
        /example/main.go:49 +0x96
Previous read by goroutine 6:
    main.incCounter()
        /example/main.go:40 +0x66

Goroutine 5 (running) created at:
    main.main()
        /example/main.go:25 +0x5c

Goroutine 6 (running) created at:
    main.main()
        /example/main.go:26 +0x73
==================
Final Counter: 2
Found 1 data race(s)
```

The race detector in listing 6.11 has pointed out the following four lines of code from our example.

Listing 6.12   Lines of code called out by the race detector

```
Line 49: counter = value
Line 40: value := counter
Line 25: go incCounter(1)
Line 26: go incCounter(2)
```

Listing 6.12 shows that the race detector has told us which goroutine is causing the data race and which two lines of code are in conflict. It's not surprising that the code that's pointed out is reading from and writing to the counter variable.

One way we can fix our example and eliminate the race condition is by using the support Go has for synchronizing goroutines by locking down shared resources.

6.4   *Locking shared resources*

Go provides traditional support to synchronize goroutines by locking access to shared resources. If you need to serialize access to an integer variable or a block of code, then the functions in the atomic and sync packages may be a good solution. We'll look at a few of the atomic package functions and the mutex type from the sync package.

6.4.1   *Atomic functions*

Atomic functions provide low-level locking mechanisms for synchronizing access to integers and pointers. We can use atomic functions to fix the race condition we created in listing 6.9.

Listing 6.13   listing13.go

```
01 // This sample program demonstrates how to use the atomic
02 // package to provide safe access to numeric types.
03 package main
```

```
04
05 import (
06      "fmt"
07      "runtime"
08      "sync"
09      "sync/atomic"
10 )
11
12 var (
13      // counter is a variable incremented by all goroutines.
14      counter int64
15
16      // wg is used to wait for the program to finish.
17      wg sync.WaitGroup
18 )
19
20 // main is the entry point for all Go programs.
21 func main() {
22      // Add a count of two, one for each goroutine.
23      wg.Add(2)
24
25      // Create two goroutines.
26      go incCounter(1)
27      go incCounter(2)
28
29      // Wait for the goroutines to finish.
30      wg.Wait()
31
32      // Display the final value.
33      fmt.Println("Final Counter:", counter)
34 }
35
36 // incCounter increments the package level counter variable.
37 func incCounter(id int) {
38      // Schedule the call to Done to tell main we are done.
39      defer wg.Done()
40
41      for count := 0; count < 2; count++ {
42          // Safely Add One To Counter.
43          atomic.AddInt64(&counter, 1)          @
44
45          // Yield the thread and be placed back in queue.
46          runtime.Gosched()
47      }
48 }
```

Compare p 140

Listing 6.14   Output for listing13.go

```
Final Counter: 4
```

On line 43 the program is now using the AddInt64 function from the atomic package. @
This function synchronizes the adding of integer values by enforcing that only one
goroutine can perform and complete this add operation at a time. When goroutines

attempt to call any atomic function, they're automatically synchronized against the variable that's referenced. Now we get the correct value of 4.

Two other useful `atomic` functions are `LoadInt64` and `StoreInt64`. These functions provide a safe way to read and write to an integer value. Here's an example using `LoadInt64` and `StoreInt64` to create a synchronous flag that can alert multiple goroutines of a special condition in a program.

Listing 6.15   listing15.go

```
01 // This sample program demonstrates how to use the atomic
02 // package functions Store and Load to provide safe access
03 // to numeric types.
04 package main
05
06 import (
07     "fmt"
08     "sync"
09     "sync/atomic"
10     "time"
11 )
12
13 var (
14     // shutdown is a flag to alert running goroutines to shutdown.
15     shutdown int64
16
17     // wg is used to wait for the program to finish.
18     wg sync.WaitGroup
19 )
20
21 // main is the entry point for all Go programs.
22 func main() {
23     // Add a count of two, one for each goroutine.
24     wg.Add(2)
25
26     // Create two goroutines.
27     go doWork("A")
28     go doWork("B")
29
30     // Give the goroutines time to run.
31     time.Sleep(1 * time.Second)
32
33     // Safely flag it is time to shutdown.
34     fmt.Println("Shutdown Now")
35     atomic.StoreInt64(&shutdown, 1)
36
37     // Wait for the goroutines to finish.
38     wg.Wait()
39 }
40
41 // doWork simulates a goroutine performing work and
42 // checking the Shutdown flag to terminate early.
43 func doWork(name string) {
44     // Schedule the call to Done to tell main we are done.
```

```
45        defer wg.Done()
46
47        for {
48            fmt.Printf("Doing %s Work\n", name)
49            time.Sleep(250 * time.Millisecond)
50
51            // Do we need to shutdown.
52            if atomic.LoadInt64(&shutdown) == 1 {        @ 144, 145
53                fmt.Printf("Shutting %s Down\n", name)
54                break
55            }
56        }
57 }
```

In this example two goroutines are launched and begin to perform some work. After @
every iteration of their respective loop, the goroutines check the value of the shutdown variable by using the LoadInt64 function on line 52. This function returns a safe
copy of the shutdown variable. If the value equals 1, the goroutine breaks out of the
loop and terminates.

The main function uses the StoreInt64 function on line 35 to safely change the   ✗
value of the shutdown variable. If any of the doWork goroutines attempt to call the
LoadInt64 function at the same time as the main function calls StoreInt64, the
atomic functions will synchronize the calls and keep all the operations safe and race
condition–free.

6.4.2 Mutexes

Another way to synchronize access to a shared resource is by using a mutex. A mutex is
named after the concept of mutual exclusion. A mutex is used to create a critical
section around code that ensures only one goroutine at a time can execute that code
section. We can also use a mutex to fix the race condition we created in listing 6.9.   139-140

Listing 6.16   listing16.go

```
01 // This sample program demonstrates how to use a mutex
02 // to define critical sections of code that need synchronous
03 // access.
04 package main
05
06 import (
07     "fmt"
08     "runtime"
09     "sync"
10 )
11
12 var (
13     // counter is a variable incremented by all goroutines.
14     counter int
15
16     // wg is used to wait for the program to finish.
17     wg sync.WaitGroup
```

```
18
19      // mutex is used to define a critical section of code.
20      mutex sync.Mutex
21  )
22
23  // main is the entry point for all Go programs.
24  func main() {
25      // Add a count of two, one for each goroutine.
26      wg.Add(2)
27
28      // Create two goroutines.
29      go incCounter(1)
30      go incCounter(2)
31
32      // Wait for the goroutines to finish.
33      wg.Wait()
34      fmt.Printf("Final Counter: %d\\n", counter)
35  }
36
37  // incCounter increments the package level Counter variable
38  // using the Mutex to synchronize and provide safe access.
39  func incCounter(id int) {
40      // Schedule the call to Done to tell main we are done.
41      defer wg.Done()
42
43      for count := 0; count < 2; count++ {
44          // Only allow one goroutine through this
45          // critical section at a time.
46          mutex.Lock()
47          {
48              // Capture the value of counter.
49              value := counter
50
51              // Yield the thread and be placed back in queue.
52              runtime.Gosched()
53
54              // Increment our local value of counter.
55              value++
56
57              // Store the value back into counter.
58              counter = value
59          }
60          mutex.Unlock()
61          // Release the lock and allow any
62          // waiting goroutine through.
63      }
64  }
```

The operations against the counter variable are now protected within a critical section defined by the calls to Lock() and Unlock() on lines 46 and 60. The use of the curly brackets is just to make the critical section easier to see; they're not necessary. Only one goroutine can enter the critical section at a time. Not until the call to the Unlock() function is made can another goroutine enter the critical section. When the thread is yielded on line 52, the scheduler assigns the same goroutine to continue running. After the program completes, we get the correct value of 4 and the race condition no longer exists.

6.5 *Channels*

Atomic functions and mutexes work, but they don't make writing concurrent programs easier, less error-prone, or fun. In Go you don't have only atomic functions and mutexes to keep shared resources safe and eliminate race conditions. You also have channels that synchronize goroutines as they send and receive the resources they need to share between each other.

When a resource needs to be shared between goroutines, channels act as a conduit between the goroutines and provide a mechanism that guarantees a synchronous exchange. When declaring a channel, the type of data that will be shared needs to be specified. Values and pointers of built-in, named, struct, and reference types can be shared through a channel.

Creating a channel in Go requires the use of the built-in function make.

Listing 6.17   Using make to create a channel

```
// Unbuffered channel of integers.
unbuffered := make(chan int)

// Buffered channel of strings.
buffered := make(chan string, 10)
```

make slice 66
make map 83

In listing 6.17 you see the use of the built-in function make to create both an unbuffered and buffered channel. The first argument to make requires the keyword chan and then the type of data the channel will allow to be exchanged. If you're creating a buffered channel, then you specify the size of the channel's buffer as the second argument.

Sending a value or pointer into a channel requires the use of the <- operator.

Listing 6.18   Sending values into a channel

```
// Buffered channel of strings.
buffered := make(chan string, 10)

// Send a string through the channel.
buffered <- "Gopher"
```

or write (string) to chan

↳ note u = binary op

In listing 6.18 we create a buffered channel of type string that contains a buffer of 10 values. Then we send the string "Gopher" through the channel. For another goroutine to receive that string from the channel, we use the same <- operator, but this time as a unary operator.

Listing 6.19   Receiving values from a channel

```
// Receive a string from the channel.
value := <-buffered
```

or read (string) from chan

↳ unary op

When receiving a value or pointer from a channel, the <- operator is attached to the left side of the channel variable, as seen in listing 6.19.

Unbuffered and buffered channels behave a bit differently. Understanding the differences will help you determine when to prefer one over the other, so let's look at each type separately.

6.5.1　Unbuffered channels

An *unbuffered channel* is a channel with no capacity to hold any value before it's received. These types of channels require both a sending and receiving goroutine to be ready at the same instant before any send or receive operation can complete. If the two goroutines aren't ready at the same instant, the channel makes the goroutine that performs its respective send or receive operation first wait. Synchronization is inherent in the interaction between the send and receive on the channel. One can't happen without the other.

In figure 6.6, you see an example of two goroutines sharing a value using an unbuffered channel. In step 1 the two goroutines approach the channel, but neither have issued a send or receive yet. In step 2 the goroutine on the left sticks its hand into the channel, which simulates a send on the channel. At this point, that goroutine is locked

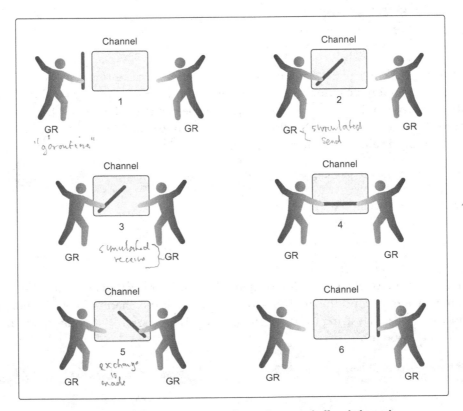

Figure 6.6　Synchronization between goroutines using an unbuffered channel

in the channel until the exchange is complete. In step 3 the goroutine on the right places its hand into the channel, which simulates a receive on the channel. That goroutine is now locked in the channel until the exchange is complete. In steps 4 and 5 the exchange is made and finally, in step 6, both goroutines are free to remove their hands, which simulates the release of the locks. They both can now go on their merry way.

To make this more clear, let's look at two complete examples that use an unbuffered channel to synchronize the exchange of data between two goroutines.

In the game of tennis, two players hit a ball back and forth to each other. The players are always in one of two states: either waiting to receive the ball, or sending the ball back to the opposing player. You can simulate a game of tennis using two goroutines and an unbuffered channel to simulate the exchange of the ball.

Listing 6.20   listing20.go

```go
01 // This sample program demonstrates how to use an unbuffered
02 // channel to simulate a game of tennis between two goroutines.
03 package main
04
05 import (
06     "fmt"
07     "math/rand"
08     "sync"
09     "time"
10 )
11
12 // wg is used to wait for the program to finish.
13 var wg sync.WaitGroup          18, 134
14
15 func init() {
16     rand.Seed(time.Now().UnixNano())          // rand
17 }
18
19 // main is the entry point for all Go programs.
20 func main() {
21     // Create an unbuffered channel.
22     court := make(chan int)
23
24     // Add a count of two, one for each goroutine.
25     wg.Add(2)          // WaitGroup: starting count
26
27     // Launch two players.
28     go player("Nadal", court)          // each goroutine takes court, a chan int, as
29     go player("Djokovic", court)          // 2nd arg
30     // Both players locked here
31     // Start the set.
32     court <- 1          // main sends 1 into court channel
33
34     // Wait for the game to finish.
35     wg.Wait()          // blocks until WaitGroup count becomes 0
36 }
37
```

```
38  // player simulates a person playing the game of tennis.
39  func player(name string, court chan int) {
40      // Schedule the call to Done to tell main we are done.
41      defer wg.Done()     // causes WaitGroup count to be decremented by 1
42
43      for {
44          // Wait for the ball to be hit back to us.
45          ball, ok := <-court     // initially, ball gets count of 1
46          if !ok {                // ok is false means channel was closed
47              // If the channel was closed we won.
48              fmt.Printf("Player %s Won\n", name)
49              return     // defer code runs here :
50          }
51
52          // Pick a random number and see if we miss the ball.
53          n := rand.Intn(100)     // n ∈ {0,1,...,99}        ?
54          if n%13 == 0 {
55              fmt.Printf("Player %s Missed\n", name)
56
57              // Close the channel to signal we lost.
58              close(court)     // Other goroutine/player is signalled
59              return           // via ok ← false
60          }
61
62          // Display and then increment the hit count by one.
63          fmt.Printf("Player %s Hit %d\n", name, ball)
64          ball++     // increment ball count          ball count
65
66          // Hit the ball back to the opposing player.
67          court <- ball¹     // stuck here unless I code receiving on court channel
68      }
69  }
```

(handwritten margin note line 53: rand *)*

When you run the program, you get the following output.

Listing 6.21 Output for listing20.go

```
Player Nadal Hit 1
Player Djokovic Hit 2
Player Nadal Hit 3
Player Djokovic Missed
Player Nadal Won
```

In the main function on line 22, an unbuffered channel of type int is created to synchronize the exchange of the ball being hit by both goroutines. Then the two goroutines that will be playing the game are created on lines 28 and 29. At this point both goroutines are locked waiting to receive the ball. On line 32 a ball is sent into the channel, and the game is played until one of the goroutines lose.

Inside the player function, you find an endless for loop on line 43. Within the loop, the game is played. On line 45 the goroutine performs a receive on the channel, waiting to receive the ball. This locks the goroutine until a send is performed on the channel. Once the receive on the channel returns, the ok flag is checked on line 46

---

1 For an unbuffered channel like court, the receive finishes before the send... so the player would play his own ball!

for `false`. A value of `false` indicates the channel was closed and the game is over. On lines 53 through 60 a random number is generated to determine if the goroutine hits or misses the ball. If the ball is hit, then on line 64 the value of the ball is incremented by one and the ball is sent back to the other player on line 67. At this point both goroutines are locked until the exchange is made. Eventually a goroutine misses the ball and the channel is closed on line 58. Then both goroutines return, the call to Done via the `defer` statement is performed, and the program terminates.

Another example that uses a different pattern to synchronize goroutines with an unbuffered channel is simulating a relay race. In a relay race, four runners take turns running around the track. The second, third, and fourth runners can't start running until they receive the baton from the previous runner. The exchange of the baton is a critical part of the race and requires synchronization to not miss a step. For this synchronization to take place, both runners who are involved in the exchange need to be ready at exactly the same time.

Listing 6.22 listing22.go

```
01 // This sample program demonstrates how to use an unbuffered
02 // channel to simulate a relay race between four goroutines.
03 package main
04
05 import (
06     "fmt"
07     "sync"
08     "time"
09 )
10
11 // wg is used to wait for the program to finish.
12 var wg sync.WaitGroup
13
14 // main is the entry point for all Go programs.
15 func main() {
16     // Create an unbuffered channel.
17     baton := make(chan int)
18
19     // Add a count of one for the last runner.
20     wg.Add(1)
21
22     // First runner to his mark.
23     go Runner(baton)
24
25     // Start the race.
26     baton <- 1
27
28     // Wait for the race to finish.
29     wg.Wait()
30 }
31
32 // Runner simulates a person running in the relay race.
33 func Runner(baton chan int) {
34     var newRunner int
```

```
35
36     // Wait to receive the baton.
37     runner := <-baton          // The runner number is set from the value
38                                // received on the baton channel
39     // Start running around the track.
40     fmt.Printf("Runner %d Running With Baton\n", runner)
41
42     // New runner to the line.
43     if runner != 4 {
44         newRunner = runner + 1       // Set up new Runner val
45         fmt.Printf("Runner %d To The Line\n", newRunner)
46         go Runner(baton)          // invoke goroutine ... which is blocked
47     }                             // until this routine writes to chan, L64
48
49     // Running around the track.
50     time.Sleep(100 * time.Millisecond)
51
52     // Is the race over.
53     if runner == 4 {
54         fmt.Printf("Runner %d Finished, Race Over\n", runner)
55         wg.Done()
56         return
57     }
58
59     // Exchange the baton for the next runner.
60     fmt.Printf("Runner %d Exchange With Runner %d\n",
61         runner,
62         newRunner)
63
64     baton <- newRunner           // go Runner (baton) called 4 times
65 }                                // baton receives vals 1, 2, 3, 4
```

When you run the program, you get the following output.
// "spent" runner returns ... only 1 runner at a time

Listing 6.23   Output for listing22.go

```
Runner 1 Running With Baton
Runner 1 Exchange With Runner 2
Runner 2 Running With Baton
Runner 2 Exchange With Runner 3
Runner 3 Running With Baton
Runner 3 Exchange With Runner 4
Runner 4 Running With Baton
Runner 4 Finished, Race Over
```

In the main function on line 17, an unbuffered channel of type int is created to synchronize the exchange of the baton. On line 20 we add a count of 1 to the WaitGroup so the main function can wait until the last runner is finished. The first runner takes to the track on line 23 with the creation of a goroutine, and then on line 26 the baton is given to the runner and the race begins. Finally, on line 29 the main function waits on the WaitGroup for the last runner to finish.

Inside the Runner goroutine, you can see how the baton is exchanged from runner to runner. On line 37 the goroutine waits to receive the baton with the receive call on the channel. Once the baton is received, the next runner takes his mark on line 46 unless the goroutine represents the fourth runner. On line 50 the runner runs around the track for 100 milliseconds. On line 55 if the fourth runner just finished running, the `WaitGroup` is decremented by the call to `Done` and the goroutine returns. If this isn't the fourth runner, then on line 64 the baton is passed to the next runner who is already waiting. At this point both goroutines are locked until the exchange is made.

In both examples we used an unbuffered channel to synchronize goroutines to simulate a tennis game and a relay race. The flow of the code was inline with the way these events and activities take place in the real world. This makes the code readable and self-documenting. Now that you know how unbuffered channels work, next you can learn how buffered channels work.

6.5.2 *Buffered channels*

A *buffered channel* is a channel with capacity to hold one or more values before they're received. These types of channels don't force goroutines to be ready at the same instant to perform sends and receives. There are also different conditions for when a send or receive does block. A receive will block only if there's no value in the channel to receive. A send will block only if there's no available buffer to place the value being sent. This leads to the one big difference between unbuffered and buffered channels: An unbuffered channel provides a guarantee that an exchange between two goroutines is performed at the instant the send and receive take place. A buffered channel has no such guarantee.

In figure 6.7 you see an example of two goroutines adding and removing items from a buffered channel independently. In step 1 the goroutine on the right is in the process of receiving a value from the channel. In step 2 that same goroutine is able to complete the receive independent of the goroutine on the left sending a new value

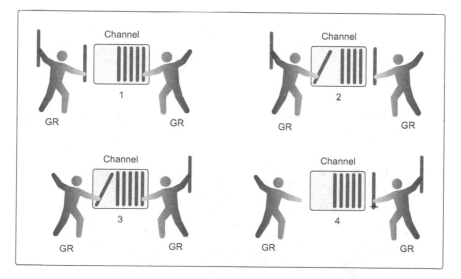

Figure 6.7 Synchronization between goroutines using a buffered channel

into the channel. In step 3 the goroutine on the left is sending a new value into the channel while the goroutine on the right is receiving a different value. Neither of these two operations in step 3 are in sync with each other or blocking. Finally, in step 4 all the sends and receives are complete and we have a channel with several values and room for more.

Let's look at an example using a buffered channel to manage a set of goroutines to receive and process work. Buffered channels provide a clean and intuitive way to implement this code.

Listing 6.24   listing24.go

```go
01 // This sample program demonstrates how to use a buffered
02 // channel to work on multiple tasks with a predefined number
03 // of goroutines.
04 package main
05
06 import (
07     "fmt"
08     "math/rand"
09     "sync"
10     "time"
11 )
12
13 const (
14     numberGoroutines = 4  // Number of goroutines to use.
15     taskLoad         = 10 // Amount of work to process.
16 )
17
18 // wg is used to wait for the program to finish.
19 var wg sync.WaitGroup
20
21 // init is called to initialize the package by the
22 // Go runtime prior to any other code being executed.
23 func init() {
24     // Seed the random number generator.
25     rand.Seed(time.Now().Unix())
26 }
27
28 // main is the entry point for all Go programs.
29 func main() {
30     // Create a buffered channel to manage the task load.
31     tasks := make(chan string, taskLoad)
32
33     // Launch goroutines to handle the work.
34     wg.Add(numberGoroutines)
35     for gr := 1; gr <= numberGoroutines; gr++ {
36         go worker(tasks, gr)
37     }
38
39     // Add a bunch of work to get done.
40     for post := 1; post <= taskLoad; post++ {
41         tasks <- fmt.Sprintf("Task : %d", post)
42     }
```

```
43
44      // Close the channel so the goroutines will quit
45      // when all the work is done.
46      close(tasks)                          @156
47
48      // Wait for all the work to get done.
49      wg.Wait()
50 }
51
52 // worker is launched as a goroutine to process work from
53 // the buffered channel.
54 func worker(tasks chan string, worker int) {
55      // Report that we just returned.
56      defer wg.Done()
57
58      for {
59          // Wait for work to be assigned.
60          task, ok := <-tasks
61          if !ok {
62              // This means the channel is empty and closed.
63              fmt.Printf("Worker: %d : Shutting Down\n", worker)
64              return
65          }
66
67          // Display we are starting the work.
68          fmt.Printf("Worker: %d : Started %s\n", worker, task)
69
70          // Randomly wait to simulate work time.
71          sleep := rand.Int63n(100)                          rand
72          time.Sleep(time.Duration(sleep) * time.Millisecond)
73
74          // Display we finished the work.
75          fmt.Printf("Worker: %d : Completed %s\n", worker, task)
76      }
77 }
```

When you run the program, you get the following output.

Listing 6.25   Output for listing24.go

```
Worker: 1 : Started Task : 1
Worker: 2 : Started Task : 2
Worker: 3 : Started Task : 3
Worker: 4 : Started Task : 4
Worker: 1 : Completed Task : 1
Worker: 1 : Started Task : 5
Worker: 4 : Completed Task : 4
Worker: 4 : Started Task : 6
Worker: 1 : Completed Task : 5
Worker: 1 : Started Task : 7
Worker: 2 : Completed Task : 2
Worker: 2 : Started Task : 8
Worker: 3 : Completed Task : 3
Worker: 3 : Started Task : 9
```

```
Worker: 1 : Completed Task : 7
Worker: 1 : Started Task : 10
Worker: 4 : Completed Task : 6
Worker: 4 : Shutting Down
Worker: 3 : Completed Task : 9
Worker: 3 : Shutting Down
Worker: 2 : Completed Task : 8
Worker: 2 : Shutting Down
Worker: 1 : Completed Task : 10
Worker: 1 : Shutting Down
```

Because of the random nature of the program and the Go scheduler, the output for this program will be different every time you run it. But the use of all four goroutines to process work from the buffered channel won't change. You can see from the output how each goroutine is receiving work distributed from the channel.

In the main function on line 31, a buffered channel of type string is created with a capacity of 10. On line 34 the WaitGroup is given the count of 4, one for each goroutine that's going to be created. Then on lines 35 through 37, four goroutines are created and passed the channel they will be receiving the work on. On lines 40 through 42, 10 strings are sent into the channel to simulate work for the goroutines. Once the last string is sent into the channel, the channel is closed on line 46 and the main function waits for all the work to be completed on line 49.

Closing the channel on line 46 is an important piece of code. When a channel is closed, goroutines can still perform receives on the channel but can no longer send on the channel. Being able to receive on a closed channel is important because it allows the channel to be emptied of all its values with future receives, so nothing in the channel is ever lost. A receive on a closed and empty channel always returns immediately and provides the zero value for the type the channel is declared with. If you also request the optional flag on the channel receive, you can get information about the state of the channel.

Inside the worker function you find an endless for loop on line 58. Within the loop, all of the received work is processed. Each goroutine blocks on line 60 waiting to receive work from the channel. Once the receive returns, the ok flag is checked to see if the channel is both empty and closed. If the value of ok is false, the goroutine terminates, which causes the defer statement on line 56 to call Done and report back to main.

If the ok flag is true, then the value received is valid. Lines 71 and 72 simulate work being processed. Once the work is done, the goroutine blocks again in the receive of the channel on line 60. Once the channel is closed, the receive on the channel returns immediately and the goroutine terminates itself.

The examples for the unbuffered and buffered channels provided a good sampling of the kind of code you can write with channels. In the next chapter we'll look at real-world concurrency patterns that you could use in your own projects.

6.6 Summary

- Concurrency is the independent execution of goroutines.
- Functions are created as goroutines with the keyword go.
- Goroutines are executed within the scope of a logical processor that owns a single operating system thread and run queue.
- A race condition is when two or more goroutines attempt to access the same resource.
- Atomic functions and mutexes provide a way to protect against race conditions.
- Channels provide an intrinsic way to safely share data between two goroutines.
- Unbuffered channels provide a guarantee between an exchange of data. Buffered channels do not.

Concurrency patterns

In this chapter

- Control the lifetime of programs   158
- Manage a pool of resources that can be reused   167
- Create a pool of goroutines that can process work   177

In chapter 6 you learned what concurrency is and how channels behave, and reviewed code that showed concurrency in action. In this chapter you'll extend that knowledge by reviewing more code. We'll review three packages that implement different concurrency patterns that you can use in your own projects. Each package provides a practical perspective on the use of concurrency and channels and how they can make concurrent programs easier to write and reason about.

7.1 Runner

The purpose of the runner package is to show how channels can be used to monitor the amount of time a program is running and terminate the program if it runs too long. This pattern is useful when developing a program that will be scheduled to run as a background task process. This could be a program that runs as a cron job, or in a worker-based cloud environment like Iron.io.

Let's take a look at the runner.go code file from the runner package.

Listing 7.1 runner/runner.go

```
01 // Example provided with help from Gabriel Aszalos.
02 // Package runner manages the running and lifetime of a process.
03 package runner
04
05 import (
06     "errors"
07     "os"
08     "os/signal"
09     "time"
10 )
11
12 // Runner runs a set of tasks within a given timeout and can be
13 // shut down on an operating system interrupt.
14 type Runner struct {
15     // interrupt channel reports a signal from the
16     // operating system.
17     interrupt chan os.Signal
18
19     // complete channel reports that processing is done.
20     complete chan error
21
22     // timeout reports that time has run out.
23     timeout <-chan time.Time
24
25     // tasks holds a set of functions that are executed
26     // synchronously in index order.
27     tasks []func(int)
28 }
29
30 // ErrTimeout is returned when a value is received on the timeout.
31 var ErrTimeout = errors.New("received timeout")
32
33 // ErrInterrupt is returned when an event from the OS is received.
34 var ErrInterrupt = errors.New("received interrupt")
35
36 // New returns a new ready-to-use Runner.
37 func New(d time.Duration) *Runner {
38     return &Runner{                               // Create 3 channels
39         interrupt: make(chan os.Signal, 1),      // buffered for 1 signal
40         complete:  make(chan error),
41         timeout:   time.After(d),
42     }
43 }
44
45 // Add attaches tasks to the Runner. A task is a function that
46 // takes an int ID.                          One or more funcs taking int arg
47 func (r *Runner) Add(tasks ...func(int)) {
48     r.tasks = append(r.tasks, tasks...)
49 }                                   the var number of func args, collected into a slice
50
51 // Start runs all tasks and monitors channel events.
52 func (r *Runner) Start() error {
53     // We want to receive all interrupt based signals.
```

↙ buffered chan for OS.Signal

```
 54      signal.Notify(r.interrupt, os.Interrupt)
 55
 56      // Run the different tasks on a different goroutine.
 57      go func() {
 58          r.complete <- r.run()
 59      }()
 60
 61      select {
 62      // Signaled when processing is done.
 63      case err := <-r.complete:
 64          return err
 65
 66      // Signaled when we run out of time.
 67      case <-r.timeout:
 68          return ErrTimeout
 69      }
 70  }
 71
 72  // run executes each registered task.
 73  func (r *Runner) run() error {
 74      for id, task := range r.tasks {
 75          // Check for an interrupt signal from the OS.
 76          if r.gotInterrupt() {
 77              return ErrInterrupt
 78          }
 79
 80          // Execute the registered task.
 81          task(id)
 82      }
 83
 84      return nil
 85  }
 86
 87  // gotInterrupt verifies if the interrupt signal has been issued.
 88  func (r *Runner) gotInterrupt() bool {
 89      select {
 90      // Signaled when an interrupt event is sent.
 91      case <-r.interrupt:
 92          // Stop receiving any further signals.
 93          signal.Stop(r.interrupt)
 95          return true
 96
 97      // Continue running as normal.
 98      default:
 99          return false
100      }
101  }
```

The program in listing 7.1 shows a concurrency pattern for task-oriented programs that run unattended on a schedule. It's designed with three possible termination points:

- The program can finish its work within the allotted amount of time and terminate normally.
- The program doesn't finish in time and kills itself.

- An operating system interrupt event is received and the program attempts to immediately shut down cleanly.

Let's walk through the code and see how each point has been implemented.

Listing 7.2 `runner/runner.go`: lines 12–28

```
12 // Runner runs a set of tasks within a given timeout and can be
13 // shut down on an operating system interrupt.
14 type Runner struct {
15     // interrupt channel reports a signal from the
16     // operating system.
17     interrupt chan os.Signal        ⓐ
18
19     // complete channel reports that processing is done.
20     complete chan error            ⓑ
21
22     // timeout reports that time has run out.
23     timeout <-chan time.Time        // Channel   ⓒ 162
24
25     // tasks holds a set of functions that are executed
26     // synchronously in index order.
27     tasks []func(int)
28 }
```

Listing 7.2 starts us off with the declaration of the struct named `Runner` on line 14. This type declares three channels that help manage the lifecycle of the program and a slice of functions that represent the different tasks to run in series.

The `interrupt` channel on line 17 sends and receives values of interface type ⓐ `os.Signal` and is used to receive interrupt events from the host operating system.

Listing 7.3 golang.org/pkg/os/#Signal

```
// A Signal represents an operating system signal. The usual underlying
// implementation is operating system-dependent: on Unix it is
// syscall.Signal.
type Signal interface {
    String() string
    Signal() // to distinguish from other Stringers   ie, I/f's implementing String()
}
```

The declaration of the `os.Signal` interface is presented in listing 7.3. This interface abstracts specific implementations for trapping and reporting events from different operating systems.

The second field is named `complete` and is a channel that sends and receives val- ⓑ ues of interface type `error`.

Listing 7.4 `runner/runner.go`: lines 19–20

```
19     // complete channel reports that processing is done.
20     complete chan error
```

This channel is called complete because it's used by the goroutine running the tasks to signal that the channel's done. If an error occurs, it's reported back via an error interface value sent through the channel. If no error occurs, the value of nil is sent as the error interface value.

© 161

The third field is named timeout and receives time.Time values.

Listing 7.5 `runner/runner.go`: lines 22–23

```
22    // timeout reports that time has run out.
23    timeout <-chan time.Time
```

This channel is used to manage the amount of time the process has to complete all its tasks. If a time.Time value is ever received on this channel, the program will attempt to shut itself down cleanly.

The final field is named tasks and is a slice of function values.

Listing 7.6 `runner/runner.go`: lines 25–27

```
25    // tasks holds a set of functions that are executed
26    // synchronously in index order.
27    tasks []func(int)
```

These function values represent functions that are run in series, one after the other. The execution of these functions happens on a single but separate goroutine from main.

With the Runner type declared, next we have two error interface variables.

Listing 7.7 `runner/runner.go`: lines 30–34

```
30 // ErrTimeout is returned when a value is received on the timeout.
31 var ErrTimeout = errors.New("received timeout")
32
33 // ErrInterrupt is returned when an event from the OS is received.
34 var ErrInterrupt = errors.New("received interrupt")
```

The first error interface variable is named ErrTimeout. This error value is returned by the Start method when a timeout event is received. The second error interface variable is named ErrInterrupt. This error value is returned by the Start method when an operating system event is received.

Now we can look at how users can create values of type Runner.

Listing 7.8 `runner/runner.go`: lines 36–43

```
36 // New returns a new ready-to-use Runner.
37 func New(d time.Duration) *Runner {
38    return &Runner{
39        interrupt: make(chan os.Signal, 1),
40        complete:  make(chan error),
```

```
41              timeout:    time.After(d),
42      }
43  }
```

// time.After returns a chan time.Time

Listing 7.8 shows a factory function called New, which accepts a value of type time.Duration and returns a pointer of type Runner. The function creates a value of type Runner and initializes each of the channel fields. The tasks field is not explicitly initialized, since the zero value for this field is a nil slice. Each channel field has a unique initialization, so let's explore each one in more detail.

The interrupt channel is initialized as a buffered channel with a buffer of 1. This guarantees at least one os.Signal value is received from the runtime. The runtime sends this event in a nonblocking way. If a goroutine isn't ready to receive this value, the value is thrown away. As an example, if the user hits Ctrl+C repeatedly, the program will receive the event only when a buffer is available in the channel and all other events will be thrown away.

The complete channel is initialized as an unbuffered channel. When the goroutine running the tasks is finished, it sends an error value or nil error value on this channel. Then it waits for main to receive it. Once main receives the error value, it's safe for the goroutine to terminate.

The final channel, timeout, is initialized using the After function from the time package. The After function returns a channel of type time.Time. The runtime will send a time.Time value on this channel after the specified duration has elapsed.

Now that you've seen how a Runner value is created and initialized, we can look at the methods associated with the Runner type. The first method, Add, is used to capture the task functions to be executed.

Listing 7.9 runner/runner.go: lines 45–49

```
45  // Add attaches tasks to the Runner. A task is a function that
46  // takes an int ID.
47  func (r *Runner) Add(tasks ...func(int)) {
48      r.tasks = append(r.tasks, tasks...)
49  }
```

Listing 7.9 shows the Add method, which is declared with a single varadic parameter named tasks. *Varadic parameters* can accept any number of values that are passed in. In this case the value must be a function that accepts a single integer value and returns nothing. The tasks parameter, once inside the code, becomes a slice of these function values.

Now let's look at the run method.

Listing 7.10 runner/runner.go: lines 72–85

```
72  // run executes each registered task.
73  func (r *Runner) run() error {
74      for id, task := range r.tasks {
```

```
75              // Check for an interrupt signal from the OS.
76              if r.gotInterrupt() {
77                  return ErrInterrupt
78              }
79
80              // Execute the registered task.
81              task(id)
82          }
83
84      return nil
85  }
```

The run method on line 73 in listing 7.10 iterates over the tasks slice and executes each function in order. Before any function is executed on line 81, the gotInterrupt method is called on line 76 to see if there are any events to receive from the operating system.

Listing 7.11   `runner/runner.go`: lines 87–101

```
87  // gotInterrupt verifies if the interrupt signal has been issued.
88  func (r *Runner) gotInterrupt() bool {
89      select {
90      // Signaled when an interrupt event is sent.
91      case <-r.interrupt:      // attempt to receive
92              // Stop receiving any further signals.
93  @           signal.Stop(r.interrupt)
95              return true
96
97      // Continue running as normal.
98      default:
99              return false
100     }
101 }
```

The gotInterrupt method in listing 7.11 shows a classic use of the select statement with a default case. On line 91, the code attempts to receive on the interrupt channel. Normally that would block if there was nothing to receive, but we have a default case on line 98. The default case turns the attempt to receive on the interrupt channel into a nonblocking call. If there's an interrupt to receive, then it's received and processed. If there's nothing to receive, the default case is then executed.

When an interrupt event is received, the code requests to stop receiving any future events by calling the Stop method on line 93. Then the function returns true. If no interrupt event is received, the method returns false on line 99. Essentially, the gotInterrupt method lets the goroutine peek for interrupt events and keep processing work if one has not been issued.

The final method in the package is called Start.

Listing 7.12   `runner/runner.go`: lines 51–70

```
51  // Start runs all tasks and monitors channel events.
52  func (r *Runner) Start() error {
```

```
53    // We want to receive all interrupt based signals.
54    signal.Notify(r.interrupt, os.Interrupt)
55
56    // Run the different tasks on a different goroutine.
57    go func() {
58        r.complete <- r.run()          // r.run() returned an error (maybe nil)
59    }()                                 // which is written to the r.complete chan
60
61    select {
62    // Signaled when processing is done.
63    case err := <-r.complete:          // event; can read an error/nil from r.complete
64        return err
65
66    // Signaled when we run out of time.
67    case <-r.timeout:                  // event; can read from r.timeout
68        return ErrTimeout               // due to
69    }
70 }
```

The Start method implements the main workflow for the program. In listing 7.12 on
line 52, Start sets up the ability for the gotInterrupt method to receive interrupt
events from the operating system. On lines 56 through 59, an anonymous function is
declared and created as a goroutine. This is the goroutine that executes the set of
assigned tasks for the program. On line 58, inside this goroutine, the run method is
called and the returned error interface value is sent on the complete channel. Once
the error interface value is received, the goroutine returns that value to the caller.

With the goroutine created, Start enters into a select statement that blocks waiting for one of two events to occur. If an error interface value is received on the
complete channel, then the goroutine either finished its work within the allotted
amount of time or an operating system interrupt event was received. Regardless, the
received error interface value is returned and the method terminates. If a time.Time
value is received on the timeout channel, then the goroutine didn't finish its work
within the allotted amount of time. In this case, the program returns the ErrTimeout
variable.

Now that you've seen the code for the runner package and learned how it works,
let's review the test program in the main.go source code file.

Listing 7.13 runner/main/main.go

```
01 // This sample program demonstrates how to use a channel to
02 // monitor the amount of time the program is running and terminate
03 // the program if it runs too long.
03 package main
04
05 import (
06     "log"
07     "time"
08
09     "github.com/goinaction/code/chapter7/patterns/runner"
10 )
```

```
11
12 // timeout is the number of second the program has to finish.
13 const timeout = 3 * time.Second
14
15 // main is the entry point for the program.
16 func main() {
17     log.Println("Starting work.")
18
19     // Create a new timer value for this run.
20     r := runner.New(timeout)
21
22     // Add the tasks to be run.
23     r.Add(createTask(), createTask(), createTask())
24
25     // Run the tasks and handle the result.
26     if err := r.Start(); err != nil {
27         switch err {
28         case runner.ErrTimeout:
29             log.Println("Terminating due to timeout.")
30             os.Exit(1)
31         case runner.ErrInterrupt:
32             log.Println("Terminating due to interrupt.")
33             os.Exit(2)
34         }
35     }
36
37     log.Println("Process ended.")
38 }
39
40 // createTask returns an example task that sleeps for the specified
41 // number of seconds based on the id.
42 func createTask() func(int) {
43     return func(id int) {
44         log.Printf("Processor - Task #%d.", id)
45         time.Sleep(time.Duration(id) * time.Second)
46     }
47 }
```

The main function can be found on line 16 in listing 7.13. On line 20 the timeout value is passed to the New function, and a pointer of type Runner is returned. Then the createTask function is added to the Runner several times on line 23. The createTask function, declared on line 42, is a function that just pretends to perform some work for a specified amount of time. Once the functions have been added, the Start method is called on line 26 and the main function waits for Start to return.

When Start returns the returned error interface value is checked. If an error did occur, the code uses the error interface variables to identify if the method terminated due to a timeout event or interrupt event. If there's no error, then the tasks finished in time. On a timeout event, the program terminates with an error code of 1. On an interrupt event, the program terminates with an error code of 2. In all other cases, the program terminates normally with error code 0.

7.2   Pooling

The purpose of the `pool` package is to show how you can use a buffered channel to pool a set of resources that can be shared and individually used by any number of goroutines. This pattern is useful when you have a static set of resources to share, such as database connections or memory buffers. When a goroutine needs one of these resources from the pool, it can acquire the resource, use it, and then return it to the pool.

Let's take a look at the pool.go code file from the pool package.

Listing 7.14   pool/pool.go

```
01 // Example provided with help from Fatih Arslan and Gabriel Aszalos.
02 // Package pool manages a user defined set of resources.
03 package pool
04
05 import (
06     "errors"
07     "log"
08     "io"
09     "sync"
10 )
11
12 // Pool manages a set of resources that can be shared safely by
13 // multiple goroutines. The resource being managed must implement
14 // the io.Closer interface.
15 type Pool struct {
16     m         sync.Mutex        146
17     resources chan io.Closer
18     factory   func() (io.Closer, error)    // to create a new resource when the
19     closed    bool  // pool is shutdown     // pool requires one
20 }                         // or being shutdown
21
22 // ErrPoolClosed is returned when an Acquire returns on a
23 // closed pool.
24 var ErrPoolClosed = errors.New("Pool has been closed.")
25
26 // New creates a pool that manages resources. A pool requires a
27 // function that can allocate a new resource and the size of
28 // the pool.
29 func New(fn func() (io.Closer, error), size uint) (*Pool, error) {
30     if size <= 0 {
31         return nil, errors.New("Size value too small.")
32     }
33
34     return &Pool{
35         factory:   fn,
36         resources: make(chan io.Closer, size),    // buffered chan of io.Closer
37     }, nil
38 }
39
40 // Acquire retrieves a resource from the pool.    // method on Pool
41 func (p *Pool) Acquire() (io.Closer, error) {
```

```
42      select {
43      // Check for a free resource.
44      case r, ok := <-p.resources:
45          log.Println("Acquire:", "Shared Resource")
46          if !ok {
47              return nil, ErrPoolClosed
48          }
49          return r, nil
50
51      // Provide a new resource since there are none available.
52      default:
53          log.Println("Acquire:", "New Resource")
54          return p.factory()
55      }
56 }
57
58 // Release places a new resource onto the pool.
59 func (p *Pool) Release(r io.Closer) {          // method on Pool
60      // Secure this operation with the Close operation.
61      p.m.Lock()
62      defer p.m.Unlock()
63
64      // If the pool is closed, discard the resource.
65      if p.closed {
66          r.Close()
67          return
68      }
69
70      select {
71      // Attempt to place the new resource on the queue.
72      case p.resources <- r:
73          log.Println("Release:", "In Queue")
74
75      // If the queue is already at capacity we close the resource.
76      default:
77          log.Println("Release:", "Closing")
78          r.Close()
79      }
80 }
81
82 // Close will shutdown the pool and close all existing resources.
83 func (p *Pool) Close() {              // method on Pool
84      // Secure this operation with the Release operation.
85      p.m.Lock()
86      defer p.m.Unlock()
87
88      // If the pool is already closed, don't do anything.
89      if p.closed {
90          return
91      }
92
93      // Set the pool as closed.
94      p.closed = true
95
96      // Close the channel before we drain the channel of its
```

```
97      // resources. If we don't do this, we will have a deadlock.
98      close(p.resources)
99
100     // Close the resources
101     for r := range p.resources {
102         r.Close()
103     }
104 }
```

The code for the `pool` package in listing 7.14 declares a struct named `Pool` that allows the caller to create as many different pools as needed. Each pool can manage any type of resource as long as the type implements the `io.Closer` interface. Let's take a look at the declaration of the `Pool` struct.

Listing 7.15   pool/pool.go: lines 12–20

```
12 // Pool manages a set of resources that can be shared safely by
13 // multiple goroutines. The resource being managed must implement
14 // the io.Closer interface.
15 type Pool struct {
16     m         sync.Mutex
17     resources chan io.Closer
18     factory   func() (io.Closer, error)
19     closed    bool
20 }
```

The `Pool` struct declares four fields, each of which helps manage the pool in a goroutine-safe way. On line 16 the struct starts off with a field of type `sync.Mutex`. This mutex is used to keep all the operations against a `Pool` value-safe for multigoroutine access. The second field is named `resources` and is declared as a channel of interface type `io.Closer`. This channel will be created as a buffered channel and will contain the resources being shared. Because an interface type is being used, the pool can manage any type of resource that implements the `io.Closer` interface.

The `factory` field is of a function type. Any function that takes no parameters and returns an `io.Closer` and an error interface value can be assigned to this field. [The purpose of this function is to create a new resource when the pool requires one. This functionality is an implementation detail beyond the scope of the `pool` package and needs to be implemented and supplied by the user using this package.] 1

The final field on line 19 is the `closed` field. This field is a flag that indicates the `Pool` is being shut down or is already shut down. Now that you've seen the declaration of the `Pool` struct, let's look at the error interface variable that's declared on line 24.

Listing 7.16   pool/pool.go: lines 22–24

```
22 // ErrPoolClosed is returned when an Acquire returns on a
23 // closed pool.
24 var ErrPoolClosed = errors.New("Pool has been closed.")
```

1   Very important "implementation detail": point of this code is that resources are limited/static so wouldn't expect a factory function to create a new resource in an unlimited way. More realistic: create a slice of resources, write them into a buffered chan of size that takes them all. Then factory function reads from chan or waits for one

Creating error interface variables is a common practice in Go. This allows the caller to identify specific returned error values from any function or method within the package. The error interface variable in listing 7.16 has been declared to report when the user calls the Acquire method and the Pool has been closed. Since the Acquire method can return multiple different errors, returning this error variable when the Pool is closed allows the caller to identify this specific error over others.

With the Pool type and the error interface variable declared, we can start to look at the functions and methods that are declared in the pool package. Let's start with the pool's factory function, named New.

Listing 7.17 pool/pool.go: lines 26–38

```
26 // New creates a pool that manages resources. A pool requires a
27 // function that can allocate a new resource and the size of
28 // the pool.
29 func New(fn func() (io.Closer, error), size uint) (*Pool, error) {
30     if size <= 0 {
31         return nil, errors.New("Size value too small.")
32     }
33
34     return &Pool{
35         factory:   fn,
36         resources: make(chan io.Closer, size),
37     }, nil
38 }
```

The New function in listing 7.17 accepts two parameters and returns two values. The first parameter, fn, is declared as a function type that accepts no parameters and returns an io.Closer and an error interface value. The function parameter represents a factory function that creates values of the resource being managed by the pool. The second parameter, size, represents the size of the buffered channel created to hold the resources.

On line 30 the value of size is checked to make sure it's not less than or equal to 0. If it is, then the code returns nil for the returned pool pointer value and then creates an error interface value on the fly for the error. Since this is the only error being returned from this function, it's not necessary to create and use an error interface variable for this error. If the size value is good, then a new Pool value is created and initialized. On line 35 the function parameter is assigned, and on line 36 the buffered channel is created using the size value. Everything can be created and initialized within the scope of the return statement. So a pointer to the new Pool value and the error interface value of nil are created and returned as the arguments.

With the ability to create and initialize a Pool value, next let's look at the Acquire method. This method allows the caller to acquire a resource from the pool.

Listing 7.18 `pool/pool.go`: lines 40–56

```
40 // Acquire retrieves a resource from the pool.
41 func (p *Pool) Acquire() (io.Closer, error) {
42     select {
43     // Check for a free resource.
44     case r, ok := <-p.resources:
45         log.Println("Acquire:", "Shared Resource")
46         if !ok {
47             return nil, ErrPoolClosed
48         }
49         return r, nil
50
51     // Provide a new resource since there are none available.
52     default:
53         log.Println("Acquire:", "New Resource")
54         return p.factory()
55     }
56 }
```

Listing 7.18 contains the code for the `Acquire` method. This method returns a resource from the pool if one is available, or creates a new one for the call. This implementation is accomplished by using a `select` / `case` statement to check if there's a resource in the buffered channel. If there is, it's received and then returned to the caller. This can be seen on lines 44 and 49. If there's no resource in the buffered channel to receive, then the `default` case is executed. In this case, on line 54 the user's factory function is executed and a new resource is created and returned.

After a resource is acquired and no longer needed, it must be released back into the pool. This is where the `Release` method comes in. But to understand the mechanics behind the code in the `Release` method, we need to look at the `Close` method first.

Listing 7.19 `pool/pool.go`: lines 82–104

```
82 // Close will shutdown the pool and close all existing resources.
83 func (p *Pool) Close() {
84     // Secure this operation with the Release operation.
85     p.m.Lock()
86     defer p.m.Unlock()
87
88     // If the pool is already closed, don't do anything.
89     if p.closed {
90         return
91     }
92
93     // Set the pool as closed.
94     p.closed = true
95
96     // Close the channel before we drain the channel of its
97     // resources. If we don't do this, we will have a deadlock.
98     close(p.resources)
99
```

```
100    // Close the resources
101    for r := range p.resources {
102        r.Close()
103    }
104 }
```

Once the program is finished with the pool, it should call the Close method. The code
for the Close method is shown in listing 7.19. The method closes and flushes the buffered channel on lines 98 and 101, closing any resources that exist until the channel is
empty. All the code in this method must be executed by only one goroutine at a time.
In fact, when this code is being executed, goroutines must also be prevented from executing code in the Release method. You'll understand why this is important soon.

On lines 85 and 86, the mutex is locked and then scheduled to be unlocked when
the function returns. On line 89 the closed flag is checked to see if the pool is already
closed. If it is, the method returns immediately, which releases the lock. If this is the
first time the method is called, then the flag is set to true and the resources channel
is closed and flushed.

Now we can look at the Release method and see how it works in coordination with
the Close method.

Listing 7.20   pool/pool.go: lines 58–80

```
58 // Release places a new resource onto the pool.
59 func (p *Pool) Release(r io.Closer) {
60     // Secure this operation with the Close operation.
61     p.m.Lock()
62     defer p.m.Unlock()
63
64     // If the pool is closed, discard the resource.
65     if p.closed {
66         r.Close()          // r implements Closer() i/f
67         return
68     }
69
70     select {
71     // Attempt to place the new resource on the queue.
72     case p.resources <- r:
73         log.Println("Release:", "In Queue")
74
75     // If the queue is already at capacity we close the resource.
76     default:
77         log.Println("Release:", "Closing")
78         r.Close()
79     }
80 }
```

The implementation of the Release method can be found in listing 7.20. The method
starts out with the locking and unlocking of a mutex on lines 61 and 62. This is the
same mutex as in the Close method. This is how both methods are prevented from
being run at the same time by different goroutines. The use of the mutex serves two

purposes. First, it protects the read on the closed flag on line 65 from happening at the same time as a write on this flag in the Close method. Second, we don't want to attempt to send on a closed channel because this will cause a panic. When the closed field is false, we know the resources channel has been closed.

On line 66, the Close method on the resource is called directly when the pool is closed. This is because there's no way to release the resource back into the pool. At this point the pool has been both closed and flushed. The reads and writes to the closed flag must be synchronized or else goroutines could be misled into thinking the pool is open and attempt to perform an invalid operation on the channel.

Now that you've seen the pool code and learned how it works, let's review the test program in the main.go source code file.

Listing 7.21 pool/main/main.go

```
01 // This sample program demonstrates how to use the pool package
02 // to share a simulated set of database connections.
03 package main
04
05 import (
06     "log"
07     "io"
08     "math/rand"
09     "sync"
10     "sync/atomic"      143
11     "time"
12
13     "github.com/goinaction/code/chapter7/patterns/pool"
14 )
15
16 const (
17     maxGoroutines   = 25 // the number of routines to use.
18     pooledResources = 2  // number of resources in the pool
19 )
20
21 // dbConnection simulates a resource to share.
22 type dbConnection struct {
23     ID int32
24 }
25
26 // Close implements the io.Closer interface so dbConnection
27 // can be managed by the pool. Close performs any resource
28 // // release management.
29 func (dbConn *dbConnection) Close() error {          // implement Closer() i/f on dbConnection
30     log.Println("Close: Connection", dbConn.ID)      // just print a line
31     return nil
32 }
33
34 // idCounter provides support for giving each connection a unique id.
35 var idCounter int32
36
37 // createConnection is a factory method that will be called by
38 // the pool when a new connection is needed.
39 func createConnection() (io.Closer, error) {
```

```
40      id := atomic.AddInt32(&idCounter, 1)
41      log.Println("Create: New Connection", id)
42
43      return &dbConnection{id}, nil        // return unitialized db Connection
44 }
45
46 // main is the entry point for all Go programs.
47 func main() {
48      var wg sync.WaitGroup
49      wg.Add(maxGoroutines)                 // 25
50
51      // Create the pool to manage our connections.
52      p, err := pool.New(createConnection, pooledResources)
53      if err != nil {                              factory function
54          log.Println(err)                    to create a new db Connection if one not
55      }                                        available in pool
56
57      // Perform queries using connections from the pool.
58      for query := 0; query < maxGoroutines; query++ {
59          // Each goroutine needs its own copy of the query
60          // value else they will all be sharing the same query
61          // variable.
62          go func(q int) {
63              performQueries(q, p)
64              wg.Done()                        // each of the 25 goroutines does its job then
65          }(query)                             // returns ... is finished
66      }
67
68      // Wait for the goroutines to finish.
69      wg.Wait()
70
71      // Close the pool.
72      log.Println("Shutdown Program.")
73      p.Close()                                a goroutine w. id ∈ {0, 1, ... 24}
74 }
75
76 // performQueries tests the resource pool of connections.
77 func performQueries(query int, p *pool.Pool) {
78      // Acquire a connection from the pool.
79      conn, err := p.Acquire()                 // conn is a db Connection
80      if err != nil {
81          log.Println(err)
82          return
83      }
84
85      // Release the connection back to the pool.
86      defer p.Release(conn)
87
88      // Wait to simulate a query response.
89      time.Sleep(time.Duration(rand.Intn(1000)) * time.Millisecond)
90      log.Printf("QID[%d] CID[%d]\n", query, conn.(*dbConnection).ID)
91 }                                            get underlying type
```

The code in main.go, shown in listing 7.21, uses the pool package to manage a simu-lated pool of database connections. The code starts out declaring two constants, maxGoroutines and pooledResources, to set the number of goroutines and resources the program is going to use. The declaration of the resource and the implementation of the io.Closer interface follows.

Listing 7.22 pool/main/main.go: lines 21–32

```
21 // dbConnection simulates a resource to share.
22 type dbConnection struct {
23     ID int32
24 }
25
26 // Close implements the io.Closer interface so dbConnection
27 // can be managed by the pool. Close performs any resource
28 // release management.
29 func (dbConn *dbConnection) Close() error {
30     log.Println("Close: Connection", dbConn.ID)
31     return nil
32 }
```

Listing 7.22 shows the declaration of the dbConnection struct and its implementation of the io.Closer interface. The dbConnection type simulates a struct that's managing a database connection and currently has one field, ID, that contains a unique ID for each connection. The Close method just reports that the connection is being closed and displays its ID.

Next we have the factory function that creates values of dbConnection.

Listing 7.23 pool/main/main.go: lines 34–44

```
34 // idCounter provides support for giving each connection a unique id.
35 var idCounter int32
36
37 // createConnection is a factory method that will be called by
38 // the pool when a new connection is needed.
39 func createConnection() (io.Closer, error) {
40     id := atomic.AddInt32(&idCounter, 1)
41     log.Println("Create: New Connection", id)
42
43     return &dbConnection{id}, nil
44 }
```

Listing 7.23 shows the implementation of the createConnection function. The function generates a new and unique ID for the connection, displays that the connection is being created, and returns a pointer to a value of type dbConnection with this unique ID. The generation of the unique ID is performed with the atomic.AddInt32 function. It's used to safely increment the value of the package level variable idCounter. Now that we have our resource and the factory function, we can use it with the pool package.

Next, let's look at the code inside the main function.

Listing 7.24   pool/main/main.go: lines 48–55

```
48      var wg sync.WaitGroup
49      wg.Add(maxGoroutines)
50
51      // Create the pool to manage our connections.
52      p, err := pool.New(createConnection, pooledResources)
53      if err != nil {
54          log.Println(err)
55      }
```

The main function starts out with declaring a WaitGroup on line 48 and setting the value of the WaitGroup to match the number of goroutines that will be created. The new Pool is created using the New function from the pool package. The factory function and the number of resources to manage are passed in. This returns a pointer to the Pool value and any possible error is checked. Now that we have a Pool, we can create goroutines that can share resources being managed by the pool.

Listing 7.25   pool/main/main.go: lines 57–66

```
57      // Perform queries using connections from the pool.
58      for query := 0; query < maxGoroutines; query++ {
59          // Each goroutine needs its own copy of the query
60          // value else they will all be sharing the same query
61          // variable.
62          go func(q int) {
63              performQueries(q, p)
64              wg.Done()
65          }(query)
66      }
```

A for loop is used in listing 7.25 to create goroutines that will use the pool. Each goroutine calls the performQueries function once and then quits. The performQueries function is provided a unique ID for logging and the pointer to the Pool. Once all the goroutines are created, the main function then waits for the goroutines to complete.

Listing 7.26   pool/main/main.go: lines 68–73

```
68      // Wait for the goroutines to finish.
69      wg.Wait()
70
71      // Close the pool.
72      log.Println("Shutdown Program.")
73      p.Close()
```

In listing 7.26, the main function waits on the WaitGroup. Once all the goroutines report they're done, the Pool is closed and the program terminates. Next, let's look at the performQueries function, which uses the pool's Acquire and Release methods.

Listing 7.27 `pool/main/main.go: lines 76–91`

```
76 // performQueries tests the resource pool of connections.
77 func performQueries(query int, p *pool.Pool) {
78     // Acquire a connection from the pool.
79     conn, err := p.Acquire()
80     if err != nil {
81         log.Println(err)
82         return
83     }
84
85     // Release the connection back to the pool.
86     defer p.Release(conn)
87
88     // Wait to simulate a query response.
89     time.Sleep(time.Duration(rand.Intn(1000)) * time.Millisecond)
90     log.Printf("QID[%d] CID[%d]\n", query, conn.(*dbConnection).ID)
91 }
```

The implementation of the performQueries function in listing 7.27 shows the use of the pool's Acquire and Release methods. The function starts out by calling the Acquire method to retrieve a dbConnection from the pool. The returned error interface value is checked, and then on line 86 a defer is used to release the dbConnection back into the pool once the function returns. On lines 89 and 90 a random amount of sleep occurs to simulate work time using the dbConnection.

7.3 Work   *// Name changes clarify the code!*

The purpose of the work package is to show how you can use an unbuffered channel to create a pool of goroutines that will perform and control the amount of work that gets done concurrently. This is a better approach than using a buffered channel of *@ 154* some arbitrary static size that acts as a queue of work and throwing a bunch of goroutines at it. Unbuffered channels provide a guarantee that data has been exchanged between two goroutines. This approach of using an unbuffered channel allows the user to know when the pool is performing the work, and the channel pushes back when it can't accept any more work because it's busy. No work is ever lost or stuck in a queue that has no guarantee it will ever be worked on.

Let's take a look at the work.go code file from the work package.

Listing 7.28 `work/work.go`

```
01 // Example provided with help from Jason Waldrip.
02 // Package work manages a pool of goroutines to perform work.
03 package work
04
05 import "sync"
06
07 // Worker must be implemented by types that want to use
08 // the work pool.    *i.e, that want to be submitted to the channel of objects of type chan Worker*
09 type Worker interface {
10     Task()
```

type Tasker interface {
Task()
}

① Approach here: Create a pool of n workers. Pool contains an unbuffered channel carrying types implementing Tasker. Each pool worker processes the range of tasks "thrown at" the channel.

```
11 }
12
13 // Pool provides a pool of goroutines that can execute any Worker
14 // tasks that are submitted.
15 type Pool struct {
16     work chan Worker
17     wg   sync.WaitGroup
18 }
19
20 // New creates a new work pool.
21 func New(maxGoroutines int) *Pool {
22     p := Pool{
23         tasks: make(chan Worker),
24     }
25
26     p.wg.Add(maxGoroutines)
27     for i := 0; i < maxGoroutines; i++ {
28         go func() {
29             for w := range p.work {
30                 w.Task()
31             }
32             p.wg.Done()
33         }()
34     }
35
36     return &p
37 }
38
39 // Run submits work to the pool.
40 func (p *Pool) Run(w Worker) {
41     p.work <- w
42 }
43
44 // Shutdown waits for all the goroutines to shutdown.
45 func (p *Pool) Shutdown() {
46     close(p.tasks)
47     p.wg.Wait()
48 }
```

Handwritten annotations:
- Line 16–18: `// tasks chan Tasker   Note: unbuffered // set to a count of the number of // goroutines "servicing" the work channel`
- Line 21: `// arg: the no. of goroutines servicing the work chann`
- Line 23–24: `// Better names    tasks : make(chan Tasker)   work :`
- Line 28: `// This goroutine pulls off work, calls its Task(), repeat`
- Line 29–30: `for t := range p.tasks.   t.Task()`
- Line 32–33: `// done when // work channel // is closed`
- Line 39–41: `// waits until a worker goroutine is available   Run (t Tasker)   p.tasks <- t`
- Left margin line 39: `better name: Submit`
- Line 46: `p.work`

The work package in listing 7.28 starts off with the declaration of an interface named
Worker and a struct named Pool.

```
07 // Worker must be implemented by types that want to use
08 // the work pool.
09 type Worker interface {
10     Task()
11 }
12
13 // Pool provides a pool of goroutines that can execute any Worker
14 // tasks that are submitted.
15 type Pool struct {
16     work chan Worker
17     wg   sync.WaitGroup
18 }
```

Handwritten annotation line 08: `// ok: any object that has Task() method that does whateve`

The `Worker` interface on line 09 in listing 7.29 declares a single method called `Task`. On line 15 a struct named `Pool` is declared, which is the type that implements the pool of goroutines and will have methods that process the work. The type declares two fields, one named `work`, which is a channel of the `Worker` interface type, and a `sync.WaitGroup` named `wg`.

Next let's look at the factory function for the work package.

Listing 7.30 work/work.go: lines 20–37

```
20 // New creates a new work pool.
21 func New(maxGoroutines int) *Pool {
22     p := Pool{
23         work: make(chan Worker),
24     }          tasks              Tasker
25
26     p.wg.Add(maxGoroutines)
27     for i := 0; i < maxGoroutines; i++ {
28         go func() {          tasks
29             for w := range p.work {
30                 w.Task()
31             }
32             p.wg.Done()
33         }()
34     }
35
36     return &p
37 }
```

Listing 7.30 shows the `New` function that's used to create work pool that's configured with a fixed number of goroutines. The number of goroutines is passed in as a parameter to the `New` function. On line 22 a value of type `Pool` is created, and the `work` field is initialized with an unbuffered channel.

Then, on line 26, the `WaitGroup` is initialized, and on lines 27 through 34 the same number of goroutines are created. The goroutines just receive interface values of type `Worker` and call the `Task` method on those values. *Each goroutine gets a Tasker/Work object and calls Task() on it*

Listing 7.31 work/work.go: lines 28–33

```
28         go func() {          p  tasks
29             for w := range p.work {          ] "infinite" loop
30                 w.Task()
31             }
32             p.wg.Done()
33         }()
```

The `for range` loop blocks until there's a `Worker` interface value to receive on the work channel. When a value is received,[1] the `Task` method is called. Once the work channel is closed, the `for range` loop ends and the call to `Done` on the `WaitGroup` is called. Then the goroutine terminates.

1   *By one of the goroutines not engaged in a Task*

Now that we can create a pool of goroutines that can wait for and execute work, let's look at how work is submitted into the pool.

Listing 7.32   work/work.go: lines 39–42

```
39 // Run submits work to the pool.
40 func (p *Pool) Run(w Worker) {
41     w.work <- w
42 }
```

(handwritten: ↳ Tasker   p.works ← w   or   p.tasks <- Tasker)

Listing 7.32 shows the Run method. This method is used to submit work into the pool. It accepts an interface value of type Worker and sends that value through the work channel. Since the work channel is an unbuffered channel, the caller must wait for a goroutine from the pool to receive it. This is what we want, because the caller needs the guarantee that the work being submitted is being worked on once the call to Run returns.

At some point, the work pool needs to be shut down. This is where the Shutdown method comes in.

Listing 7.33   work/work.go: lines 44–48

```
44 // Shutdown waits for all the goroutines to shutdown.
45 func (p *Pool) Shutdown() {
46     close(p.work)
47     p.wg.Wait()
48 }
```

The Shutdown method in listing 7.33 does two things. First, it closes the work channel, which causes all of the goroutines in the pool to shut down and call the Done method on the WaitGroup. Then the Shutdown method calls the Wait method on the WaitGroup, which causes the Shutdown method to wait for all the goroutines to report they have terminated.

Now that you've seen the code for the work package and learned how it works, let's review the test program in the main.go source code file.

Listing 7.34   work/main/main.go

```
01 // This sample program demonstrates how to use the work package
02 // to use a pool of goroutines to get work done.
03 package main
04
05 import (
06     "log"
07     "sync"
08     "time"
09
10     "github.com/goinaction/code/chapter7/patterns/work"
11 )
12
```

```go
13  // names provides a set of names to display.
14  var names = []string{
15      "steve",
16      "bob",
17      "mary",
18      "therese",
19      "jason",
20  }
21
22  // namePrinter provides special support for printing names.
23  type namePrinter struct {
24      name string
25  }
26
27  // Task implements the Worker interface...  on namePrinter
28  func (m *namePrinter) Task() {
29      log.Println(m.name)
30      time.Sleep(time.Second)
31  }
32
33  // main is the entry point for all Go programs.
34  func main() {
35      // Create a work pool with 2 goroutines.
36      p := work.New(2)        // New is a function defined in work package
37
38      var wg sync.WaitGroup
39      wg.Add(100 * len(names))    // 100 x 5
40
41      for i := 0; i < 100; i++ {
42          // Iterate over the slice of names.
43          for _, name := range names {
44              // Create a namePrinter and provide the
45              // specific name.
46              np := namePrinter{
47                  name: name,
48              }
49
50              go func() {
51                  // Submit the task to be worked on. When Run
52                  // returns we know it is being handled.
53                  p.Run(&np)
54                  wg.Done()
55              }()
56          }
57      }
58
59      wg.Wait()
60
61      // Shutdown the work pool and wait for all existing work
62      // to be completed.
63      p.Shutdown()
64  }
```

Handwritten annotations:

Line 27: "on namePrinter"

Line 36: "// New is a function defined in work package"

Line 39: "// 100 x 5"

Lines 41–44: "// Note: there are 500 (anon) goroutines created to submit Tasks (namePrinters) to the work queue but 2 goroutines engaged in pulling off Tasks and executing them"

Lines 46–50 (right side):
"i: 0 namePrntr for 'steve' namePrntr for 'bob' namePrntr for 'jason' } 5"
"i: 1 namePrntr for 'steve' } 5"

Line 51: "Run"

Lines 59–60: "// waits until all 500 anon goroutines have called p.Run(&np): i.e, // have been able to submit a Task-implementor to the work queue"

Listing 7.34 shows the test program that uses the work package to perform the displaying of names. The code starts out on line 14 with the declaration of a package level variable named names, which is declared as a slice of strings. The slice is also initialized with five names. Then a type named namePrinter is declared.

Listing 7.35   work/main/main.go: lines 22–31

```
22 // namePrinter provides special support for printing names.
23 type namePrinter struct {
24     name string
25 }
26
27 // Task implements the Worker interface.
28 func (m *namePrinter) Task() {
29     log.Println(m.name)
30     time.Sleep(time.Second)
31 }
```

On line 23 in listing 7.35, the namePrinter type is declared and the implementation of the Worker interface follows. The purpose of the work is to display names to the screen. The type contains a single field, name, that will contain the name to display. The implementation of the Worker interface uses the log.Println function to display the name and then waits a second before returning. The second wait is just to slow the test program down so you can see the concurrency is action.

With the implementation of the Worker interface, we can look at the code inside the main function.

Listing 7.36   work/main/main.go: lines 33–64

```
33 // main is the entry point for all Go programs.
34 func main() {
35     // Create a work pool with 2 goroutines.
36     p := work.New(2)
37
38     var wg sync.WaitGroup
39     wg.Add(100 * len(names))
40
41     for i := 0; i < 100; i++ {
42         // Iterate over the slice of names.
43         for _, name := range names {
44             // Create a namePrinter and provide the
45             // specific name.
46             np := namePrinter{
47                 name: name,
48             }
49
50             go func() {
51                 // Submit the task to be worked on. When RunTask
52                 // returns we know it is being handled.
53                 p.Run(&np)     // blocked here until a goroutine in
                                   // the pool receives &np, pointer to Tasker
```

```
54                    wg.Done()
55                }()
56            }
57        }
58
59        wg.Wait()
60
61        // Shutdown the work pool and wait for all existing work
62        // to be completed.
63        p.Shutdown()
64 }
```

On line 36 in listing 7.36, the New function from the work package is called to create the work pool. The number 2 is passed into the call, indicating the pool should only contain two goroutines. On lines 38 and 39 a WaitGroup is declared and initialized to each goroutine that will be created. In this case, a goroutine for each name in the names slice will be created 100 times. This is to create a lot of goroutines competing to submit work to the pool.

On lines 41 and 43 inner and outer for loops are declared to create all the goroutines. Inside each iteration of the inner loop, a value of type namePrinter is created and provided with a name to print. Then, on line 50, an anonymous function is declared and created as a goroutine. The goroutine calls the Run method against the work pool to submit the namePrinter value to the pool. Once a goroutine from the work pool receives the value, the call to Run returns. This in turn causes the goroutine to decrement the WaitGroup count and terminate.

. Once all the goroutines are created, the main function calls Wait on the Wait-Group. The function will wait until all the goroutines that were created submit their work. Once Wait returns, the work pool is shut down by calling the Shutdown method This method won't return until all the work is complete. In our case, there would be only two outstanding pieces of work by this time.] *All 500 submits to the work queue have been accomplished... the 2 workers in the pool must be executing Task(s) for the last 2 pieces of work*

7.4 Summary

- You can use channels to control the lifetime of programs.
- A select statement with a default case can be used to attempt a nonblocking send or receive on a channel.
- Buffered channels can be used to manage a pool of resources that can be reused.
- The coordination and synchronization of channels is taken care of by the runtime.
- Create a pool of goroutines to perform work using unbuffered channels.
- Any time an unbuffered channel can be used to exchange data between two goroutines, you have guarantees you can count on.

Standard library

What is the *Go standard library* and why is it important? The Go standard library is a set of core packages that enhance and extend the language. These packages add to the number of different types of programs you can write without the need to build your own packages or download packages others have published. Since these packages are tied to the language, they come with some special guarantees:

- They will always exist for each minor release of the language.
- They will honor the backward-compatibility promise.
- They are part of the dev, build, and release process for Go.
- They are maintained and reviewed by Go contributors.
- They are tested and benchmarked with each new release of the language.

These guarantees make the standard library special and something you want to leverage as much as possible. By using packages from the standard library, you make it easier to manage your code and ensure that it's reliable. This is because you don't have to worry if your program is going to break between release cycles, nor do you have to manage third-party dependencies.

All these benefits would be useless if the standard library didn't contain all the great packages that it does. Go developers in the community depend on these packages more so than in other languages. This is because they are well designed and provide more functionality than is normally found in traditional standard libraries. In the end, the Go community relies on the standard library for lots of things that developers in other languages do not, such as networking, HTTP, image processing, and cryptology.

In this chapter we'll take a high-level look at the current set of packages that are a part of the standard library. Then we'll explore in greater detail three packages that come in handy for many different programs: log, json, and io. These packages also show off some of the great things that Go has to offer.

8.1 Documentation and source code

The standard library is filled with so many packages that it would be impossible to cover them all in the scope of one chapter. Currently there are well over 100 packages organized within 38 categories.

Listing 8.1 Set of top-level folders and packages in the standard library

```
archive    bufio      bytes      compress   container   crypto    database
debug      encoding   errors     expvar     flag        fmt       go
hash       html       image      index      io          log       math
mime       net        os         path       reflect     regexp    runtime
sort       strconv    strings    sync       syscall     testing   text
time       unicode    unsafe
```

Many of the categories in listing 8.1 are also packages themselves. For a detailed description and a look at all the available packages, the Go team maintains documentation on the Go website at http://golang.org/pkg/.

The pkg section of the golang website provides the godoc documentation for each package. Figure 8.1 shows an example of the package documentation on the golang website for the io package.

```
type Writer

    type Writer interface {
            Write(p []byte) (n int, err error)
    }

Writer is the interface that wraps the basic Write method.

Write writes len(p) bytes from p to the underlying data stream. It returns the number of bytes written from p (0 <
if it returns n < len(p). Write must not modify the slice data, even temporarily.
```

Figure 8.1 golang.org/pkg/io/#Writer

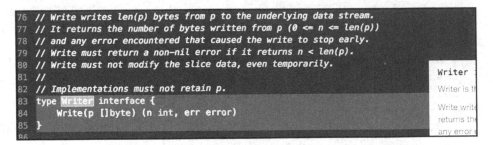

```
76  // Write writes len(p) bytes from p to the underlying data stream.
77  // It returns the number of bytes written from p (0 <= n <= len(p))
78  // and any error encountered that caused the write to stop early.
79  // Write must return a non-nil error if it returns n < len(p).
80  // Write must not modify the slice data, even temporarily.
81  //
82  // Implementations must not retain p.
83  type Writer interface {
84      Write(p []byte) (n int, err error)
85  }
86
```

Figure 8.2   sourcegraph.com/code.google.com/p/go/.GoPackage/io/.def/Writer

If you want documentation that you can interact with, Sourcegraph has indexed all the code for the standard library and many of the public repositories that contain Go code. Figure 8.2 shows an example of the package documentation on the Sourcegraph website (https://sourcegraph.com/)for the io package.

No matter how you installed Go, all the source code for the standard library can be found on your development machine in the $GOROOT/src/pkg folder. Having the source code for the standard library is important for the Go tooling to work. Tools like godoc, gocode, and even go build read this source code to perform their functions. If this source code is not on your machine and accessible through the $GOROOT variable, you'll get errors when trying to build your programs.

The source code for the standard library is precompiled as part of your Go distribution package. These precompiled files, called *archive files*, can be found in the $GOROOT/pkg folder for each target platform and operating system you have installed. In figure 8.3 you can see files with an .a extension, which are the archive files.

These files are special static Go libraries that the Go build tools create and use when compiling and linking your final programs together. This helps the build process to be fast. But there's no way to specify these files when performing a build, so you can't share them. The Go tooling knows when it can use an existing .a file and when it needs to rebuild one from the source code on your machine.

With this background in place, let's take a look at a few of the packages in the standard library and see how you can consume them in your own programs.

include	.DS_Store	html
lib	darwin_amd64	html.a
LICENSE	linux_amd64	image
misc	obj	image.a
PATENTS	tool	index
pkg		io
README		io.a
robots.txt		log
src		log.a
test		math
VERSION		math.a

Figure 8.3   View of the archive files inside the pkg folder

8.2 Logging

Your programs have bugs, even if they haven't shown themselves yet. That's the nature of software development. Logging is a way to find those bugs and learn more about how your program is functioning. Logs can be your eyes and ears, providing code tracing, profiling, and analytics. With this in mind, the standard library provides a log package that can be used with some basic configuration. You can also create custom loggers to implement your own specific logging needs.

Logging has a long history in UNIX, and this has carried over into the `log` package. Traditional CLI (command-line interface) programs write their output to the `stdout` device. This device exists on all operating systems and is the default destination for standard text output. Terminals are configured by default to display text written to this device. Using this single destination works great until you have a program that needs to write both output and details about how the program is functioning. When you want to write logging information, you want to write that to a different destination so your output and logging won't be mixed together.

To solve this problem, UNIX architects added a device called `stderr`. This device was created to be the default destination for logging. It allows developers to separate their programs' output from their logging. For a user to see both the output and the logging when running a program, terminal consoles are configured to display what's written to both `stdout` and `stderr`. But if your program only writes logs, then it's common practice to write general logging information to `stdout` and errors or warnings to `stderr`.

8.2.1 Log package

Let's start with the base functionality provided by the `log` package before you learn how to create your own custom loggers. The purpose of logging is to get a trace of what the program is doing, where it's happening, and when. This is some of the information that you can write on every log line with some configuration.

Listing 8.2 Sample trace line

```
TRACE: 2009/11/10 23:00:00.000000 /tmpfs/gosandbox-/prog.go:14: message
```

In listing 8.2 you see a log entry produced by the `log` package. This log entry contains a prefix, a datetime stamp, the full path to the source code writing to the log, the line of code performing the write, and finally the message. Let's look at a program that allows you to configure the `log` package to write such a line.

Listing 8.3 listing03.go

```
01 // This sample program demonstrates how to use the base log package.
02 package main
03
04 import (
```

```
05       "log"
06 )
07
08 func init() {
09      log.SetPrefix("TRACE: ")
10      log.SetFlags(log.Ldate | log.Lmicroseconds | log.Llongfile)
11 }
12
13 func main() {
14      // Println writes to the standard logger.
15      log.Println("message")
16
17      // Fatalln is Println() followed by a call to os.Exit(1).
18      log.Fatalln("fatal message")
19
20      // Panicln is Println() followed by a call to panic().
21      log.Panicln("panic message")
22 }
```

If you run the program from listing 8.3, you should get something close to the same output from listing 8.2. Let's break down the code and see how it works.

Listing 8.4   listing03.go: lines 08–11

```
08 func init() {                                        assumes L, Ltime
09      log.SetPrefix("TRACE: ")
10      log.SetFlags(log.Ldate | log.Lmicroseconds | log.Llongfile)
11 }
```

On lines 08 through 11, we have a function called init(). This function is executed before main() as part of the program initialization. It's common to set the log configuration inside of init() so the log package can be used immediately when the program starts. In our program on line 09, we set the string to be used as a prefix for each line. This should be a string that allows you to identify a log line over normal program output. Traditionally this string is written in capital letters.

There are several flags associated with the log package that control other information that can be written on each log line. The following listing shows the flags that currently exist.

Listing 8.5   golang.org/src/log/log.go

```
const (
    // Bits or'ed together to control what's printed. There is no control
    // over the order they appear (the order listed here) or the format
    // they present (as described in the comments).  A colon appears after
    // these items:
    //   2009/01/23 01:23:23.123123 /a/b/c/d.go:23: message
    //                 1          2          3
    // the date: 2009/01/23
    Ldate = 1 << iota

    // the time: 01:23:23
```

1: log.Ldate] or log.LstdFlags
2: log.Ltime]
              or log.Lmicroseconds

3: log.Longfile

```
*   Ltime

    // microsecond resolution: 01:23:23.123123. assumes Ltime
    Lmicroseconds

    // full file name and line number: /a/b/c/d.go:23
*   Llongfile

    // final file name element and line number: d.go:23
    // overrides Llongfile
    Lshortfile

    // initial values for the standard logger
    LstdFlags = Ldate | Ltime
)
```

Listing 8.5 comes right out of the source code for the log package. These flags are declared as constants, and the first constant in this block is called Ldate, which is declared with special syntax.

Listing 8.6 Declaration of the Ldate constant

```
// the date: 2009/01/23
    Ldate = 1 << iota
```

The iota keyword has a special purpose when it comes to declaring a block of constants. It instructs the compiler to duplicate the expression for every constant until the block ends or an assignment statement is found. Another function of the iota keyword is that the value of iota for each preceding constant gets incremented by 1, with an initial value of 0. Let's look at this more closely.

Listing 8.7 Use of the keyword iota

```
const (
    Ldate = 1 << iota,  // 1 << 0 = 000000001 = 1
    Ltime =     •       // 1 << 1 = 000000010 = 2
    Lmicroseconds = •   // 1 << 2 = 000000100 = 4
    Llongfile  •        // 1 << 3 = 000001000 = 8
    Lshortfile •        // 1 << 4 = 000010000 = 16
    ...
)
```

Listing 8.7 shows what's happening behind the scenes with the constant declarations. The << operator performs a left bitwise shift of the bits represented by the value on the left side of the operator. In each case the bit pattern for the value of 1 is shifted to the left iota position. This has the effect of giving each constant its own unique bit position, which you'll see is perfect when working with flags.

The LstdFlags constant shows the purpose behind giving each constant its own unique bit position.

Listing 8.8   Declaration of the `LstdFlags` constant

```
const (
  ...
  LstdFlags = Ldate(1) | Ltime(2) = 00000011 = 3
)
```

In listing 8.8 you see the `LstdFlags` constant break the `iota` chain because of the use of the assignment operator. The `LstdFlags` constant is assigned the value of 3, thanks to the fact that the pipe operator (|) is used to or bits together. Or'ing bits is equivalent to joining bits so each individually set bit is then represented in the final value. When bits 1 and 2 are `ored` together, they form the value of 3.

Let's look again at how we set the log flags we wanted applied.

Listing 8.9   listing03.go: lines 08–11

```
08 func init() {
09     ...
10     log.SetFlags(log.Ldate | log.Lmicroseconds | log.Llongfile)
11 }
```

OR'd

Here we piped the `Ldate`, `Lmicroseconds`, and `Llongfile` flags together and passed the value of that operation to the `SetFlags` function. These flags, when piped together, represent the value 13 and bits 4, 3, and 1 (00001101). Since each constant represents an individual bit, flags can be joined together using the pipe operator to create a value that represents all the log options we want applied. The `log` package then takes that integer value we passed and inspects which bits are set to apply the correct attributes we requested.

With the `log` package initialized, you can look at `main()` and see how to write messages.

Listing 8.10   listing03.go: lines 13–22

```
13 func main() {                        // standard logger writes to stderr
14     // Println writes to the standard logger.
15     log.Println("message")
16
17     // Fatalln is Println() followed by a call to os.Exit(1).
18     log.Fatalln("fatal message")
19
20     // Panicln is Println() followed by a call to panic().
21     log.Panicln("panic message")
22 }
```

Listing 8.10 shows how to write log messages using three different functions: `Println`, `Fatalln`, and `Panicln`. These functions have a format version, as well, that end with the letter `f` instead of the letters `ln`. The `Fatal` family of functions is used to write a log message and then terminate the program using the `os.Exit(1)` function call. The

Panic family of functions is used to write a log message and then issue a panic, which unless recovered, will cause the program to terminate and stack trace. The Print family of functions is the standard way to write log messages.

One nice thing about the log package is that loggers are multigoroutine-safe. This means that multiple goroutines can call these functions from the same logger value at the same time without the writes colliding with each other. The standard logger and any customized logger you may create will have this attribute.

Now that you know how to use the log package and configure it, let's explore how to create customized loggers so you can have different logging levels that can write logs to different destinations.

8.2.2 Customized loggers

Creating customized loggers require that you create your own Logger type values. Each logger you create can be configured for a unique destination and set with its own prefix and flags. Let's look at an example program that creates different Logger type pointer variables to support different logging levels.

Listing 8.11 listing11.go

```
01 // This sample program demonstrates how to create customized loggers.
02 package main
03
04 import (
05     "io"
06     "io/ioutil"
07     "log"
08     "os"
09 )
10
11 var (
12     Trace   *log.Logger // Just about anything
13     Info    *log.Logger // Important information
14     Warning *log.Logger // Be concerned
15     Error   *log.Logger // Critical problem
16 )
17
18 func init() {
19     file, err := os.OpenFile("errors.txt",
20         os.O_CREATE|os.O_WRONLY|os.O_APPEND, 0666)
21     if err != nil {
22         log.Fatalln("Failed to open error log file:", err)
23     }
24
25     Trace = log.New(ioutil.Discard,
26         "TRACE: ",
27         log.Ldate|log.Ltime|log.Lshortfile)
28
29     Info = log.New(os.Stdout,
30         "INFO: ",
31         log.Ldate|log.Ltime|log.Lshortfile)
32
```

*[handwritten annotations: used line 37; // pkg-level vars; // Set up logging in init(); os.Create 209; io.Writer like /dev/null; @193; var Logvar *log.Logger; Logvar = log.New (to, prefix, flags); io.Writer]*

```
33     Warning = log.New(os.Stdout,
34         "WARNING: ",
35         log.Ldate|log.Ltime|log.Lshortfile)
36
37     Error = log.New(io.MultiWriter(file, os.Stderr),
38         "ERROR: ",
39         log.Ldate|log.Ltime|log.Lshortfile)
40 }
41
42 func main() {
43     Trace.Println("I have something standard to say")
44     Info.Println("Special Information")
45     Warning.Println("There is something you need to know about")
46     Error.Println("Something has failed")
47 }
```

Listing 8.11 shows a complete program that creates four different `Logger` type pointer variables. They're named `Trace`, `Info`, `Warning`, and `Error`. Each variable is configured differently because of the importance each represents. Let's break down the code so you can learn how all this works.

On lines 11 through 16 we declare the four `Logger` type pointer variables for our different logging levels.

Listing 8.12   listing11.go: lines 11–16

```
11 var (
12     Trace    *log.Logger // Just about anything
13     Info     *log.Logger // Important information
14     Warning  *log.Logger // Be concerned
15     Error    *log.Logger // Critical problem
16 )
```

In listing 8.12 you see the declaration of the `Logger` type pointer variables. We've given each logger a short but descriptive variable name. Next, let's look at the code in `init()` that creates and assigns the address of each `Logger` type value to each variable.

Listing 8.13   listing11.go: lines 25–39

```
25     Trace = log.New(ioutil.Discard,
26         "TRACE: ",
27         log.Ldate|log.Ltime|log.Lshortfile)
28
29     Info = log.New(os.Stdout,
30         "INFO: ",
31         log.Ldate|log.Ltime|log.Lshortfile)
32
33     Warning = log.New(os.Stdout,
34         "WARNING: ",
35         log.Ldate|log.Ltime|log.Lshortfile)
36
37     Error = log.New(io.MultiWriter(file, os.Stderr),
38         "ERROR: ",
39         log.Ldate|log.Ltime|log.Lshortfile)
```

To create each logger, we use the New function from the log package, which creates a properly initialized Logger type value. The New function returns the address to the newly created value. Before the New function can create a value, we need to pass it some parameters.

Listing 8.14 golang.org/src/log/log.go

```
// New creates a new Logger. The out variable sets the
// destination to which log data will be written.
// The prefix appears at the beginning of each generated log line.
// The flag argument defines the logging properties.
func New(out io.Writer, prefix string, flag int) *Logger {
    return &Logger{out: out, prefix: prefix, flag: flag}
}
```

@ 191

✗

Listing 8.14 shows the declaration of the New function from the source code for the log package. The first parameter is the destination we want the logger to write to. This is provided as a value that implements the io.Writer interface. The second parameter is the prefix that you saw before, and log flags comprise the final parameter.

In our program, the Trace logger uses the Discard variable from the ioutil package as the destination to write to.

Listing 8.15 listing11.go: lines 25–27

```
25      Trace = log.New(ioutil.Discard,
26          "TRACE: ",
27          log.Ldate|log.Ltime|log.Lshortfile)
```

The Discard variable has some very interesting properties.

Listing 8.16 golang.org/src/io/ioutil/ioutil.go

```
// devNull is a named type using int as its base type.
type devNull int

// Discard is an io.Writer on which all Write calls succeed
// without doing anything.
var Discard io.Writer = devNull(0)

// Implementation of the io.Writer interface.
func (devNull) Write(p []byte) (int, error) {
    return len(p), nil
}
```

✗

Listing 8.16 shows the declaration of the Discard variable and the implementation surrounding it. The Discard variable is declared to be of interface type io.Writer and is given a value of 0 of type devNull. Anything written to this variable is discarded based on the implementation of the Write method for the devNull type. Using the Discard variable is a technique you can use to disable a logging level when the output for that level is not required.

✗

The Info and Warning loggers both use the stdout destination.

Listing 8.17   listing11.go: lines 29–35

```
29    Info = log.New(os.Stdout,
30       "INFO: ",
31       log.Ldate|log.Ltime|log.Lshortfile)
32
33    Warning = log.New(os.Stdout,
34       "WARNING: ",
35       log.Ldate|log.Ltime|log.Lshortfile)
```

The declaration of the Stdout variable is also interesting.

Listing 8.18   golang.org/src/os/file.go

```
// Stdin, Stdout, and Stderr are open Files pointing to the standard
// input, standard output, and standard error file descriptors.
var (
    Stdin  = NewFile(uintptr(syscall.Stdin), "/dev/stdin")
    Stdout = NewFile(uintptr(syscall.Stdout), "/dev/stdout")
    Stderr = NewFile(uintptr(syscall.Stderr), "/dev/stderr")
)

os/file_unix.go

// NewFile returns a new File with the given file descriptor and name.
func NewFile(fd uintptr, name string) *File {
```

*[handwritten notes: Stdin is a *File. File implements io.Writer I/f. ↑ fd. ↑ name]*

In listing 8.18 you can see the declaration for the three variables that represent the standard destinations that exist on all operating systems: Stdin, Stdout, and Stderr. All these variables are declared to be pointers of type File, which implements the io.Writer interface. This leads us to the final logger, Error.

Listing 8.19   listing11.go: lines 37–39

```
37    Error = log.New(io.MultiWriter(file, os.Stderr),
38       "ERROR: ",
39       log.Ldate|log.Ltime|log.Lshortfile)
```

In listing 8.19 you can see that the first parameter to the New function comes from a special function called MultiWriter from the io package.

Listing 8.20   Declaration of the MultiWriter function in the io package

```
io.MultiWriter(file, os.Stderr)
```

Listing 8.20 isolates the call to the MultiWriter function, which returns an interface type value of io.Writer that contains both the file that we opened and the stderr destination. The MultiWriter function is a variadic function that accepts any number of values that implement the io.Writer interface. The function returns a single io.Writer value that bundles all of the io.Writer values that are passed in. This allows functions like `log.New` to accept multiple writers within a single writer. Now when we write a log using the `Error` logger, the output will be written to both the file and `stderr`.

Now that you know how to create custom loggers, let's look at how you can use them to write messages.

Listing 8.21 listing11.go: lines 42–47

```
42 func main() {
43     Trace.Println("I have something standard to say")
44     Info.Println("Special Information")
45     Warning.Println("There is something you need to know about")
46     Error.Println("Something has failed")
47 }
```

Listing 8.21 shows the `main()` function from listing 8.11. On lines 43 through 46 we write a single message for each logger that we created. Each logger variable contains a set of methods that are identical to the set of functions that are implemented by the `log` package.

Listing 8.22 Declarations of the different logging methods

```
func (l *Logger) Fatal(v ...interface{})
func (l *Logger) Fatalf(format string, v ...interface{})
func (l *Logger) Fatalln(v ...interface{})
func (l *Logger) Flags() int                          // retrieve flags
func (l *Logger) Output(calldepth int, s string) error
func (l *Logger) Panic(v ...interface{})
func (l *Logger) Panicf(format string, v ...interface{})
func (l *Logger) Panicln(v ...interface{})
func (l *Logger) Prefix() string                      // retrieve prefix
func (l *Logger) Print(v ...interface{})
func (l *Logger) Printf(format string, v ...interface{})
func (l *Logger) Println(v ...interface{})
func (l *Logger) SetFlags(flag int)
func (l *Logger) SetPrefix(prefix string)
```

Listing 8.22 shows all the methods that have been implemented for the `Logger` type.

8.2.3 Conclusion

The `log` package has been implemented with the long history and understanding of the purpose of logging and how it has been applied in practice. Writing output to `stdout` and logging to `stderr` has long been the tradition of many CLI-based programs. But when your program is only outputting logs, then using `stdout`, `stderr`, and files is perfectly acceptable.

The `log` package from the standard library has everything you need for logging and its use is recommended. You can trust the implementation not only because it's part of the standard library, but because it's used widely by the community.

8.3   *Encoding/Decoding*

Many applications, whether they're using databases, making web calls, or working within a distributed system, need to consume and publish data. If your application is working with either XML or JSON, the standard library has packages called xml and json that make working with these data formats trivial. If you have your own data formats that need to be encoded and decoded, the implementation of these packages is a great road map of how to implement your own packages.

Working with and using JSON is more common nowadays than working with XML. This is primarily because using JSON requires less markup than working with XML. This means less data per message needs to be sent over the network, which helps with the overall performance of the system. Also, JSON can be transformed into BSON (Binary JavaScript Object Notation), which reduces the size of each message even further. In view of this, we'll explore how to consume and publish JSON in Go applications. But working with XML is very similar.

8.3.1   *Decoding JSON*

The first aspect of working with JSON we'll explore is using the NewDecoder function and Decode method from the json package. If you're consuming JSON from a web response or a file, this is the function and method you want to use. Let's look at an example that works with the http package to perform a Get request against the Google search API that returns results in JSON. The next listing shows what the response looks like.

Listing 8.23   Google search API sample JSON response

```
{
    "responseData": {
        "results": [
            {
                "GsearchResultClass": "GwebSearch",
                "unescapedUrl": "https://www.reddit.com/r/golang",
                "url": "https://www.reddit.com/r/golang",
                "visibleUrl": "www.reddit.com",
                "cacheUrl": "http://www.google.com/search?q=cache:W...",
                "title": "r/\u003cb\u003eGolang\u003c/b\u003e - Reddit",
                "titleNoFormatting": "r/Golang - Reddit",
                "content": "First Open Source \u003cb\u003eGolang\u003e\u..."
            },
            {
                "GsearchResultClass": "GwebSearch",
                "unescapedUrl": "http://tour.golang.org/",
                "url": "http://tour.golang.org/",
                "visibleUrl": "tour.golang.org",
                "cacheUrl": "http://www.google.com/search?q=cache:O...",
                "title": "A Tour of Go",
                "titleNoFormatting": "A Tour of Go",
                "content": "Welcome to a tour of the Go programming ..."
            }
        }
```

```
            ]
        }
    }
```

Here's the example that retrieves and decodes the response into a struct type.

Listing 8.24   listing24.go

```
01 // This sample program demonstrates how to decode a JSON response
02 // using the json package and NewDecoder function.
03 package main
04
05 import (
06     "encoding/json"          // encode or decode
07     "fmt"
08     "log"
09     "net/http"
10 )
11
12 type (
13     // gResult maps to the result document received from the search.
14     gResult struct {
15         GsearchResultClass string `json:"GsearchResultClass"`      hold annotations
16         UnescapedURL       string `json:"unescapedUrl"`
17         URL                string `json:"url"`
18         VisibleURL         string `json:"visibleUrl"`
19         CacheURL           string `json:"cacheUrl"`
20         Title              string `json:"title"`
21         TitleNoFormatting  string `json:"titleNoFormatting"`
22         Content            string `json:"content"`
23     }
24
25     // gResponse contains the top level document.
26     gResponse struct {
27         ResponseData struct {       // struct containing slice of results.  cap R.
28             Results []gResult `json:"results"`     // slice of gResult,    cap R
29         } `json:"responseData"`
30     }
31 )
32
33 func main() {
34     uri := "http://ajax.googleapis.com/ajax/services/search/web?
                                      v=1.0&rsz=8&q=golang"
35
36     // Issue the search against Google.
37     resp, err := http.Get(uri)          // retrieve a json doc from google
38     if err != nil {
39         log.Println("ERROR:", err)
40         return
41     }
42     defer resp.Body.Close()
43
44     // Decode the JSON response into our struct type.
45     var gr gResponse               implements io. Reader 204
46     err = json.NewDecoder(resp.Body).Decode(&gr)      @ 198
```

JSON is body of response

Alt: decoder = json.NewDecoder(resp.Body)
     err = decoder.Decode(&gr)

// json bytes → struct
// like python: json.load()
// DECODE

```
47     if err != nil {
48          log.Println("ERROR:", err)
49          return
50     }
51
52     fmt.Println(gr)        // print struct
53 }
```

@ 197

The code on line 37 in listing 8.24 shows a program that makes an HTTP Get call that retrieves a JSON document from Google. Then, using the NewDecoder function and Decode method on line 46, the JSON document from the response is decoded into a variable of the struct type that's declared on line 26. On line 52 the value of the variable is written to stdout.

If you look at the type declarations for gResponse and gResult on lines 26 and 14, you'll notice strings declared at the end of each field. These are called *tags*, and they're the mechanism to provide metadata about the field mapping between the JSON document and the struct type. If tags are not present, the decoding and encoding process will attempt to match against the field names directly in a case-insensitive way. When a mapping can't be made, the field in the struct value will contain its zero value.

Thanks to the standard library, all of the technical aspects of performing HTTP Get calls and decoding JSON into struct types are taken care of. Let's look at the declaration of both the NewDecoder function and Decode method.

Listing 8.25 golang.org/src/encoding/json/stream.go

```
// NewDecoder returns a new decoder that reads from r.
//
// The decoder introduces its own buffering and may
// read data from r beyond the JSON values requested.
func NewDecoder(r io.Reader) *Decoder
                                 return

// Decode reads the next JSON-encoded value from its
// input and stores it in the value pointed to by v.
//
// See the documentation for Unmarshal for details about
// the conversion of JSON into a Go value.
func (dec *Decoder) Decode(v interface{}) error
          recv                  v a pointer ?
```

In listing 8.25 you can see that the NewDecoder function accepts any value whose type implements the io.Reader interface. In the next section you'll learn more about the io.Reader and io.Writer interfaces. For now, understand that many different types from within the standard library implement these interfaces, including types from the http package. When types implement these particular interfaces, you get a lot of support and functionality for free.

The NewDecoder function returns a pointer value of type Decoder. Since Go supports compound statement calls, the return value from the NewDecoder function can be used to call the Decode method immediately without the need to declare a variable first. In listing 8.25 you can see that the `Decode` method accepts a value of type `interface{}` and returns an error.

As described in chapter 5, the empty interface is an interface implemented by every type. This means the `Decode` method can accept values of any type. Through the use of reflection, the `Decode` method will inspect the type information about the value you pass in. Then as it reads the JSON response, it will decode the response into a value of that type. This means you don't need to create values yourself; `Decode` can do this for you.

Listing 8.26 Use of the Decode method

```
var gr *gResponse
err = json.NewDecoder(resp.Body).Decode(&gr)
```

In listing 8.26 we pass the address of a pointer variable of type `gResponse`, with the value of `nil`, to the `Decode` method. After the method call, the value of the pointer variable will be assigned to a value of type `gResponse` and initialized based on the JSON document being decoded.

Sometimes the JSON documents you're working with come to you as a `string` value. In these cases, you need to convert the `string` into a byte slice (`[]byte`) and use the `Unmarshal` function from the `json` package.

Listing 8.27 listing27.go

```
01 // This sample program demonstrates how to decode a JSON string.
02 package main
03
04 import (
05     "encoding/json"
06     "fmt"
07     "log"
08 )
09
10 // Contact represents our JSON string.
11 type Contact struct {
12     Name    string `json:"name"`
13     Title   string `json:"title"`
14     Contact struct {
15         Home string `json:"home"`
16         Cell string `json:"cell"`
17     } `json:"contact"`
18 }
19
20 // JSON contains a sample string to unmarshal.
21 var JSON = `{
22     "name": "Gopher",
23     "title": "programmer",
24     "contact": {
25         "home": "415.333.3333",
26         "cell": "415.555.5555"
```

```
27        }
28 }`
29
30 func main() {
31     // Unmarshal the JSON string into our variable.
32     var c Contact
33     err := json.Unmarshal([]byte(JSON), &c)
34     if err != nil {
35         log.Println("ERROR:", err)
36         return
37     }
38
39     fmt.Println(c)
40 }
```

[handwritten: JSON contained in string]

[handwritten: // C is a zero struct — convert string → []byte]

[handwritten: // json string → bytes → struct]
[handwritten: // like python json.loads()]
[handwritten: // DECODE]

[handwritten: addr of struct]

[handwritten: @ 199] In listing 8.27 we have an example that takes a JSON document inside of a `string` variable and uses the `Unmarshal` function to decode the JSON into a struct type value. If you run the program, you'll get the following output.

Listing 8.28   Output for listing27.go

```
{Gopher programmer {415.333.3333 415.555.5555}}
```

[handwritten: ✳] Sometimes it's not possible to declare a struct type and you need more flexibility to work with the JSON document. In these cases you can decode or unmarshal the JSON document into a `map` variable.

Listing 8.29   listing29.go

```
01 // This sample program demonstrates how to decode a JSON string.
02 package main
03
04 import (
05     "encoding/json"
06     "fmt"
07     "log"
08 )
09
10 // JSON contains a sample string to unmarshal.
11 var JSON = `{
12     "name": "Gopher",
13     "title": "programmer",
14     "contact": {
15         "home": "415.333.3333",
16         "cell": "415.555.5555"
17     }
18 }`
19
20 func main() {
21     // Unmarshal the JSON string into our map variable.
22     var c map[string]interface{}
23     err := json.Unmarshal([]byte(JSON), &c)
24     if err != nil {
```

[handwritten: JSON contained in string]

[handwritten: ✳ 22]

[handwritten: C is a map]

[handwritten: addr of map]

[handwritten: convert string to byte slice]

```
25              log.Println("ERROR:", err)
26              return
27      }
28
29      fmt.Println("Name:", c["name"])
30      fmt.Println("Title:", c["title"])
31      fmt.Println("Contact")
32      fmt.Println("H:", c["contact"].(map[string]interface{})["home"])
33      fmt.Println("C:", c["contact"].(map[string]interface{})["cell"])
34 }
```

[handwritten: interface{}]

[handwritten: v.(T) construct: convert i/f value to underlying value @]

In listing 8.29 we've changed the program from listing 8.27 to use a map variable instead of our struct type variable. The map variable is declared as a map with a key of type string and a value of type interface{}. This means the map can store any type of value for any given key. Though this gives you great flexibility when working with JSON documents, it has one minor drawback. Look at the syntax required to access the home field from the contact subdocument.

Listing 8.30   Syntax for accessing a field from an unmarshaled map

```
fmt.Println("\tHome:", c["contact"].(map[string]interface{})["home"])
```

[handwritten: type conversion]

Because the value for each key is of type interface{}, you need to convert the value to the proper native type in order to work with the value. Listing 8.30 shows how you need to convert the value of the contact key to another map with a key of type string and a value of type interface{}. This can make using maps that contain JSON documents sometimes unfriendly to work with. But if you never need to dig into the JSON documents you're working with or you plan to do very little manipulation, using a map can be fast, and then there's no need to declare new types. *[handwritten: @]*

8.3.2   Encoding JSON

[handwritten: Want to convert a go struct/map into JSON string]

The second aspect of working with JSON we'll explore is using the MarshalIndent function from the json package. This comes in handy when you want to publish a pretty-printed JSON document from a Go map or struct type value. *Marshaling* is the process of transforming data into a JSON string. Here's an example that converts a map type into a JSON string. *[handwritten: ~ python: json_dumps]*

Listing 8.31   listing31.go

```
01 // This sample program demonstrates how to marshal a JSON string.
02 package main
03
04 import (
05      "encoding/json"
06      "fmt"
07      "log"
08 )
09
10 func main() {
```

```
11        // Create a map of key/value pairs.
12        c := make(map[string]interface{})
13        c["name"] = "Gopher"
14        c["title"] = "programmer"
15        c["contact"] = map[string]interface{}{
16            "home": "415.333.3333",
17            "cell": "415.555.5555",
18        }
19
20        // Marshal the map into a JSON string.
21        data, err := json.MarshalIndent(c, "", "  ")
22        if err != nil {
23            log.Println("ERROR:", err)
24            return
25        }
26
27        fmt.Println(string(data))
28 }
```

[handwritten annotations: "// data is []byte", "val/if prefix indent", "// struct → json as []byte", "// like python: json.dumps ()", "// ENCODE", "// convert json bytes to string and print"]

Listing 8.31 shows how to use the MarshalIndent function from the json package to convert a map to a JSON string. The MarshalIndent function returns a byte slice that represents the JSON string and an error value. Here's a look at the declaration of the MarshalIndent function from the json package.

> **Listing 8.32   golang.org/src/encoding/json/encode.go**

```
// MarshalIndent is like Marshal but applies Indent to format the output
func MarshalIndent(v interface{}, prefix, indent string)
                                                ([]byte, error) {
```

You can see the use of the empty interface type again as the parameter to the Marshal-Indent function. The MarshalIndent function uses reflection to determine how to transform the map type into a JSON string.

If you don't need the pretty-print formatting for your JSON encoding, the json package also provides a function called Marshal. This function is good for producing JSON that could be returned in a network response, like a web API. The Marshal function works the same as the MarshalIndent function, but without the parameters for prefix and indent.

8.3.3   *Conclusion*

If you're working with JSON or even XML, all the support you need to decode, unmarshal, and marshal data in these formats is provided to you already by the standard library. With each new release of Go, these packages get faster and faster, making working with JSON and XML a great choice. Thanks to the reflection package and the support for tags, it's easy to declare struct types and map those fields to the document fields you need to consume and publish. Since the json and xml packages provide support for the io.Reader and io.Writer interfaces, it doesn't matter where your JSON and XML documents are coming from. Everything is supported to make working with JSON and XML painless.

8.4 *Input and output*

One of the things that makes the UNIX-based operating systems so great is the idea that the output of one program can be the input for another. This philosophy has created a suite of simple programs that do only one thing and do it really well. Then, by composing programs together, scripts can be created to do some amazing things. In this world the `stdout` and `stdin` devices serve as the conduits to move data between processes.

This same idea has been extended to the io package, and the functionality that it provides is amazing. The package supports working with streams of data very efficiently, regardless of what the data is, where it's coming from, or where it's going. Instead of `stdout` and `stdin`, you have two interfaces called `io.Writer` and `io.Reader`. Values from types that implement these interfaces can be used against all the functionality provided by the `io` package or any function and method in any other package that also accepts values of these interface types. That's the real beauty of creating functionality and APIs from interfaces types. Developers can compose on top of existing functionality, take advantage of what exists, and focus on the business problems they're trying to solve.

With this in mind, let's start by looking at the declaration for the `io.Writer` and `io.Reader` interfaces and then examine code examples that showcase some of the amazing functionality of the `io` package.

8.4.1 *Writer and Reader interfaces*

The `io` package is built around working with values from types that implement the `io.Writer` and `io.Reader` interfaces. The functions and methods that make up the `io` package have no understanding about the type of data nor how that data is physically read and written. This is thanks to the abstraction that the `io.Writer` and `io.Reader` interfaces provide. Let's start by looking at the declaration of the `io.Writer` interface.

Listing 8.33   Declaration of the `io.Writer` interface

```
type Writer interface {
        Write(p []byte) (n int, err error)
}
```

Listing 8.33 shows the declaration of the `io.Writer` interface. The interface declares a single method called `Write` that accepts a byte slice and returns two values. The first value is the number of bytes written, and the second value is an `error`. The rules for implementing this method are as follows.

Listing 8.34   Documentation for the `io.Writer` interface

```
Write writes len(p) bytes from p to the underlying data stream. It
returns the number of bytes written from p (0 <= n <= len(p)) and any
error encountered that caused the write to stop early. Write must
return a non-nil error if it returns n < len(p). Write must not modify
the slice data, even temporarily.
```

The rules in listing 8.34 come from the standard library. They mean that the implementation of the Write method should attempt to write the entire length of the byte slice that's passed in. But if that isn't possible, then the method must return an error. The number of bytes reported as written can be less than the length of the byte slice, but never more. Finally, the byte slice must never be modified in any way.

Let's look at the declaration of the Reader interface.

Listing 8.35   Declaration of the io.Reader interface

```
type Reader interface {
        Read(p []byte) (n int, err error)
}
```

The io.Reader interface in listing 8.35 declares a single method, Read, that accepts a byte slice and returns two values. The first value is the number of bytes read and the second value is an error. The rules for implementing this method are as follows.

Listing 8.36   Documentation for the io.Reader interface

```
(1) Read reads up to len(p) bytes into p. It returns the number of bytes
read (0 <= n <= len(p)) and any error encountered. Even if Read returns
n < len(p), it may use all of p as scratch space during the call. If
some data is available but not len(p) bytes, Read conventionally
returns what is available instead of waiting for more.

(2) When Read encounters an error or end-of-file condition after
successfully reading n > 0 bytes, it returns the number of bytes read.
It may return the (non-nil) error from the same call or return the
error (and n == 0) from a subsequent call. An instance of this general
case is that a Reader returning a non-zero number of bytes at the end
of the input stream may return either err == EOF or err == nil. The next
Read should return 0, EOF regardless.

(3) Callers should always process the n > 0 bytes returned before
considering the error err. Doing so correctly handles I/O errors that
happen after reading some bytes and also both of the allowed EOF
behaviors.

(4) Implementations of Read are discouraged from returning a zero byte
count with a nil error, and callers should treat that situation as a
no-op.
```

There are four rules listed in the standard library about implementing the Read method. The first rule states that the implementation should attempt to read the entire length of the byte slice that's passed in. It's okay to read less than the entire length, and it shouldn't wait to read the entire length if that much data isn't available at the time of the call.

The second rule provides guidance about end of file (EOF) read conditions. When the last byte is read, two options are available. Read either returns the final bytes with the proper count and EOF for the error value, or returns the final bytes with the proper count and `nil` for the error value. In the latter case, the next read must return no bytes with the count of 0 and `EOF` for the error value.

The third rule is a suggestion for those who make the `Read` call. Any time the `Read` method returns bytes, those bytes should be processed first before checking the error value for an EOF or other error value. Finally, the fourth rule requests that implementations of the `Read` method never return a 0 byte read count with an error value of `nil`. Reads that result in no bytes read should always return an error.

Now that you know what the `io.Writer` and `io.Reader` interfaces look like and how they're expected to behave, let's look at some examples of how you can use these interfaces and the `io` package in your programs.

8.4.2 Working together

This example shows how different packages from the standard library work together by providing support for values from types that implement the `io.Writer` interface. The example uses the `bytes`, `fmt`, and `os` packages to buffer, concatenate, and write a string to stdout.

Listing 8.37 listing37.go

```
01 // Sample program to show how different functions from the
02 // standard library use the io.Writer interface.
03 package main
04
05 import (
06     "bytes"
07     "fmt"
08     "os"
09 )
10
11 // main is the entry point for the application.
12 func main() {
13     // Create a Buffer value and write a string to the buffer.
14     // Using the Write method that implements io.Writer.
15     var b bytes.Buffer        // Use a bytes.Buffer as underlying stream
16     b.Write([]byte("Hello ")) // a string is converted to a byte slice, and written to the buffer
17                               // &b is io.Writer
18     // Use Fprintf to concatenate a string to the Buffer.
19     // Passing the address of a bytes.Buffer value for io.Writer.
20     fmt.Fprintf(&b, "World!")      // Concatenate to buffer
21                                    // io.writer
22     // Write the content of the Buffer to the stdout device.
23     // Passing the address of a os.File value for io.Writer.
24     b.WriteTo(os.Stdout)
25 }
                                // io.Writer
```

When you run the program in listing 8.37, you'll get the following output.

Listing 8.38 Output for listing37.go

```
Hello World!
```

This program is using three packages from the standard library to write "Hello World!" to the terminal window. The program starts on line 15 by declaring a variable of type Buffer from the bytes package, which is initialized to its zero value. On line 16 a byte slice is created and initialized with the string "Hello". The byte slice is passed into the Write method and becomes the initial content for the buffer.

Line 20 uses the Fprintf function from the fmt package to append the string "World!" to the buffer. Let's look at the declaration of the Fprintf function.

Listing 8.39   golang.org/src/fmt/print.go

```
// Fprintf formats according to a format specifier and writes to w. It
// returns the number of bytes written and any write error encountered.
func Fprintf(w io.Writer, format string, a ...interface{})
                                                    (n int, err error)
```

What's important to note is the first parameter of the Fprintf function. It accepts values from types that implement the io.Writer interface. This means that the Buffer type from the bytes package must implement this interface since we're able to pass the address of a variable of that type through. In the source code for the bytes package, we should then find the Write method declared for the Buffer type.

Listing 8.40   golang.org/src/bytes/buffer.go

```
// Write appends the contents of p to the buffer, growing the buffer
// as needed. The return value n is the length of p; err is always
// nil. If the buffer becomes too large, Write will panic with ...
func (b *Buffer) Write(p []byte) (n int, err error) {
    b.lastRead = opInvalid     ?
    m := b.grow(len(p))
    return copy(b.buf[m:], p), nil
}
```

Listing 8.40 shows the current implementation of the Write method for the Buffer type that implements the io.Writer interface. Because of the implementation of this method, we can pass pointers of type Buffer as the first parameter to Fprintf. We use the Fprintf function in our example to append the string "World!" to the internal buffer of the Buffer type variable via the implementation of the Write method.

Let's review the last line of listing 8.37, which writes the entire buffer to stdout.

Listing 8.41   listing37.go: lines 22–25

```
22 // Write the content of the Buffer to the stdout device.
23     // Passing the address of a os.File value for io.Writer.
24     b.WriteTo(os.Stdout)          // os.Stdout is type File (207) which implements
25 }                                 // the os. Writer i/f
```

On line 24 of listing 8.37, the contents of the Buffer type variable are written to stdout using the WriteTo method. This method accepts a value that implements the io.Writer interface. In our program we pass the value of the Stdout variable from the os package.

Listing 8.42   golang.org/src/os/file.go

```
var (
    Stdin  = NewFile(uintptr(syscall.Stdin),  "/dev/stdin")
    Stdout = NewFile(uintptr(syscall.Stdout), "/dev/stdout")
    Stderr = NewFile(uintptr(syscall.Stderr), "/dev/stderr")
)
```

The declaration of these variables comes from the type returned by the NewFile function.

Listing 8.43   golang.org/src/os/file_unix.go

```
// NewFile returns a new File with the given file descriptor and name.
func NewFile(fd uintptr, name string) *File {
    fdi := int(fd)
    if fdi < 0 {
        return nil
    }
    f := &File{&file{fd: fdi, name: name}}
    runtime.SetFinalizer(f.file, (*file).close)
    return f
}
```

As you can see in listing 8.43, the NewFile function returns a pointer of type File. This is the type of the Stdout variable. Since we can pass pointers of this type as a parameter to the WriteTo method, it must implement the io.Writer interface. In the source code for the os package, we should find the Write method.

Listing 8.44   golang.org/src/os/file.go

```
// Write writes len(b) bytes to the File.
// It returns the number of bytes written and an error, if any.
// Write returns a non-nil error when n != len(b).
func (f *File) Write(b []byte) (n int, err error) {
    if f == nil {
        return 0, ErrInvalid
    }
    n, e := f.write(b)
    if n < 0 {
        n = 0
    }
    if n != len(b) {
        err = io.ErrShortWrite
    }

    epipecheck(f, e)

    if e != nil {
```

```
        err = &PathError{"write", f.name, e}
    }
    return n, err
}
```

Sure enough, listing 8.44 shows the implementation of the io.Writer interface for pointers of type File. Look again at line 24 from listing 8.37.

Listing 8.45 listing37.go: lines 22–25

```
22      // Write the content of the Buffer to the stdout device.
23      // Using the io.Writer implementation for os.File.
24      b.WriteTo(os.Stdout)
25 }
```

You see that the WriteTo method is able to write the contents of the buffer to stdout which results in the string "Hello World!" being displayed on our terminal window. The method will use the implementation of the Write method from the File type via the interface value.

This example shows the beauty of interfaces and the power they bring to the language. Thanks to the implementation of the interface by both the bytes.Buffer and os.File types, we were able to reuse functionality in the standard library and have these types work together to implement a solution. Next let's look at an example that's a bit more practical.

8.4.3 *Simple curl*   also 102

A command-line tool called curl can be found on both Linux and Mac OS X systems. The tool allows you to specify a URL, and it will perform an HTTP request and save the content. By using the http, io, and os packages, you can write your own version of curl in just a few lines of code.

Let's take a look at an example that implements a basic version of curl.

Listing 8.46 listing46.go

```
01 // Sample program to show how to write a simple version of curl using
02 // the io.Reader and io.Writer interface support.
03 package main
04
05 import (
06     "io"
07     "log"
08     "net/http"
09     "os"
10 )
11
12 // main is the entry point for the application.
13 func main() {
14     // r here is a response, and r.Body is an io.Reader.
15     r, err := http.Get(os.Args[1])
```
a URL

```
16      if err != nil {
17          log.Fatalln(err)
18      }
19
20      // Create a file to persist the response.
21      file, err := os.Create(os.Args[2])          os.OpenFile   191
22      if err != nil {                        File name
23          log.Fatalln(err)
24      }
25      defer file.Close()
26
27      // Use MultiWriter so we can write to stdout and      @
28      // a file on the same write operation.
29      dest := io.MultiWriter(os.Stdout, file)
30
31      // Read the response and write to both destinations.
32      io.Copy(dest, r.Body)        // io.Copy (dest, src)
33      if err := r.Body.Close(); err != nil {
34          log.Println(err)
35      }
36  }
```

Listing 8.46 shows a very bare-bones implementation of curl that can be used to download, display, and save the content of any HTTP Get request. The example will write the response to a file and to stdout at the same time. To keep the example small, the program doesn't check for valid command-line arguments, nor provide switches for advanced options.   Go in Practice

On line 15 the program takes the first argument from the command line and performs an HTTP Get. If the first argument is a URL and there are no errors, the variable r contains the response. On line 21 we open a file based on the second command-line parameter. If we're successful in opening the file, then on line 25 we schedule the closing of the file with the defer statement.

Since we want to write the content of the request to both stdout and to our file,   (a) on line 29 we combine the file and stdout values together into a single io.Writer value by using the MultiWriter function from the io package. On line 33 we use the Copy function from the io package to read the content from the response body and to write that to both destinations. With one call to Copy, thanks to the value provided by the MultiWriter function we can use a single call that writes the content to both destinations.

Thanks to the support already provided by the io package and the implementation of the io.Writer and io.Reader interfaces by the http and os packages, we don't need to write any code to perform these lower-level functions. We can leverage everything that already exists and just focus on the problem we're trying to solve. If we support these interfaces with our own types, we get a huge amount of functionality for free.

8.4.4   *Conclusion*

There's an incredible amount of functionality that can be found in the io package, and it can all be accessed through values from types that implement the io.Writer and io.Reader interfaces. Other packages such as the http package follow a similar pattern, declaring interfaces as part of the packages API and providing support for using the io package as well. It's worth your time to explore what's provided by the standard library and how it's implemented—not only to save you from reinventing the wheel, but also to learn idiomatic Go from the language designers for your own packages and APIs.

8.5   *Summary*

- The standard library comes with special guarantees and is widely used by the community.
- Using packages from the standard library makes it easier to manage and trust your code.
- Well over 100 packages are organized within 38 different categories.
- The log package from the standard library has everything you need for logging.
- The standard library has two packages called xml and json that make working with these data formats trivial.
- The io package supports working with streams of data very efficiently.
- Interfaces allow your code to compose with existing functionality.
- Reading code from the standard library is a great way to get a feel for idiomatic Go.

Testing and benchmarking

In this chapter

- Writing unit tests to validate your code
- Mocking HTTP-based requests and responses using httptest
- Documenting your packages with example code
- Examining performance with benchmarks

Testing your code is not something that you should wait to do until after you're finished developing your program. With Go's testing framework, unit testing and benchmarking can happen during the development process. Just like the go build command, there's a go test command to execute explicit test code that you write. All you need to do is follow a few guidelines, and you can integrate tests into your project and continuous integration systems seamlessly.

9.1   *Unit testing*

A *unit test* is a function that tests a specific piece or set of code from a package or program. The job of the test is to determine whether the code in question is working as expected for a given scenario. One scenario may be a positive-path test, where the test is making sure the normal execution of the code doesn't produce an error. This could be a test that validates that the code can insert a job record into the database successfully.

Other unit tests may test negative-path scenarios to make sure the code produces not only an error, but the expected one. This could be a test that makes a query against a database where no results are found, or performs an invalid update against a database. In both cases, the test would validate that the error is reported and the correct error context is provided. In the end, the code you write must be predictable no matter how it's called or executed.

There are several ways in Go to write unit tests. *Basic tests* test a specific piece of code for a single set of parameters and result. *Table tests* also test a specific piece of code, but the test validates itself against multiple parameters and results. There are also ways to mock external resources that the test code needs, such as databases or web servers. This helps to simulate the existence of these resources during testing without the need for them to be available. Finally, when building your own web services, there are ways to test calls coming in to the service without ever needing to run the service itself.

9.1.1   *Basic unit test*

Let's start with an example of a unit test.

> Listing 9.1   listing01_test.go

```
01 // Sample test to show how to write a basic unit test.
02 package listing01
03
04 import (
05     "net/http"
06     "testing"
07 )
08
09 const checkMark = "\u2713"        //  ✓
10 const ballotX = "\u2717"          //  ✗
11
12 // TestDownload validates the http Get function can download content.
13 func TestDownload(t *testing.T) {
14     url := "http://www.goinggo.net/feeds/posts/default?alt=rss"
15     statusCode := 200
16
17     t.Log("Given the need to test downloading content.")
18     {
19         t.Logf("\tWhen checking \"%s\" for status code \"%d\"",
20             url, statusCode)
21         {
```

```
22              resp, err := http.Get(url)
23              if err != nil {
24                  t.Fatal("\t\tShould be able to make the Get call.",
25                      ballotX, err)
26              }
27              t.Log("\t\tShould be able to make the Get call.",
28                  checkMark)
29
30              defer resp.Body.Close()
31
32              if resp.StatusCode == statusCode {
33                  t.Logf("\t\tShould receive a \"%d\" status. %v",
34                      statusCode, checkMark)
35              } else {
36                  t.Errorf("\t\tShould receive a \"%d\" status. %v %v",
37                      statusCode, ballotX, resp.StatusCode)
38              }
39          }
40      }
41 }
```

Listing 9.1 shows a unit test that's testing the Get function from the http package. It's testing that the goinggo.net RSS feed can be downloaded properly from the web. When we run this test by calling go test -v, where -v means *provide verbose output*, we get the test results shown in figure 9.1.

go test [-v]

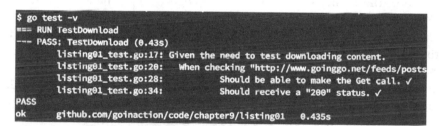

```
$ go test -v
=== RUN TestDownload
--- PASS: TestDownload (0.43s)
        listing01_test.go:17: Given the need to test downloading content.
        listing01_test.go:20:   When checking "http://www.goinggo.net/feeds/posts
        listing01_test.go:28:       Should be able to make the Get call. ✓
        listing01_test.go:34:       Should receive a "200" status. ✓
PASS
ok      github.com/goinaction/code/chapter9/listing01    0.435s
```

Figure 9.1 Output from the basic unit test

A lot of little things are happening in this example to make this test work and display the results as it does. It all starts with the name of the test file. If you look at the top of listing 9.1, you'll see that the name of the test file is listing01_test.go. The Go testing tool will only look at files that end in _test.go. If you forget to follow this convention, running go test inside of a package may report that there are no test files. Once the testing tool finds a testing file, it then looks for testing functions to run.

@ 212

Let's take a closer look at the code in the listing01_test.go test file.

Listing 9.2 listing01_test.go: lines 01–10

```
01 // Sample test to show how to write a basic unit test.
02 package listing01
03
```

```
04 import (
05     "net/http"
06     "testing"
07 )
08
09 const checkMark = "\u2713"        // ✓
10 const ballotX = "\u2717"          // ✗
```

In listing 9.2, you can see the import of the testing package on line 06. The testing package provides the support we need from the testing framework to report the output and status of any test. Lines 09 and 10 provide two constants that contain the characters for the check mark and X mark that will be used when writing test output.

Next, let's look at the declaration of the test function.

Listing 9.3　listing01_test.go: lines 12–13

```
12 // TestDownload validates the http Get function can download content.
13 func TestDownload(t *testing.T) {
```

The name of the test function is TestDownload, and you can see it on line 13 in listing 9.3. A test function must be an exported function that begins with the word Test. Not only must the function start with the word Test, it must have a signature that accepts a pointer of type testing.T and returns no value. If we don't follow these conventions, the testing framework won't recognize the function as a test function and none of the tooling will work against it.

The pointer of type testing.T is important. It provides the mechanism for reporting the output and status of each test. There's no one standard for formatting the output of your tests. I like the test output to read well, which does follow the Go idioms for writing documentation. For me, the testing output is documentation for the code. The test output should document why the test exists, what's being tested, and the result of the test in clear complete sentences that are easy to read. Let's see how I accomplish this as we review more of the code.

Listing 9.4　listing01_test.go: lines 14–18

```
14     url := "http://www.goinggo.net/feeds/posts/default?alt=rss"
15     statusCode := 200
16
17     t.Log("Given the need to test downloading content.")
18     {
```

You see on lines 14 and 15 in listing 9.4 that two variables are declared and initialized. These variables contain the URL we want to test and the status we expect back from the response. On line 17 the t.Log method is used to write a message to the test output. There's also a format version of this method called t.Logf. If the verbose option (-v) isn't used when calling go test, we won't see any test output unless the test fails.

Each test function should state why the test exists by explaining the *given need* of the test. For this test, the given need is to test downloading content. After declaring the given need of the test, the test should then state *when* the code being tested would execute, and how.

Listing 9.5 listing01_test.go: lines 19–21

```
19          t.Logf("\tWhen checking \"%s\" for status code \"%d\"",
20              url, statusCode)
21          {
```

You see the when clause on line 19 in listing 9.5. It states specifically the values for the test. Next, let's look at the code being tested using these values.

Listing 9.6 listing01_test.go: lines 22–30

```
22          resp, err := http.Get(url)          // Using Get func in http pkg for actual call
23          if err != nil {
24              t.Fatal("\t\tShould be able to make the Get call.",
25                  ballotX, err)
26          }
27          t.Log("\t\tShould be able to make the Get call.",
28              checkMark)
29
30          defer resp.Body.Close()
```

The code in listing 9.6 uses the Get function from the http package to make a request to the goinggo.net web server to pull down the RSS feed file for the blog. After the Get (XML) call returns, the error value is checked to see if the call was successful or not. In either case, we state what the result of the test *should* be. If the call failed, we write an *X* as well to the test output along with the error. If the test succeeded, we write a check mark.

If the call to Get does fail, the use of the t.Fatal method on line 24 lets the testing framework know this unit test has failed. The t.Fatal method not only reports the unit test has failed, but also writes a message to the test output and then stops the execution of this particular test function. If there are other test functions that haven't run yet, they'll be executed. A formatted version of this method is named t.Fatalf.

When we need to report the test has failed but don't want to stop the execution of the particular test function, we can use the t.Error family of methods.

Listing 9.7 listing01_test.go: lines 32–41

```
32          if resp.StatusCode == statusCode {
33              t.Logf("\t\tShould receive a \"%d\" status. %v",
34                  statusCode, checkMark)
35          } else {
36              t.Errorf("\t\tShould receive a \"%d\" status. %v %v",
37                  statusCode, ballotX, resp.StatusCode)
38          }
39      }
40  }
41 }
```

2   If there were more checks/tests to be made after line 38; even if t.Errorf reports an error they would be executed.

```
$ go test -v
=== RUN TestDownload
--- PASS: TestDownload (0.43s)
        listing01_test.go:17: Given the need to test downloading content.
        listing01_test.go:20:   When checking "http://www.goinggo.net/feeds/posts
        listing01_test.go:28:           Should be able to make the Get call. ✓
        listing01_test.go:34:           Should receive a "200" status. ✓
PASS
ok      github.com/goinaction/code/chapter9/listing01    0.435s
```

Figure 9.2   Output from the basic unit test

One line 32 in listing 9.7, the status code from the response is compared with the status code we expect to receive. Again, we state what the result of the test should be. If the status codes match, then we use the t.Logf method; otherwise, we use the t.Errorf method. Since the t.Errorf method doesn't stop the execution of the test function, if there were more tests to conduct after line 38, the unit test would continue to be executed. If the t.Fatal or t.Error functions aren't called by a test function, the test will be considered as passing.

If you look at the output of the test one more time (see figure 9.2), you can see how it all comes together.

In figure 9.2 you see the complete documentation for the test. Given the need to download content, when checking the URL for the statusCode (which is cut off in the figure), we should be able to make the call and should receive a status of 200. The testing output is clear, descriptive, and informative. We know what unit test was run, that it passed, and how long it took: 435 milliseconds.

9.1.2   Table tests

When you're testing code that can accept a set of different parameters with different results, a table test should be used. A *table test* is like a basic unit test except it maintains a table of different values and results. The different values are iterated over and run through the test code. With each iteration, the results are checked. This helps to leverage a single test function to test a set of different values and conditions. Let's look at an example table test.

Listing 9.8   listing08_test.go

```
01 // Sample test to show how to write a basic unit table test.
02 package listing08
03
04 import (
05     "net/http"
06     "testing"
07 )
08
09 const checkMark = "\u2713"
10 const ballotX = "\u2717"
11
12 // TestDownload validates the http Get function can download
```

```
13 //   content and handles different status conditions properly.
14 func TestDownload(t *testing.T) {
15     var urls = []struct {
16         url        string
17         statusCode int
18     }{
19         {
20             "http://www.goinggo.net/feeds/posts/default?alt=rss",
21             http.StatusOK,
22         },
23         {
24             "http://rss.cnn.com/rss/cnn_topstbadurl.rss",
25             http.StatusNotFound,
26         },
27     }
28
29     t.Log("Given the need to test downloading different content.")
30     {
31         for _, u := range urls {
32             t.Logf("\tWhen checking \"%s\" for status code \"%d\"",
33                 u.url, u.statusCode)
34             {
35                 resp, err := http.Get(u.url)
36                 if err != nil {
37                     t.Fatal("\t\tShould be able to Get the url.",
38                         ballotX, err)
39                 }
40                 t.Log("\t\tShould be able to Get the url",
41                     checkMark)
42
43                 defer resp.Body.Close()
44
45                 if resp.StatusCode == u.statusCode {
46                     t.Logf("\t\tShould have a \"%d\" status. %v",
47                         u.statusCode, checkMark)
48                 } else {
49                     t.Errorf("\t\tShould have a \"%d\" status %v %v",
50                         u.statusCode, ballotX, resp.StatusCode)
51                 }
52             }
53         }
54     }
55 }
```

In listing 9.8, we've taken the basic unit test and converted it to a table test. Now we can use a single test function to test different URLs and status codes against the http.Get function. We don't need to create a new test function for each URL and status code we want to test. Let's look at the changes.

Listing 9.9   listing08_test.go: lines 12–27

```
12 // TestDownload validates the http Get function can download
13 //   content and handles different status conditions properly.
14 func TestDownload(t *testing.T) {
```

```
15      var urls = []struct {
16          url        string
17          statusCode int
18      }{
19          {
20              "http://www.goinggo.net/feeds/posts/default?alt=rss",
21              http.StatusOK,
22          },
23          {
24              "http://rss.cnn.com/rss/cnn_topstbadurl.rss",
25              http.StatusNotFound,
26          },
27      }
```

In listing 9.9 you see the same test function, `TestDownload`, accepting a pointer of type `testing.T`. But this version of `TestDownload` is slightly different. On lines 15 through 27, you see the implementation of the table. The first field of the table is a URL to a given resource on the internet, and the second field is the status we expect to receive when we make the request for the resource.

Currently, we've configured the table with two values. The first value is the goinggo.net URL with a status of OK, and the second value is a different URL with a status of NotFound. The second URL has been misspelled to cause the server to return a NotFound error. When we run this test, we get the test output shown in figure 9.3.

```
$ go test -v
=== RUN TestDownload
--- PASS: TestDownload (0.72s)
        listing02_test.go:29: Given the need to test downloading different conten
        listing02_test.go:33:   When checking "http://www.goinggo.net/feeds/posts/
        listing02_test.go:41:           Should be able to Get the url. ✓
        listing02_test.go:47:           Should have a "200" status. ✓
        listing02_test.go:33:   When checking "http://rss.cnn.com/rss/cnn_topstbad
        listing02_test.go:41:           Should be able to Get the url. ✓
        listing02_test.go:47:           Should have a "404" status. ✓
PASS
ok      github.com/goinaction/code/chapter9/listing02    0.724s
```

Figure 9.3   Output from the table test

The output in figure 9.3 shows how the table of values is iterated over and used to conduct the test. The output looks the same as the basic unit test except we tested two different URLs this time. Once again, the test passes.

Let's look at the changes we made to make the table test work.

Listing 9.10   listing08_test.go: lines 29–34

```
29      t.Log("Given the need to test downloading different content.")
30      {
31          for _, u := range urls {
32              t.Logf("\tWhen checking \"%s\" for status code \"%d\"",
33                  u.url, u.statusCode)
34              {
```

The for range loop on line 31 in listing 9.10 allows the test to iterate over the table and run the test code for each different URL. The original code from the basic unit test is the same except for the use of the table values.

Listing 9.11   listing08_test.go: lines 35–55

```
35                     resp, err := http.Get(u.url)
36                     if err != nil {
37                         t.Fatal("\t\tShould be able to Get the url.",
38                             ballotX, err)
39                     }
40                     t.Log("\t\tShould be able to Get the url",
41                         checkMark)
42
43                     defer resp.Body.Close()
44
45                     if resp.StatusCode == u.statusCode {
46                         t.Logf("\t\tShould have a \"%d\" status. %v",
47                             u.statusCode, checkMark)
48                     } else {
49                         t.Errorf("\t\tShould have a \"%d\" status %v %v",
50                             u.statusCode, ballotX, resp.StatusCode)
51                     }
52                 }
53             }
54     }
55 }
```

Listing 9.11 shows how, on line 35, the code uses the u.url field for the URL to call. On line 45 the u.statusCode field is used to compare the actual status code from the response. In the future, new URLs and status codes can be added to the table and the core of the test doesn't need to change.

9.1.3   Mocking calls

The unit tests we wrote are great, but they do have a couple of flaws. First, they require access to the internet in order for the tests to run successfully. Figure 9.4 shows what happens when we run the basic unit test again without an internet connection—the test fails.

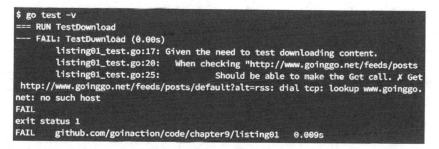

Figure 9.4   Failed test due to having no internet connection

You shouldn't always assume the computer you have to run tests on can access the internet. Also, it's not good practice to have tests depend on servers that you don't own or operate. Both of these things can have a great impact on any automation you put into place for continuous integration and deployment. Suddenly you can't deploy a new build because you lost your access to the outside world. If the tests fail, you can't deploy.

To fix this situation, the standard library has a package called httptest that will let you mock HTTP-based web calls. Mocking is a technique many developers use to simulate access to resources that won't be available when tests are run. The httptest package provides you with the ability to mock requests and responses from web resources on the internet. By mocking the http.Get response in our unit test, we can solve the problem we saw in figure 9.4. No longer will our test fail because we don't have an internet connection. Yet the test can validate that our http.Get call works and handles the expected response. Let's take the basic unit test and change it to mock a call to the goinggo.net RSS feed.

Listing 9.12   listing12_test.go: lines 01–41

```
01 // Sample test to show how to mock an HTTP GET call internally.
02 // Differs slightly from the book to show more.
03 package listing12
04
05 import (
06     "encoding/xml"
07     "fmt"
08     "net/http"
09     "net/http/httptest"
10     "testing"
11 )
12
13 const checkMark = "\u2713"
14 const ballotX = "\u2717"
15
16 // feed is mocking the XML document we except to receive.
17 var feed = `<?xml version="1.0" encoding="UTF-8"?>
18 <rss>
19 <channel>
20     <title>Going Go Programming</title>
21     <description>Golang : https://github.com/goinggo</description>
22     <link>http://www.goinggo.net/</link>
23     <item>
24         <pubDate>Sun, 15 Mar 2015 15:04:00 +0000</pubDate>
25         <title>Object Oriented Programming Mechanics</title>
26         <description>Go is an object oriented language.</description>
27         <link>http://www.goinggo.net/2015/03/object-oriented</link>
28     </item>
29 </channel>
30 </rss>`
31
32 // mockServer returns a pointer to a server to handle the get call.
33 func mockServer() *httptest.Server {
```

```
34      f := func(w http.ResponseWriter, r *http.Request) {
35          w.WriteHeader(200)
36          w.Header().Set("Content-Type", "application/xml")
37          fmt.Fprintln(w, feed)
38      }
39
40      return httptest.NewServer(http.HandlerFunc(f))
41 }
```

Listing 9.12 shows how we can mock a call to the goinggo.net website to simulate the downloading of the RSS feed. On line 17 a package-level variable named feed is declared and initialized with a literal string that represents the RSS XML document we'll receive from our mock server call. It's a small snippet of the actual RSS feed document and is enough to conduct our test. On line 32 we have the declaration of a function named mockServer that leverages the support inside the httptest package to simulate a call to a real server on the internet.

Listing 9.13   listing12_test.go: lines 32–40

```
32 func mockServer() *httptest.Server {
33      f := func(w http.ResponseWriter, r *http.Request) {
34          w.WriteHeader(200)
35          w.Header().Set("Content-Type", "application/xml")
36          fmt.Fprintln(w, feed)
37      }
38
39      return httptest.NewServer(http.HandlerFunc(f))
40 }
```

The mockServer function in listing 9.13 is declared to return a pointer of type httptest.Server. The httptest.Server value is the key to making all of this work. The code starts out with declaring an anonymous function that has the same signature as the http.HandlerFunc function type.

Listing 9.14   golang.org/pkg/net/http/#HandlerFunc

```
type HandlerFunc func(ResponseWriter, *Request)
```

The HandlerFunc type is an adapter to allow the use of ordinary functions as HTTP handlers. If f is a function with the appropriate signature, HandlerFunc(f) is a Handler object that calls f

This makes the anonymous function a handler function. Once the handler function is declared, then on line 39 it's used as a parameter for the httptest.NewServer function call to create our mock server. Then the mock server is returned via a pointer on line 39.

We'll be able to use this mock server with our http.Get call to simulate hitting the goinggo.net web server. When the http.Get call is made, the handler function is actually executed and used to mock the request and response. On line 34 the handler function first sets the status code; then, on line 35, the content type is set; and finally, on line 36, the XML string named feed that represents the response is returned as the response body.

Now, let's look at how the mock server is integrated into the basic unit test and how the http.Get call is able to use it.

Listing 9.15   listing12_test.go: lines 43–74

```
43 // TestDownload validates the http Get function can download content
44 // and the content can be unmarshaled and clean.
45 func TestDownload(t *testing.T) {
46     statusCode := http.StatusOK
47
48     server := mockServer()
49     defer server.Close()
50
51     t.Log("Given the need to test downloading content.")
52     {
53         t.Logf("\tWhen checking \"%s\" for status code \"%d\"",
54             server.URL, statusCode)
55         {
56             resp, err := http.Get(server.URL)
57             if err != nil {
58                 t.Fatal("\t\tShould be able to make the Get call.",
59                     ballotX, err)
60             }
61             t.Log("\t\tShould be able to make the Get call.",
62                 checkMark)
63
64             defer resp.Body.Close()
65
66             if resp.StatusCode != statusCode {
67                 t.Fatalf("\t\tShould receive a \"%d\" status. %v %v",
68                     statusCode, ballotX, resp.StatusCode)
69             }
70             t.Logf("\t\tShould receive a \"%d\" status. %v",
71                 statusCode, checkMark)
72         }
73     }
74 }
```

In listing 9.15 you see the TestDownload function once more, but this time it's using the mock server. On lines 48 and 49 a call to the mockServer function is made, and a call to the Close method is deferred for when the test function returns. After that, the test code looks identical to the basic unit test except for one thing.

Listing 9.16   listing12_test.go: line 56

```
56         resp, err := http.Get(server.URL)
```

This time the URL to call is provided to by the httptest.Server value. When we use the URL provided by the mocking server, the http.Get call runs as expected. The http.Get call has no idea it's not making a call over the internet. The call is made and

```
$ go test -v
=== RUN TestDownload
--- PASS: TestDownload (0.00s)
        listing03_test.go:51: Given the need to test downloading content.
        listing03_test.go:54:   When checking "http://127.0.0.1:52065" for status code "200"
        listing03_test.go:62:       Should be able to make the Get call. ✓
        listing03_test.go:71:       Should receive a "200" status. ✓
        listing03_test.go:79:       Should be able to unmarshal the response. ✓
        listing03_test.go:83:       Should have "1" item in the feed. ✓
PASS
ok      github.com/goinaction/code/chapter9/listing03   0.007s
```

Figure 9.5 Successful test without having an internet connection

our handler function is executed underneath, resulting in a response of our RSS XML document and a status of http.StatusOK.

When we run the test now without an internet connection, we see the test runs and passes, as shown in figure 9.5. This figure shows how the test is passing again. If you look at the URL used to make the call, you can see it's using the localhost address with port number 52065. That port number will change every time we run the test. The http package, in conjunction with the httptest package and our mock server, knows to route that URL to our handler function. Now, we can test our calls to the goinggo.net RSS feed without ever hitting the actual server.

9.1.4 Testing endpoints

If you're building a web API, you'll want to test all of your endpoints without the need to start the web service. The httptest package provides a facility for doing just this. Let's take a look at a sample web service that implements a single endpoint, and then you can see how to write a unit test that mocks an actual call.

Listing 9.17 listing17.go

```
01 // This sample code implement a simple web service.
02 package main
03
04 import (
05     "log"
06     "net/http"
07
08     "github.com/goinaction/code/chapter9/listing17/handlers"
09 )
10
11 // main is the entry point for the application.
12 func main() {
13     handlers.Routes()
14
15     log.Println("listener : Started : Listening on :4000")
16     http.ListenAndServe(":4000", nil)
17 }
```

Listing 9.17 shows the code file for the entry point of the web service. Inside the `main` function on line 13, the code calls the `Routes` function from the internal `handlers` package. This function sets up the routes for the different endpoints the web service is hosting. On lines 15 and 16 the `main` function displays the port the service is listening on and starts the web service, waiting for requests.

Now, let's look at the code for the `handlers` package.

Listing 9.18   handlers/handlers.go

```
01 // Package handlers provides the endpoints for the web service.
02 package handlers
03
04 import (
05     "encoding/json"
06     "net/http"
07 )
08
09 // Routes sets the routes for the web service.
10 func Routes() {
11     http.HandleFunc("/sendjson", SendJSON)
12 }
13
14 // SendJSON returns a simple JSON document.
15 func SendJSON(rw http.ResponseWriter, r *http.Request) {
16     u := struct {
17         Name  string
18         Email string
19     }{
20         Name:  "Bill",
21         Email: "bill@ardanstudios.com",
22     }
23
24     rw.Header().Set("Content-Type", "application/json")
25     rw.WriteHeader(200)
26     json.NewEncoder(rw).Encode(&u)
27 }
```

The code for the `handlers` package in listing 9.18 provides the implementation of the handler function and sets up the routes for the web service. On line 10 you see the `Routes` function, which uses the default `http.ServeMux` from inside the `http` package to configure the routing between the URLs and the corresponding handler code. On line 11 we bind the `/sendjson` endpoint to the `SendJSON` function.

Starting on line 15, we have the implementation of the `SendJSON` function. The function has the same signature as the `http.HandlerFunc` function type that you saw in listing 9.14. On line 16 an anonymous struct type is declared, and a variable named `u` is created with some values. On lines 24 and 25 the content type and status code for the response is set. Finally, on line 26 the `u` value is encoded into a JSON document and sent back to the client.

If we build the web service and start the server, we see the JSON document served up, as in figures 9.6 and 9.7.

Figure 9.6 Running the web service

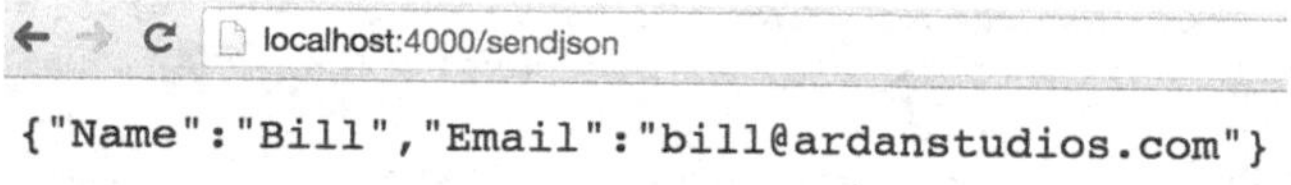

{"Name":"Bill","Email":"bill@ardanstudios.com"}

Figure 9.7 Web service serving up the JSON document

Now that we have a functioning web service with an endpoint, we can write a unit test to test the endpoint.

Listing 9.19 handlers/handlers_test.go

```
01 // Sample test to show how to test the execution of an
02 // internal endpoint.
03 package handlers_test
04
05 import (
06     "encoding/json"
07     "net/http"
08     "net/http/httptest"
09     "testing"
10
11     "github.com/goinaction/code/chapter9/listing17/handlers"
12 )
13
14 const checkMark = "\u2713"
15 const ballotX - "\u2717"
16
17 func init() {
18     handlers.Routes()
19 }
20
21 // TestSendJSON testing the sendjson internal endpoint.
22 func TestSendJSON(t *testing.T) {
23     t.Log("Given the need to test the SendJSON endpoint.")
24     {
25         req, err := http.NewRequest("GET", "/sendjson", nil)
26         if err != nil {
27             t.Fatal("\tShould be able to create a request.",
28                 ballotX, err)
29         }
30         t.Log("\tShould be able to create a request.",
31             checkMark)
32
33         rw := httptest.NewRecorder()
34         http.DefaultServeMux.ServeHTTP(rw, req)
35
36         if rw.Code != 200 {
37             t.Fatal("\tShould receive \"200\"", ballotX, rw.Code)
38         }
39         t.Log("\tShould receive \"200\"", checkMark)
40
```

```
41          u := struct {
42              Name  string
43              Email string
44          }{}
45
46          if err := json.NewDecoder(rw.Body).Decode(&u); err != nil {
47              t.Fatal("\tShould decode the response.", ballotX)
48          }
49          t.Log("\tShould decode the response.", checkMark)
50
51          if u.Name == "Bill" {
52            t.Log("\tShould have a Name.", checkMark)
53          } else {
54            t.Error("\tShould have a Name.", ballotX, u.Name)
55          }
56
57          if u.Email == "bill@ardanstudios.com" {
58              t.Log("\tShould have an Email.", checkMark)
59          } else {
60              t.Error("\tShould have an Email.", ballotX, u.Email)
61          }
62      }
63 }
```

Listing 9.19 shows a unit test for the /sendjson endpoint. On line 03 you see the name of the package is different from the other tests.

Listing 9.20 handlers/handlers_test.go: lines 01–03

```
01 // Sample test to show how to test the execution of an
02 // internal endpoint.
03 package handlers_test
```

This time, as you can see in listing 9.20, the package name also ends with _test. When the package name ends like this, the test code can only access exported identifiers. This is true even if the test code file is in the same folder as the code being tested.

Just like when running the service directly, the routes need to be initialized.

Listing 9.21 handlers/handlers_test.go: lines 17–19

```
17 func init() {
18     handlers.Routes()
19 }
```

On line 17 in listing 9.21, an init function is declared to initialize the routes. If the routes aren't initialized before the unit tests are run, then the tests will fail with an http.StatusNotFound error. Now we can look at the unit test for the /sendjson endpoint.

Listing 9.22 handlers/handlers_test.go: lines 21–34

```
21  // TestSendJSON testing the sendjson internal endpoint.
22  func TestSendJSON(t *testing.T) {
23      t.Log("Given the need to test the SendJSON endpoint.")
24      {
25          req, err := http.NewRequest("GET", "/sendjson", nil)
26          if err != nil {
27              t.Fatal("\tShould be able to create a request.",
28                  ballotX, err)
29          }
30          t.Log("\tShould be able to create a request.",
31              checkMark)
32
33          rw := httptest.NewRecorder()
34          http.DefaultServeMux.ServeHTTP(rw, req)
```

Listing 9.22 shows the declaration of the `TestSendJSON` test function. The test starts off logging the given need of the test, and then on line 25 it creates an `http.Request` value. The request value is configured to be a `GET` call against the `/sendjson` endpoint. Since this is a `GET` call, `nil` is passed as the third parameter for the post data.

Then, on line 33, the `httptest.NewRecorder` function is called to create an `http.ResponseRecorder` value. With the `http.Request` and `http.ResponseRecorder` values, a call to the `ServerHTTP` method against the default server multiplexer (mux) is made on line 34. Calling this method mocks a request to our `/sendjson` endpoint as if it were being made from an external client.

Once the `ServeHTTP` method call completes, the `http.ResponseRecorder` value contains the response from our `SendJSON` function handler. Now we can test the response.

Listing 9.23 handlers/handlers_test.go: lines 36–39

```
36          if rw.Code != 200 {
37              t.Fatal("\tShould receive \"200\"", ballotX, rw.Code)
38          }
39          t.Log("\tShould receive \"200\"", checkMark)
```

First, the status of the response is checked on line 36. With any successful endpoint call, a status of 200 is expected. If the status is 200, then the JSON response is decoded into a Go value.

Listing 9.24 handlers/handlers_test.go: lines 41–49

```
41          u := struct {
42              Name  string
43              Email string
44          }{}
45
46          if err := json.NewDecoder(rw.Body).Decode(&u); err != nil {
47              t.Fatal("\tShould decode the response.", ballotX)
48          }
49          t.Log("\tShould decode the response.", checkMark)
```

On line 41 in listing 9.24, an anonymous struct type is declared, and a variable named u is created and initialized to its zero value. On line 46 the json package is used to decode the JSON document from the response into the u variable. If the decode fails, the unit test is ended; otherwise, we validate the values that were decoded.

Listing 9.25   `handlers/handlers_test.go`: lines 51–63

```
51          if u.Name == "Bill" {
52            t.Log("\tShould have a Name.", checkMark)
53          } else {
54            t.Error("\tShould have a Name.", ballotX, u.Name)
55          }
56
57          if u.Email == "bill@ardanstudios.com" {
58              t.Log("\tShould have an Email.", checkMark)
59          } else {
60              t.Error("\tShould have an Email.", ballotX, u.Email)
61          }
62      }
63 }
```

Listing 9.25 shows both checks for each value we expect to receive. On line 51 we check that the value of the Name field is "Bill", and then on line 57 the value of the Email field is checked for "bill@ardanstudios.com". If these values match, then the unit test passes; otherwise, the unit test fails. These two checks use the Error method to report failure, so all the fields are checked.

9.2   *Examples*

Go is very focused on having proper documentation for the code you write. The *godoc* tool was built to produce documentation directly from your code. In chapter 3 we talked about the use of the godoc tool to produce package documentation. Another feature of the godoc tool is example code. Example code adds another dimension to both testing and documentation.

If you use your browser to navigate to the Go documentation for the json package, you'll see something like figure 9.8.

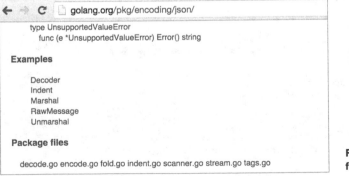

Figure 9.8   Listing of examples for the `json` package

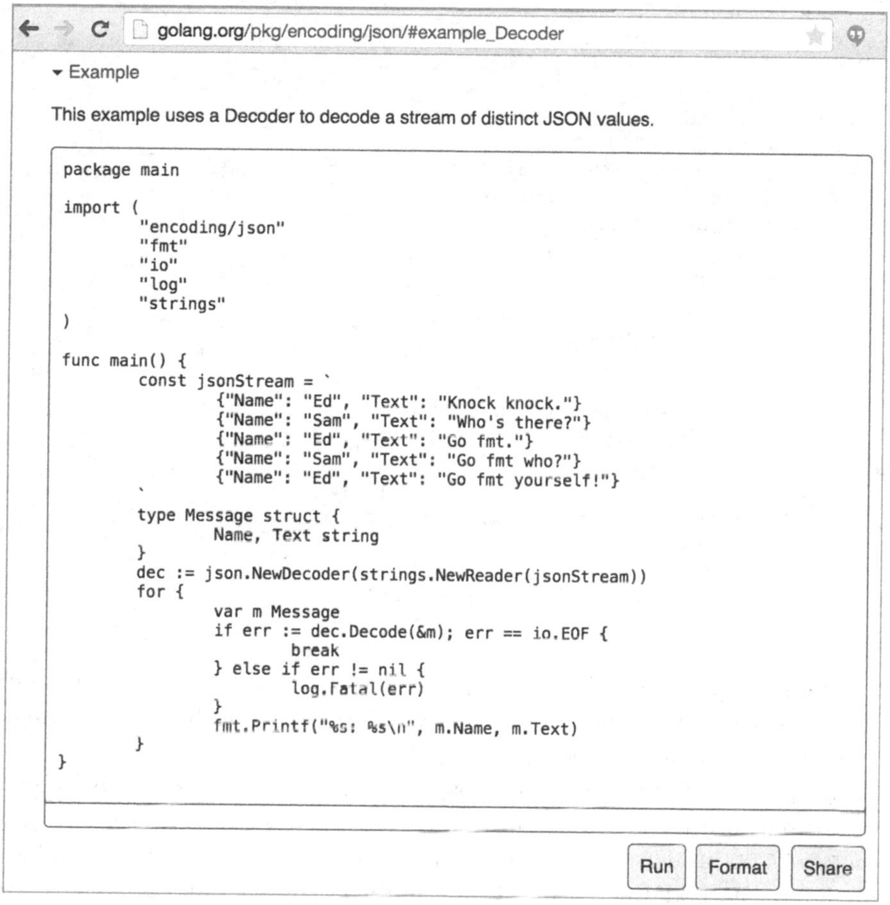

Figure 9.9 A view of the Decoder example in the Go documentation

The json package has five examples, and they show in the Go documentation for the package. If you select the first example, you see a view of the example code, as in figure 9.9.

You can create your own examples and have them show up in the Go documentation for your packages. Let's look at an example for the SendJSON function from our previous example.

Listing 9.26 handlers_example_test.go

```
01 // Sample test to show how to write a basic example.
02 package handlers_test
03
04 import (
05     "encoding/json"
06     "fmt"
07     "log"
```

```
08      "net/http"
09      "net/http/httptest"
10  )
11
12  // ExampleSendJSON provides a basic example.
13  func ExampleSendJSON() {
14      r, _ := http.NewRequest("GET", "/sendjson", nil)
15      rw := httptest.NewRecorder()
16      http.DefaultServeMux.ServeHTTP(rw, r)
17
18      var u struct {
19          Name  string
20          Email string
21      }
22
23      if err := json.NewDecoder(w.Body).Decode(&u); err != nil {
24          log.Println("ERROR:", err)
25      }
26
27      // Use fmt to write to stdout to check the output.
28      fmt.Println(u)
29      // Output:
30      // {Bill bill@ardanstudios.com}
31  }
```

Examples are based on existing functions or methods. Instead of starting the function with the word Test, we need to use the word Example. On line 13 in listing 9.26, the name of the example is ExampleSendJSON.

There's one rule you need to follow with examples. An example is always based on an existing exported function or method. Our example test is for the exported function SendJSON inside the handlers package. If you don't use the name of an existing function or method, the test won't show in the Go documentation for the package.

The code you write for an example is to show someone how to use the specific function or method. To determine if the test succeeds or fails, the test will compare the final output of the function with the output listed at the bottom of the example function.

Listing 9.27   handlers_example_test.go: lines 27–31

```
27      // Use fmt to write to stdout to check the output.
28      fmt.Println(u)
29      // Output:
30      // {Bill bill@ardanstudios.com}
31  }
```

On line 28 in listing 9.27, the code uses fmt.Println to write the value of u to stdout. The value of u is initialized from making a call to the /sendjson endpoint earlier in the function. On line 29 we have a comment with the word Output:.

The Output: marker is used to document the output you expect to have after the test function is run. The testing framework knows how to compare the final output

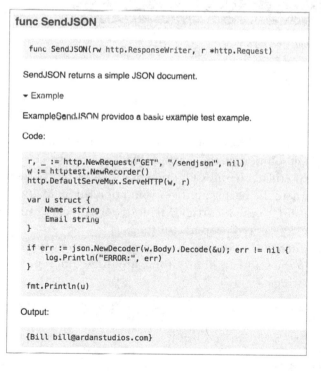

Figure 9.10   godoc view of the handlers package

from stdout against this output comment. If everything matches, the test passes, and you have an example that works inside the Go documentation for the package. If the output doesn't match, the test fails.

If you start a local godoc server (godoc -http=":3000") and navigate to the handlers package, you can see this all come together, as in figure 9.10.

You can see in figure 9.10 that the documentation for the handlers package shows the example for the SendJSON function. If you select the SendJSON link, the documentation will show the code, as in figure 9.11.

func SendJSON

```
func SendJSON(rw http.ResponseWriter, r *http.Request)
```

SendJSON returns a simple JSON document.

▾ Example

ExampleSendJSON provides a basic example test example.

Code:

```
r, _ := http.NewRequest("GET", "/sendjson", nil)
w := httptest.NewRecorder()
http.DefaultServeMux.ServeHTTP(w, r)

var u struct {
    Name  string
    Email string
}

if err := json.NewDecoder(w.Body).Decode(&u); err != nil {
    log.Println("ERROR:", err)
}

fmt.Println(u)
```

Output:

```
{Bill bill@ardanstudios.com}
```

Figure 9.11   A full view of the example in godoc

```
$ go test -v -run="ExampleSendJSON"
=== RUN: ExampleSendJSON
--- PASS: ExampleSendJSON (0.00s)
PASS
ok       github.com/goinaction/code/chapter9/listing17/handlers  0.008s
```

Figure 9.12   Running the example

Figure 9.11 shows a complete set of documentation for the example, including the code and the expected output. Since this is also a test, you can run the example function with the go test tool, as in figure 9.12.

After running the test, you see the test passes. This time when the test is run, the specific function ExampleSendJSON is specified with the -run option. The -run option takes any regular expression to filter the test functions to run. It works with both unit tests and example functions. When an example fails, it looks like this figure 9.13.

```
$ go test -v -run="ExampleSendJSON"
=== RUN: ExampleSendJSON
--- FAIL: ExampleSendJSON (0.00s)
got:
{Lisa lisa@gmail.com}
want:
{Bill bill@ardanstudios.com}
FAIL
exit status 1
FAIL    github.com/goinaction/code/chapter9/listing17/handlers  0.006s
```

Figure 9.13   Running an example that fails

When an example fails, go test shows the output that was produced and what was expected.

9.3   *Benchmarking*

Benchmarking is a way to test the performance of code. It's useful when you want to test the performance of different solutions to the same problem and see which solution performs better. It can also be useful to identify CPU or memory issues for a particular piece of code that might be critical to the performance of your application. Many developers use benchmarking to test different concurrency patterns or to help configure work pools to make sure they're configured properly for the best throughput.

Let's look at a set of benchmark functions that reveal the fastest way to convert an integer value to a string. In the standard library, there are three different ways to convert an integer value to a string.

Listing 9.28   listing28_test.go: lines 01–10

```
01 // Sample benchmarks to test which function is better for converting
02 // an integer into a string. First using the fmt.Sprintf function,
03 // then the strconv.FormatInt function and then strconv.Itoa.
```

```
04 package listing28_test
05
06 import (
07     "fmt"
08     "strconv"
09     "testing"
10 )
```

Listing 9.28 shows the initial code for the listing28_test.go benchmarks. As with unit test files, the file name must end in _test.go. The testing package must also be imported. Next, let's look at one of the benchmark functions.

Listing 9.29   listing28_test.go: lines 12–22

```
12 // BenchmarkSprintf provides performance numbers for the
13 // fmt.Sprintf function.
14 func BenchmarkSprintf(b *testing.B) {
15     number := 10
16
17     b.ResetTimer()
18
19     for i := 0; i < b.N; i++ {
20         fmt.Sprintf("%d", number)
21     }
22 }
```

On line 14 in listing 9.29, you see the first benchmark, named BenchmarkSprintf. Benchmark functions begin with the word Benchmark and take as their only parameter a pointer of type testing.B. In order for the benchmarking framework to calculate performance, it must run the code over and over again for a period of time. This is where the for loop comes in.

Listing 9.30   listing28_test.go: lines 19–22

```
19     for i := 0; i < b.N; i++ {
20         fmt.Sprintf("%d", number)
21     }
22 }
```

The for loop on line 19 in listing 9.30 shows how to use the b.N value. On line 20 we have the call to the Sprintf function from the fmt package. This is the function we're benchmarking to convert an integer value into a string.

By default, the benchmarking framework will call the benchmark function over and over again for at least one second. Each time the framework calls the benchmark function, it will increase the value of b.N. On the first call, the value of b.N will be 1. It's important to place all the code to benchmark inside the loop and to use the b.N value. If this isn't done, the results can't be trusted.

If we just want to run benchmark functions, we need to use the -bench option.

Listing 9.31   Running the benchmark test

```
go test -v -run="none" -bench="BenchmarkSprintf"
```

In our call to go test, we specified the -run option passing the string "none" to make sure no unit tests are run prior to running the specified benchmark function. Both of these options take a regular expression to filter the tests to run. Since there's no unit test function that has none in its name, none eliminates any unit tests from running. When we issue this command, we get the output shown in figure 9.14.

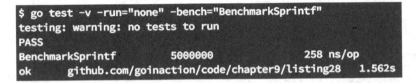

```
$ go test -v -run="none" -bench="BenchmarkSprintf"
testing: warning: no tests to run
PASS
BenchmarkSprintf          5000000                   258 ns/op
ok        github.com/goinaction/code/chapter9/listing28    1.562s
```

Figure 9.14   Running a single benchmark

The output starts out specifying that there are no tests to run and then proceeds to run the BenchmarkSprintf benchmark. After the word PASS, you see the result of running the benchmark function. The first number, 5000000, represents the number of times the code inside the loop was executed. In this case, that's five million times. The next number represents the performance of the code based on the number of nanoseconds per operation, so using the Sprintf function in this context takes 258 nanoseconds on average per call.

The final output from running the benchmark shows *ok* to represent the benchmark finished properly. Then the name of the code file that was executed is displayed, and finally, the total time the benchmark ran. The default minimum run time for a benchmark is 1 second. You can see how the framework still ran the test for approximately a second and a half. You can use another option called -benchtime if you want to have the test run longer. Let's run the test again using a bench time of three seconds (see figure 9.15).

This time the Sprintf function was run twenty million times for a period of 5.275 seconds. The performance of the function didn't change much. This time the performance was 256 nanoseconds per operation. Sometimes by increasing the bench time, you can get a more accurate reading of performance. For most tests, increasing the bench time over three seconds tends to not provide any difference for an accurate reading. But each benchmark is different.

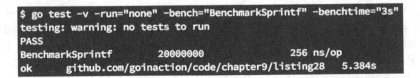

```
$ go test -v -run="none" -bench="BenchmarkSprintf" -benchtime="3s"
testing: warning: no tests to run
PASS
BenchmarkSprintf         20000000                   256 ns/op
ok        github.com/goinaction/code/chapter9/listing28    5.384s
```

Figure 9.15   Running a single benchmark with the -benchtime option

Let's look at the other two benchmark functions and then run all three benchmarks together to see what's the fastest way to convert an integer value to a string.

> **Listing 9.32   listing28_test.go: lines 24–46**

```
24 // BenchmarkFormat provides performance numbers for the
25 // strconv.FormatInt function.
26 func BenchmarkFormat(b *testing.B) {
27     number := int64(10)
28
29     b.ResetTimer()
30
31     for i := 0; i < b.N; i++ {
32         strconv.FormatInt(number, 10)
33     }
34 }
35
36 // BenchmarkItoa provides performance numbers for the
37 // strconv.Itoa function.
38 func BenchmarkItoa(b *testing.B) {
39     number := 10
40
41     b.ResetTimer()
42
43     for i := 0; i < b.N; i++ {
44         strconv.Itoa(number)
45     }
46 }
```

Listing 9.32 shows the other two benchmark functions. The `BenchmarkFormat` function benchmarks the use of the `FormatInt` function from the `strconv` package. The `BenchmarkItoa` function benchmarks the use of the `Itoa` function from the same `strconv` package. You can see the same pattern in these two other benchmark functions as in the `BenchmarkSprintf` function. The call is inside the `for` loop using `b.N` to control the number of iterations for each call.

One thing we skipped over was the call to `b.ResetTimer`, which is used in all three benchmark functions. This method is useful to reset the timer when initialization is required before the code can start executing the loop. To have the most accurate benchmark times you can, use this method.

When we run all the benchmark functions for a minimum of three seconds, we get the result shown in figure 9.16.

```
$ go test -v -run="none" -bench=. -benchtime="3s"
testing: warning: no tests to run
PASS
BenchmarkSprintf       20000000                257 ns/op
BenchmarkFormat 100000000                45.9 ns/op
BenchmarkItoa   100000000                49.4 ns/op
ok      github.com/goinaction/code/chapter9/listing28   15.057s
```

Figure 9.16   Running all three benchmarks

The results show that the `BenchmarkFormat` test function runs the fastest at 45.9 nanoseconds per operation. The `BenchmarkItoa` comes in a close second at 49.4 nanoseconds per operation. Both of those benchmarks were much faster than using the `Sprintf` function.

Another great option you can use when running benchmarks is the `-benchmem` option. It will provide information about the number of allocations and bytes per allocation for a given test. Let's use that option with the benchmark (see figure 9.17).

```
$ go test -v -run="none" -bench=. -benchtime="3s" -benchmem
testing: warning: no tests to run
PASS
BenchmarkSprintf        20000000            255 ns/op        16 B/op      2 allocs/op
BenchmarkFormat 100000000             45.8 ns/op       2 B/op      1 allocs/op
BenchmarkItoa   100000000             49.5 ns/op       2 B/op      1 allocs/op
ok      github.com/goinaction/code/chapter9/listing28    15.008s
```

Figure 9.17 Running a benchmark with the `-benchmem` option

This time with the output you see two new values: a value for `B/op` and one for `allocs/op`. The `allocs/op` value represents the number of heap allocations per operation. You can see the `Sprintf` functions allocate two values on the heap per operation, and the other two functions allocate one value per operation. The `B/op` value represents the number of bytes per operation. You can see that those two allocations from the `Sprintf` function result in 16 bytes of memory being allocated per operation. The other two functions only allocated 2 bytes per operation.

There are many different options you can use when running tests and benchmarks. I suggest you explore all those options and leverage this testing framework to the fullest extent when writing your packages and projects. The community expects package authors to provide comprehensive tests when publishing packages for open use by the community.

9.4   Summary

- Testing is built into the language and Go provides all the tooling you need.
- The `go test` tool is used to run tests.
- Test files always end with the _test.go file name.
- Table tests are a great way to leverage a single test function to test multiple values.
- Examples are both tests and documentation for a package.
- Benchmarks provide a mechanism to reveal the performance of code.

index

Symbols

_ (blank identifier) 44
:= (short variable declaration operator) 17, 90

A

AddInt64 function 143
anonymous functions 20
API, testing endpoints for 223–228
append function 38, 71–72, 79
archive files 186
arrays
  accessing elements in 60
  copying 61–62
  declaring 58–59
  internals of 58
  multidimensional 62–64
  of pointers 60–61
  passing between functions 64–65
atomic functions 142–145

B

basic tests 212–216
-bench option 233
BenchmarkFormat function
  235
benchmarking 232–236
BenchmarkItoa function 235
-benchmem option 236
-benchtime option 234
blank identifier (_) 44
bool type 88
BSON (Binary JavaScript Object Notation) 196
Buffer type 206

buffered channels 153–156
build command 41, 46
built-in types 96–97
bytes package 206

C

C/C++ 2, 6–7
chan keyword 147
channels
  buffered 153–156
  defined 129
  overview 4–5, 147–148
  unbuffered 148–153
Chdir method 101
clean command 46
CLI (command-line interface) 187
close method 25
comments 50
communicating sequential processes. *See* CSP
compilation 3
composition 5
concrete types 104
concurrency
  channels 4–5
    buffered 153–156
    overview 147–148
    unbuffered 148–153
  goroutines 3–4, 132–139
  locking shared resources
    atomic functions 142–145
    mutexes 145–147
  overview 3
  parallelism vs. 129–132
  patterns for
    pool package 167–177

concurrency, patterns for (continued)
  runner package 158–166
  work package 177–183
  race conditions 139–142
constants 23
cookiejar package 40
CSP (communicating sequential processes) 129
curl program 102, 208–209

D

data feeds example program
  main package 11–13
  program architecture
    10–11
  RSS matcher 32–38
  search package
    default.go file 26–32
    feed.go file 22–26
    match.go file 26–32
    search.go file 14–22
Decode method 25, 36
decoding JSON 196–201
default case 164
defer keyword 25, 134, 151, 209
delete function 85
dependencies
  gb build tool and 54–56
  general discussion 52
  using godep tool 52–53
distributed version control systems. *See* DVCS
doc command 49
documentation
  of code 50
  for standard library 185–186
  test examples in 228–232
Done method 31
duck typing 6
Duration type 91
DVCS (distributed version control systems) 42
dynamic languages 3

E

empty slices 67–68
encoding JSON 201–202
endpoints, testing 223–228
env package 97
EOF (end of file) 204
Errorf method 36, 216
exporting identifiers 119–127

F

Fatal method 17, 215
Fatalf method 215
Fatalln method 190
File type 100
float32 type 88
fmt package 36, 48, 103, 206
for range statements 19, 31, 76, 219
Fprintf function 103, 206
func keyword 16, 92–93
functions
  anonymous 20
  documenting 51
  passing arrays between 64–65
  passing maps between 86–87
  passing slices between 80–81

G

gb build tool 54–56
get command 43
Get function 102
Go
  concurrency support
    channels 4–5
    goroutines 3–4
    overview 3
  development speed 3
  Hello, World! example 7–8
  memory management 7
  overview 1–2
  type system
    interface system 6–7
    overview 5–6
    simplicity of 6
go command
  doc command 49
  fmt command 48
  godoc command 49–51
  overview 45–47
  running goroutines using 4
  vet command 47–48
Go Playground 8
godep tool 52–53
godoc command
  example code from 228–232
  overview 49–51
GOMAXPROCS function 137
GOPATH environment variable 14, 42
GOROOT environment variable 14
$GOROOT variable 186
goroutines
  concurrency using 132–139

goroutines *(continued)*
    defined 20
    overview 3–4

H

handlers package 224
header values 97
Hello, World! example 7–8
HOB (high order bits) 82
http package 36, 102
httptest package 220–221, 223

I

import statements
    gb build tool and 54
    overview 42
    remote packages 42–43
    renaming import 43–44
init functions 13, 31, 44–45
inner types 111
int type 89
int64 type 88
interface type 25, 27
interfaces
    implementing 104
    method sets 105–109
    overview 6–7
    polymorphic behavior using 109–111
    in standard library 102–104
io package 101
    functions implementing Writer interface
        205–208
    implementing curl program using 208–209
    overview 203, 210
    Reader interface 204–205
    Writer interface 203–204
iota keyword 189
isShellSpecialVar function 97

J

JSON (JavaScript Object Notation)
    decoding 196–201
    encoding 201–202
json package 23, 229

L

Ldate constant 189
LoadInt64 function 144–145
LOB (low order bits) 82

Lock function 146
locking shared resources
    atomic functions 142–145
    mutexes 145–147
log package
    creating customized loggers 191–195
    overview 14, 187–191, 195
low order bits. *See* LOB

M

main function 11–12, 41
main package 40–41
main thread 129
make function 15, 18, 66–67, 147
maps
    converting to JSON strings 202
    creating 83–84
    defined 81
    internals of 81–83
    passing between functions 86–87
    working with 84–86
MarshalIndent function 201–202
memory management 7
method sets 105–109
methods 92–96
mocks 219–223
multidimensional arrays 62–64
multidimensional slices 79–80
MultiWriter function 194, 209
mutexes 145–147

N

named imports 43
NewDecoder function 25, 36
NewRecorder function 227
nil slices 67–68
NumCPU function 137

O

Open function 100
operator 60, 63, 66–68
os package 103
outer types 111
Output: marker 230

P

package keyword 14
packages
    creating repositories for sharing 51–52

packages *(continued)*
  dependencies
    gb build tool and 54–56
    general discussion 52
    using godep tool 52–53
  exporting and unexporting identifiers in
      119–127
  import statements
    overview 42
    remote packages 42–43
    renaming import 43–44
  init functions in 44–45
  main 40–41
  naming conventions 40
  overview 40
  standard library 185
  _test suffix 226
  using go command with
    doc command 49
    fmt command 48
    godoc command 49–51
    overview 45–47
    vet command 47–48
Panicln function 190
parallelism 129–132
pointers, arrays of 60–61
polymorphism 101, 109–111
pool package 167–177
Println function 190
Python 2

R

race conditions 139–142
range keyword 19, 30, 76–77
Reader interface 204–205
reference types 97–98
reflect package 25
regexp package 38
remote packages 42–43
repositories, creating 51–52
ResetTimer method 235
ResponseRecorder type 227
Routes function 224
Ruby 2
run command 47
-run option 232
runner package 158–166
runtime package 133, 137

S

select statements 164–165, 171
ServeHTTP method 227

SetFlags function 190
SetMaxThreads function 131
sharing code 8
short variable declaration operator (:=) 17, 90
slices
  append operations on 71–72
  assigning values in 68
  creating
    make function 66–67
    nil and empty slices 67–68
  defined 65
  internals of 65
  iterating over 76–78
  multidimensional 79–80
  passing between functions 80–81
  slicing 68–71
  three-index slices 72–76
Sourcegraph 186
standard library
  documentation 185–186
  interfaces in 102–104
  io package
    functions implementing Writer interface
        205–208
    implementing curl program using 208–209
    overview 203, 210
    Reader interface 204–205
    Writer interface 203–204
  JSON
    decoding 196–201
    encoding 201–202
  log package
    creating customized loggers 191–195
    overview 187–191, 195
Start method 165
stderr device 187
stdin device 203
stdout device 187, 203
Stop method 164
StoreInt64 function 144–145
strings package 97
struct keyword 89, 98–101
sync package 18

T

table tests 216–219
test command 213–214
testing
  benchmarking 232–236
  documentation examples 228–232
  unit testing
    API endpoints 223–228
    basic tests 212–216

testing, unit testing *(continued)*
    mocks 219–223
    overview 212
    table tests 216–219
testing package 214, 233
threads 129
three-index slices 72–76
time package 91, 99
Time type 99–100
Trim function 97
type embedding 111–119
type keyword 89
type system
  built-in types 96–97
  exporting and unexporting identifiers in
      packages 119–127
  interfaces 6–7
    implementing 104
    method sets 105–109
    polymorphic behavior using 109–111
    in standard library 102–104
  methods 92–96
  overview 5–6
  reference types 97–98
  simplicity of 6
  struct types 98–101
  type embedding 111–119
  user defined types 89–92

U

unbuffered channels 148–153
unexporting identifiers 119–127
unit testing
  API endpoints 223–228
  basic tests 212–216
  mocks 219–223
  overview 212
  table tests 216–219
Unlock function 146
Unmarshal function 199–200
user-defined types 89–92

V

-v option 213–214
values 88
var keyword 14, 37, 89–90
vendored code 55
verbose output 213
vet command 47–48

W

Wait method 31
WaitGroup 18, 134
when clause 215
work package 177–183
Writer interface
  functions implementing
    205–208
  overview 203–204
WriteTo method 206–208

X

xml package 36, 196, 202

MORE TITLES FROM MANNING

Java 8 in Action
Lambdas, streams, and
functional-style programming
by Raoul-Gabriel Urma, Mario Fusco,
  and Alan Mycroft

ISBN: 9781617291999
424 pages
$49.99
August 2014

Groovy in Action, Second Edition
by Dierk König, Paul King,
  Guillaume Laforge, Hamlet D'Arcy,
  Cédric Champeau, Erik Pragt,
  and Jon Skeet

ISBN: 9781935182443
912 pages
$59.99
June 2015

For ordering information go to www.manning.com

MORE TITLES FROM MANNING

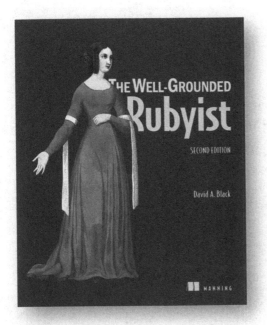

The Well-Grounded Rubyist,
Second Edition
by David A. Black

  ISBN: 9781617291692
  536 pages
  $44.99
  June 2014

The Quick Python Book,
Second Edition
Revised edition of The Quick Python Book by
Daryl K. Harms and Kenneth M. McDonald
by Naomi R. Ceder

  ISBN: 9781935182207
  360 pages
  $39.99
  January 2010

For ordering information go to www.manning.com